D1478498

The Citizen's Guide to Zoning

Herbert H. Smith

Planners Press
American Planning Association
Washington, D.C.   Chicago, Ill.

Copyright 1983 by the American Planning Association
1313 E. 60th St., Chicago, IL 60637

ISBN 918286–28–X
Library of Congress Catalog Card Number 82–062237
Printed in the United States of America

To Nancy, who has taught
me more of the meaning
of love by loving.

Table of Contents

Foreword

When Frank So, the Deputy Executive Director of the American Planning Association, asked me to consider a revised edition of this book, originally published over 16 years ago, my first reaction was that drastic rewriting would be required because of the changes in zoning practices. Having decided to accept the assignment, I dug out of my archives a copy of the edition now out of print and began to thumb through it. It soon became apparent that, while innovations have occurred, techniques have changed, and there has been a constant search for means of making zoning a more flexible tool; amazingly, the fundamentals have remained the same.

Regardless of numerous continuing challenges and the development of fancy new terms like growth management, zoning continues to be the legal means of land-use regulation. Few, if any, state statutes have been revised to the point of suggesting that the control of private property by local ordinances can stray far from the fundamentals of zoning that evolved during the early part of this century. Courts, while insisting more and more that sustainable zoning action must be supported by comprehensive planning studies, repeatedly hold that zoning is the acceptable tool for applying police power controls to the development of land. Just as was the case 15 years ago, and even before that, there has been good zoning and bad zoning, honest administration and dishonest favor granting, more understanding of the idea of zoning and, yet, a surprising lack of an involved, concerned citizenry. Many cities and towns are much more livable for having zoning, but there are those that would have been better off without it because of the way it has been used. Based on these reflections, I found myself reaching several conclusions.

In spite of the many detractors and "government regulation haters," the influence and the importance of zoning have vastly increased over the past three-quarters of this century, and there is no reason to assume that this trend will not continue in the foreseeable future. The standards and principles of the system have withstood the test of time. Zoning will continue to be the recognized method of expressing the interest of the community in the private development of land and the shaping of urban form. Its influence on the lives and economic development of individuals, both those developing and those having to live with what is developed, will be even greater as the unavoidable changes in the life style of our society takes place. The most obvious and greatest need consistently evident in my musings about the elapsed years was that of citizen support of sound principles and demand for effective administration and enforcement.

It is my hope that what is said in these pages can help to convince a few students and members of the tax-paying public that the use or misuse of zoning is important enough to their lives and the future that they will learn more about it, be concerned, and get involved. If anyone has a copy of the first edition, they will find that I have taken generously from it, but I have also updated it and added to it where necessary. Those who read this edition will find that the value of citizen involvement in good zoning and the influence of this process on the lives of all of us—now and in the future—is a subject about which I feel very strongly.

Herbert H. Smith
Denver, Colorado
April 1982

1

So You Want to Know About Zoning

There is no doubt of the presumptuousness of that chapter heading, and yet it is a most appropriate way to start. It might have been even better to have said, "You should want to know about zoning." Although there are many reading this—and millions who never will read it— who may question that statement, I suggest that there is no single governmental function, other than taxation, that has a more direct bearing on our day-to-day lives than the thing called zoning. Don't think you can stop reading here if you happen to live in a place without zoning, since the lack of such a process leaves you wide open to even more drastic and adverse effects. After some 30 years of being involved with communities and their development, I believe that any organized community in the United States that does not have zoning is shortchanging itself and that there is no town or city that has zoning that could not be doing a better job with it.

We Know All About It—Or Do We?

The interesting point is how much the word zoning is thrown around, how many more people know the term than did 16 years ago when I wrote the first edition of this book, and how few really understand what it is all about and how important it is. True, it has gotten to be one of the "in" words you hear bandied about, even at cocktail parties and church socials. Usually this occurs when a rumor has leaked out about someone proposing to ask for a zone change to permit apartments or a business in what has been thought of as a single-family residential area. The reaction then, unless you are the developer or stand to gain in some way from the change, is that "they" can't do this to our neighborhood. Understanding the process and being concerned about its day-to-day administration in the total community is another matter. In this case, the attitude is usually that "they" can take care of it as long as I am not personally affected.

In a community having no zoning, the first rumor that lights the fire of discussion is the one that "they" are proposing some law that will tell us what we can do with our land or that someone is planning to build a drag strip or locate a junkyard in our neighborhood, and "they" aren't doing anything to stop it. Both here and in places with zoning, it is evident that there is no middle ground of feeling about the idea. Usually, if the reaction is total opposition to the idea of zoning, it is based on the leftover pioneer mentality that believes that ownership of land carries with it the "right" to do anything that the possessor of a deed wants to do, that government has no right to interfere, and that the concept of an increasingly complex society requiring adjustment of this attitude is the fictitious creation of a communistic conspiracy. The necessity for changing this attitude is an important matter about which more will be said later.

In those who say that something should be done before disaster strikes, we see evidence of the prime reason we have difficulty with long-range planning in our communities. Over the years, we have developed psychologically into a re-active society and never accepted the necessity for, or durability of, a pre-active approach to problem prevention. Just let a proposal come along that we feel will adversely affect our space or our values, and we are all for governmental intervention and jump to criticize our elected officials for not having taken action to prevent this travesty. Even when this kind of situation develops, there are those not directly affected who still strongly oppose the idea of government regulation of land use. After all, if they should support this proposition just because an undesirable use may occur in another neighborhood, it might result in a regulation that would interfere with something they may want to do with their land at a later time.

We Know a Controversial
Issue When We See It

This illustrates the point of zoning being a vibrant, often controversial issue with very few middle-ground or indifferent reactions, either in places considering undertaking it or in those where it has been around for years. This can be understood easily upon reflecting that it is the only readily identified governmental control of the speculative aspect of land ownership, although there are many other less visible ways that land development can be affected by government action. Nevertheless, the process of zoning, because of its required public hearings and the fact that we are directly confronted with it where it exists, is in the forefront of the attention given to local government functions.

During the time of my tenure as city manager of Albuquerque, New Mexico, the one thing we could always count on was that the City Commission Chamber would be packed with people any time there was a major rezoning proposal on the agenda. Unfortunately, the people attending, other than the applicant, were from the immediate neighborhood only and were usually aroused by inaccurate rumors and convinced that militant action was the only way to save their property values. Most had never attended any other zoning hearing or discussion (or for that matter, any commission meeting) and probably never would again. When the matter of their immediate personal concern had been concluded, they always left, angry or pleased, regardless of the remaining items on the agenda or the importance of any of them. I still remember a meeting that included discussion of a controversial zoning amendment, after which the adoption of a phase of the comprehensive master plan and the next year's city budget of over $85 million was to be considered. Some 200 people left the room after "their" zoning issue had been settled, ignoring the larger issues.

In spite of this, it is my opinion that zoning, or some similar form of land-use regulation, is going to be with us for the foreseeable future. One need only to reflect on the increasing population, the sprawl of urbanization, and our dwindling resources and assets to accept the logic of that statement. We should not spend valuable time arguing about whether we will have zoned communities or whether the town without zoning should have it; rather, we should devote much more time to understanding it and the importance for the future of good zoning throughout our community. This understanding must come from knowledge, which, in spite of the broad prevalence of the zoning process, there is an amazing lack of by those most affected—the general public.

We May Not Know Why We Need to Know

Fully understanding zoning means knowing why it should be a tool of government at all. The next step is to learn and understand the purpose of good zoning: what it includes, how it is supposed to work, how it should be administered, and who is involved in its effective administration. Each day decisions are being made by elected representatives and appointed officials in numerous areas that have a bearing on the economic well being, the general welfare, and the character of the community in which we live. None of these surpasses in importance those decisions related to how land is to be used, how it is developed, and how that development relates to the interests of the community and its citizens. A few of the arguments in support of my conviction that zoning is vitally important to every citizen, whether they now live in a community with zoning or one without, are worthy of further exploration.

First of all, an irrefutable fact is that zoning, through its regulation of the private use of land, is a major factor in shaping community character. Building villages, towns, and cities is very much like putting together a jigsaw puzzle. Separately, each piece has a unique shape. No piece will fit with another unless the maker of the puzzle has planned for it to do so, and, when all the parts are in the right place, you have an orderly, coordinated, attractive picture. So it is with land development. Each lot and its use, each individual structure, is a part of the total community, determining what it will look like, how it will work, and, most important of all, its character.

As we think about land development and its importance to the future, it is easy to see that, while property ownership by individuals is a freedom we enjoy, there is a community interest in how that property is used. This has become increasingly important as society and our urban structures have become more and more complex. You cannot reach the density of population of the state of New Jersey, Chicago, Philadelphia, Albuquerque, or even Durango, Colorado, for example, without being forced to accept the fact, if you are realistic, that collective society has a stake in and a responsibility for how those pieces of the jigsaw puzzle are going to fit together. This responsibility for determining the character and the quality of the sum of the parts is the proprietary interest society has that necessitates the establishment of reasonable and equitable controls over private land development. This common interest in how land is used is a long-standing principle of our legal system, yet one we seem to have forgotten, overlooked, or neglected.

Fundamental to the guidance zoning should provide the community is the necessity of having an organized scheme, understood and supported by the public, of the desirable future character and pattern of development. The basis for this is comprehensive, long-range planning, the results of which are included in a well-documented master plan. No zoning will successfully guide and direct the private development of land toward a desirable overall quality and character without just such a solid foundation. More will be said about this later.

We Know We Like Money and Profit

Long before the period of inflation present at the time of writing this, and long before the average price of a single-family home was approaching $80,000, it was a fact that the largest single investment most of us ever make is in a home. The great American dream has been to own a home, to own land, and to be able to invest in real estate. In so doing, we expect the value of that property to increase continuously, and, if we sell it, we expect to make a nice profit. It is astonishing how much we take for granted that this is the way it should be and this is the way it is going to be.

Not only do we want these tangible assets to increase in their marketability and worth, we expect someone to protect our private domain and make certain that nothing will happen to threaten or endanger it. Even more, we are ready to fight if a loss in value should result from anything that others do with their land or that the public sector undertakes that affects *our* land. It is then that we have a tendency to say, "They have got to do something about this." Then, we forget how we listened to the rumor that zoning was undemocratic and how we joined the group that killed the idea of doing community planning and having a zoning ordinance. If any action that might adversely affect our property values happens in a city or town that has had zoning, most of us would not recall that we failed to attend all those public hearings on zoning changes or neglected to be involved enough to be sure that we have honest, effective administration of the ordinance.

The truth of the matter is that things can and do happen that will change our dream into a nightmare if no adequate protection is provided by the strength of collective community action expressed through the legal tool of zoning. A neighbor, following the philosophy of doing what you please with your land, could decide that it would be nice for extra income to dismantle and rebuild junk automobiles in the back yard. Someone else could decide to turn his or her first floor into a discotheque and apply for a liquor license. Farther away, the so-called business district has grown into a poorly arranged hodgepodge, with commercial and industrial uses allowed to string out in strip configuration along the main traffic arteries. Little attention is paid to the relationship of land development to the infrastructure of utilities, services, schools, and the general efficiency of traffic circulation.

Even though we take pride in our independence and self-sufficiency, we must recognize that, when it comes to the worth of the property we hold, we are interdependent. We are all dependent upon our neighbors, the people in the next block, the investors in apartments and businesses, and those elected to office who are the policy makers. When we buy a home or any piece of property, we are not just investing money in that lot or that building, we are investing in the community and its future. Even in inflationary times, the market value of property is determined more by the character of the area in which that property is located—and the overall public investment in and public policy for maintaining community quality—than in what we may do to improve an individual parcel of land.

I once heard a friend in real estate say that the market value of any property is determined by three things. These are: location, location, location! When we look at why this is so, we find that we are dependent upon all elements of our community structure working together to make every parcel of land "a good location." We begin to understand that public investment in streets, parks, libraries, utilities, and services is one major factor in determining the value of any property in a given jurisdiction. We see that attitude and concern for the future on the part of the people we elect, and the effectiveness of their administration of government is another factor. And, finally, we recognize that the presence or lack of standards of quality of the built environment, resulting from the investment of the private sector, can determine whether our investment in any community is a wise one.

We Know We Don't Like Taxes

As much as we are concerned about our individual property values, there is another aspect of societal living to which we assign almost equal importance. I refer, of course, to the cost of government and to taxes. We may yell about these, about "big government," and applaud those who advocate "getting government off our backs"; however, the fact remains that, in a collective society, some organized system of government is necessary. The only alternative is anarchy. What we really need to turn our attention to, particularly at the local level, is the economy and efficiency of the delivery of necessary services by government. Most people readily agree with this, even though they may have trouble agreeing on what these necessary services are. But they show a frightening lack of understanding of the relationship between the cost-effectiveness of the delivery of services and the land-use patterns that are permitted to evolve.

Regardless of where we live or work, whether we are property owners or not, we take for granted the delivery of what has come to be thought of as essential governmental services. When we turn on a water faucet, we expect an ample supply of water to come gushing forth, pure enough to drink. When we feel the call of nature, in urban society, we assume it to be a "right" that we don't have to go outside to a privy and that sewage is going to go somewhere and be taken care of once a toilet is flushed. In most areas, we expect the city to provide the means for picking up and disposing of our tons of solid waste. We don't want our kids to have to be bused to school at all, but, if they are, it shouldn't be far. If we are told the costs of providing these services are going up, we become convinced that someone is just trying to "rip us off" and immediately determine that we had better work to see that "they" don't get reelected.

The interesting, and somewhat alarming, point is that the same people who agree completely with the idea of economy and efficiency of government have never considered how much effect good or bad zoning has on both of these. After all these years of zoning controls, there is little understanding that the patterns of permitted land use determine the demand for services, the efficiency of those services, and the economy of the costs of delivering those services, as well as the economic base that will pay for them. Each time commercial development is permitted to line the edges of a major traffic arterial in an extended strip pattern, each time a housing development leapfrogs over vacant land, and each time a more intensive development is allowed by ordinance change or variance, a servicing cost factor is built in that can only be met by public subsidy.

Scattered development, as exemplified in most of our urban sprawl, is inefficient and uneconomical, so much so that it could not happen without all of us who pay taxes subsidizing it with public funds. The most expensive and least cost-efficient development of all is the leap-frogging subdivision. Whether it be residential, commercial, or industrial, land development permitted to locate in areas without existing service delivery systems will be a drain on the public purse. So, too, is the commercial strip that adds miles to utility lines and increases the need for police and fire protection. As a city manager in a city whose policy makers were enamored with the idea of growth at all cost—resulting in a horizontal, spread-out city—I saw the effects of this first hand. For every new low-density subdivision approved, the city provided a goodly proportion of the cost of the new infrastructure. Expensive miles of streets were added, to be swept and maintained. Additional refuse trucks and school buses were needed, and the public had to pay the cost of getting them from one place to another.

Any place that bases zoning on good comprehensive planning can avoid this. If we recall the comparison of community building to putting the pieces of a jigsaw puzzle together and if we recognize that underneath that total picture must be an elaborate system of utilities and on top must be a circulation pattern that is the means of providing additional essential services, we can begin to understand the importance of guiding and shaping land use through zoning to relate to the capability to deliver those services and the cost of doing so. Zoning is important because it is the only legal means we have of seeking economy and efficiency in this vital function of local government.

We Know We Like to Breathe

As much as we are interested in and concerned about finances and costs—and, logically, we should be—there is yet another area in which zoning can play an important role. In spite of political trends, it is my belief that the vast majority of our people recognize the need for us to do more to protect our environment and preserve our natural resources. If this recognition were not already expanding—and I believe it is—there is little question that the circumstances around us would soon force an awareness of our situation. We cannot continue degrading our natural environment at the rate we have been and depleting or exploiting irreplaceable natural resources as if there were no tomorrow.

Collective society and organized government have a responsibility to future generations that demands a much greater sense of stewardship of our land, resources, and environment than we have yet shown in this country. In addition, we are beginning to be held accountable by the rest of the world for our abusive misuse of resources and our contribution to the despoliation of environment.

We need to think in terms of two types of environments as we look at our communities and our own lives. First, there is the environment of nature—the air we breathe, the land, tree, water, and wildlife. If we look around at what we have done to this type of environment, it would be easy to conclude that we have been relentlessly carrying out a death wish. One of our biggest environmental problems is air pollution. No major metropolitan area and few urban places of any size in the country is without a serious problem with air quality. The major cause of air pollution has been proven to be the automobile, but the excessive number of automobiles and the concomitant polluting miles driven are attributable to the land-use patterns and urban sprawl we have permitted to occur.

We in Colorado are an outstanding example of how difficult, if not impossible, it is for those of us in this country to learn and benefit from past mistakes of others. With 104,247 square miles of area, ranking eighth in size in the nation and approaching 3 million in statewide population, the metropolitan morass around Denver is one of the most polluted areas in the country. Through the prevalence of a misguided concept that "bigger is better," coupled with slipshod zoning and the lack of a "planning attitude," urban sprawl is not only still being permitted, it is being encouraged. Like the relentless flow of volcanic lava seeking the lines of least resistance, subdivisions, shopping centers, and office parks continue to eat up thousands of acres of land each year with little thought being given to the consequences for the environment and air quality. It is a most awesomely depressing experience to drive east from the Rockies, the sky still a clear blue, and see the beginning of a huge brown cloud forming in the distance. Then, topping the last rise before dropping out of the foothills, spread before you is the panorama epitomizing what is meant by "man's inhumanity to man and nature"—the metropolis developing along Colorado's Front Range.

As if this were not enough to prove our lack of concern for the future and our insensitivity to the importance of guiding land development through well thought-out land-use policies and zoning action, we are passively facing the potential of total despoliation of the Colorado

Western Slope. The largest deposits of coal and oil shale remaining in the U.S. are located there. This is where Exxon, Tosco, ARCO, and others, with encouragement from the federal government and the Bureau of Land Management, plan to produce some 8 million barrels of synfuel per day. When fully developed, this activity, together with the resulting ancillary development, will mean an influx of between 1.25 and 1.5 million people to the area. The production of synfuel is a complicated process that is replete with environmental costs. To produce one barrel of usable oil requires two to three barrels of water— something the Rocky Mountain West does not have in abundance. The Environmental Protection Agency (before its throat was cut) estimated that, if the total development planned took place, the resulting pollution on the Western Slope would be 15 percent more than that presently over Manhattan Island and 40 percent more than that now above Denver, due to the built-in polluting factors in the synfuel production, as well as from people and vehicles. Even in the face of this, we have counties and cities in the area refusing to even consider long-range planning or land-use control action. The argument is put forward still that zoning is "un-American." In addition, the Colorado state legislature gleefully kills every attempt to strengthen the state's land-use policy, refuses to increase the minerals and resources severance tax to provide much-needed capital improvement funds, and recently eliminated the Division of State Planning. In the meantime, 20,000 people connected with the preliminary construction work already live in Battlement Mesa—a once-peaceful and pristine mountain valley. (Since writing this just a few months ago, synfuel production attempts were suddenly put on hold, and Colorado has once again been subjected to a "boom and bust" cycle.

We Should Know We Have Not Learned from Past Mistakes

This story of the failure to understand the importance of pre-active planning and sensible zoning is not unique to Colorado. The same situation exists in Montana, Utah, Wyoming, and New Mexico. If you live in one of the more developed states, don't take too much comfort. If you are concerned and look around carefully, whether it's New Jersey, Ohio, California, or Hawaii, you will find places where poor zoning or inept administration are costing you money, good environment, and an improved quality of life. This relates to both manmade and natural environments. You can see it in misplaced and poorly designed structures. It is equally obvious in the lack of humanistic amenities and human scale in central business districts. It is overwhelming in the inattention to open space, urban parks, and green areas as local officials are coerced by developers to permit the squeezing out of every inch of usable space, the short-sighted (and fallacious) rationale being that "economic ratables" or job opportunities will be created.

We see thousands of acres of land best suited for agriculture gobbled up each year by development and shrug our shoulders helplessly, thinking that nothing can be done. Housing and other uses are allowed to be built in floodplains, encroach on stream basins, deplete underground water tables, and disrupt stream flows. When the floods come or expensive public steps must be taken to overcome the lack of potable water or to clear up a polluted stream, we again shrug our shoulders and shell out public money—a public subsidy of private myopia—to let the people move back into their homes in the flood area or supply the corrective remedy through costly public improvements. Seldom do we consider that a little far-sighted planning carried out by equitable, but strictly enforced zoning could have prevented all this, saved us all money, and avoided the pain involved for the people directly affected.

We cannot go on as we have been going. We can no longer accept, or even tolerate, the outmoded philosophy "It's my land, and I'll do as I damned well please with it." The legally acceptable way, the proven and tested way, of doing something about this is through community-organized, people-supported, land development controls, through zoning based upon careful planning. Accomplishing this takes a strong commitment to the future and firm cooperative action on the part of all levels of government—municipal, county, state, and federal. The role of the federal and state governments is primarily that of policy setting, leadership, enabling legislation, and cooperation. Local governments, at present, have the responsibility for effective action pertaining to land use under these acceptable broad policies and those determined by their constituency. Until our philosophy about metropolitan, regional, and statewide land-use controls changes, municipal and county officials are the ones shaping our urban form, and they must be determined to bite the bullet in order to make things better.

We Know—"Ain't Nobody Gonna Do It But Us!"

It is vital that we all become involved and insist that the community interest in land development be constantly protected through the best zoning possible. A good environment and a good community do not just happen. They are built—and protected and preserved—by what we as a collective society choose to do, both as part of the public sector and the private sector. Part of that choosing is whether we are going to recognize and accept the importance of the community investment in every parcel of land developed, the need for that investment to be protected, and the fact that, in most cases, it won't be protected without governmental regulations and restrictions. This is why zoning is far more important to all of us than many of us have realized. It can make the difference between an urban form that just happened and one that makes physical, societal, and economic sense while providing an improved quality of life.

What is always so perplexing to me is why so many of us are willing to leave something of such importance to so few—usually the policy makers, the administrators, and the vested interests. My contention is that we cannot afford to do this. We each have a responsibility to ourselves and to the future to be informed and involved. We need to understand the importance of zoning as a process, to know the difference between good and bad zoning, and to insist that we get better community development leadership from those we elect. The remainder of this book seeks to provide the understanding and knowledge that will help in doing this.

2

The Changing Philosophy of Land Ownership

The Indian view is that man is part of a delicately balanced universe in which all components—all like forms and natural elements—interrelate and interact, with no part being more or less important than another. Further, it is believed that only man can upset this balance.

Tom Bahti,
Southwestern Indian Ceremonials,
1971

From Stewardship to Exploitation

We have all heard the expression, "Land is a precious commodity." The question is, a precious commodity for whom? The society living on it and for which it provides life support? The individual having a piece of paper that says the title of a small portion of it is vested in her or him? In this country over the past 180 or so years, we have taken the dictionary definition of the word commodity as what we want it to mean in conjunction with land and as applying to the individual. A careful study of that definition, which according to Webster is "that which affords convenience or profit, especially in commerce, including everything movable, that is bought and sold (goods, wares, merchandise, produce of land, etc.)," gives cause for reflection as to the propriety of applying the term to land. Land is certainly not movable, unless dug, mined, or hauled, and, even then, a base remains that is part of the overall land form. Yet, we have accepted and enshrined the idea that land ownership carries with it the "right" to profit by the individual.

Mirror, Mirror, on the Wall

A further look back in time can give us some idea of just how much the philosophy has changed about the land upon which we in the United States now live. The Native Americans revered the land and considered it an asset—an asset for the tribe as a whole, not for any one individual. Even with far vaster areas available for exploitation than we have now, the Indian realized the importance of land and nature to human life and its survival. "Take care of the land and be kind to nature, and the land will take care of you and nature will reward you" was a well-accepted credo. The Indians knew that, if one person abused the land or took from it unnecessarily, the entire tribal community would pay the consequences. Tribal law reflected this attitude. Our Indian forerunners had a respect for land and collective society's stake in it being well-treated that we would have been wise to continue.

The early white settlers saw this and did practice the same principles as to land ownership, if not in the protection of woods, streams, and wildlife. Granted, the original settlements were on royal grants and leaseholds, but around each village was found common land for grazing and agricultural purposes for the benefit of the entire community. In their earliest days, St. Augustine, Florida; Savannah, Georgia; and Williamsburg, Virginia; were examples reflecting this sense of the value of land as a communal asset. The wholesale clearing of forests and other attacks on the natural environment we would now consider abusive were of far less consequence then in view of the vastness of the countryside and the small numbers of people.

There Goes the Neighborhood

As more and more people came, as settlements grew into villages and towns, and as the Indians were pushed farther off the land, our ancestors set about obtaining more freedom and establishing an independent nation at about the same time that they were getting carried away over the "vast, unlimited resources" of this great land. With the successful revolution, the creation of a new country, and the freedom from monarchy came the thirst for more individual land ownership and ownership of larger and larger areas. "It's my land" became the driving motivation of almost everyone in the young nation. People fought and died over land, and it was not always the Indians who were driven off of property that might prove to be valuable.

It is interesting to note that value did not derive from the land itself, it came from what was on it or under it as a result of an action of nature. It was the preciousness of water, the potential price of a stock of timber, or, later on, the mineral deposits, that determined the worth of the land. It was not until land became a diminishing resource itself because of its location, its sheer existence as a piece of earth, that its value was to become of paramount importance to its owner. In the meantime, society had begun to accept the idea of the commodity aspect that applied to the products of land—that which is to be bought and sold for a profit—as applying to land itself without regard to the resulting effect upon any other nearby property.

The country was in the mood for expansion. Additional people were coming, and there was that vast area to the west that was still uncertain and yet to be made part of the Union. With the coming of the nineteenth century and the completion of the Louisiana Purchase, the wheels were set in motion for acquiring the territory to the Pacific Ocean by conquest or purchase. With the discovery of gold and the Gold Rush, land, again because of what nature had put there, became even more "a precious commodity." The year 1862 saw the passage of the Homestead Act by Congress authorizing the sale of public land to homesteaders in 160-acre tracts, and the concept of speculative ownership of land was carved indelibly in the American mind. In 1864, the Civil War over; the Industrial Revolution was well under way; and the last of the nineteenth century expansion to the west—aided by the transcontinental railroad—saw the last spike driven into the heart of the idea that the community had a right to control how private land was used—or abused—at least for awhile.

Don't Fence Me In!

Two psychological traits developed in those early days had a bearing on land use and ownership, along with the growth of population and technological advances. The first is the basic resistance to and dislike of monarchical control developed prior to the American Revolution. As the country was developing, this was reflected in an aversion on the part of individuals to government restrictions of any sort on private action and private land. The second was added to our collective attitude by the "conquering" of the West. The pioneer spirit that carried men and women across rivers and over mountains to find a place to live and call their own was not compatible with the idea of government having any control over what they did on their land.

Today, as I drive tricky, but modern, paved highways over mountain passes through the Rockies, I never fail to be impressed and awed by the courage of the first people who managed to make it across. They deserve our admiration, and some leftover feeling of that pioneer spirit can be understood. Frequently, in speeches in communities in Colorado, Utah, New Mexico, Texas, and even New Jersey, I have been confronted by someone who is a modern incarnation of these pioneers, and you can almost visualize a Colt 45 on their hips or in their hands as they say, "Buster, nobody's gonna tell me what I can or can't do with my land."

This attitude exists today in all parts of the country, and, while its spirit of independence can be admired, the facts are that the world around us has drastically changed. When the next neighbor was 80 miles away and land and resources vastly exceeded the demand, at least in the short range, it mattered little what you did with or on your property. With dwindling resources, with an ever-decreasing supply of land suitable for development without destroying our agriculture capability, and with combustion engine vehicles spewing more pollutants than the air and atmosphere can absorb without endangering all forms of life, it matters in any community, regardless of how small, what we do with our property.

It Grew Just Like Topsy

Small villages have a way of growing into towns, and towns into cities. Rural development is more concentrated, and few are the truly isolated rural areas that are habitable. Even though not all of us live in a densely developed metropolitan area, we do live in an ever-growing, urban society. Sheer weight of numbers and the increasing demands of land use prevent us from enjoying the privilege—and that it is, not a right—of maintaining the attitude that we can do as we damned well please, whether it be in ownership of land or individual human relations. The philosophy, mistakenly applied or otherwise, that land itself is either a commodity or an individual asset carrying with it the right of unlimited individual profit regardless of the fall-out effect on the cost to others—the community—is a luxury our society can no longer afford.

This is not to say that I am advocating reducing the meaningfulness of individual ownership of property or even taking the potential for fair profit out of that ownership. We can continue to consider land as a commodity as long as we are willing to recognize that both the private owner and the community have a legitimate interest in that commodity. The community's interest comes from two very important aspects. The first is that, although there are some builders and developers with an interest in the effect of what they do on the future, organized society—government—has the responsibility for relating every piece of property into a sensible, coordinated pattern. It is the representatives of the public who are charged with the responsibility of seeing that the development of any parcel of land will contribute to, not detract from, the betterment of the total living organism that is the city, town, or village.

The second, and more important, reason for the recognition of a community interest goes back to statements made earlier about location being the principal factor affecting the value of property. The public sector's actions contribute greatly to the quality of any location by what has been invested in services, cultural facilities, and general community character. It is nonsensical for that public sector to permit itself the delusion that development standards would infringe on individual rights. It is even worse for public officials to do nothing that meets with opposition from those developing land or to set no standards other than those agreeable to the people seeking the greatest profit. The argument usually given by those who take this position is that standards will drive away or stop all of this building that is bringing in economic ratables and increasing our tax base. Hogwash!

Translated into truth, this really says that all the public money supplied by our taxpayers and used to finance capital improvements in our city in the past, all the public money necessary to be spent in the future to correct the problems caused by developer-dictated development, is a long-range subsidy for maximizing the short-term profit for individual landowners. It also says that, even if this unguided growth creates more problems and costs more than it benefits, future generations will have to worry about it and pay for it. The present elected representatives' term of office will be over, and they will get off scot-free. A city that has created value by its public investment is entitled to some value recapture on each parcel of land developed or redeveloped—even if this value recapture is only community-interest-based, well-conceived standards guiding that development.

And Moses Came from the Mount
and Proclaimed . . .

Just prior to writing this, I attended a meeting of an advisory committee formed by an organization known as The Denver Partnership. The Partnership represents downtown businesses and others interested in the development of the center city area. At the moment, Denver is enjoying a fantastic boom in downtown office construction due to the interest in the energy sources in Colorado mentioned earlier. Since 1975, some 14 high-rise structures have been built or are under construction, all in a 20- to 25-block area downtown. At the same time, the Regional Transportation District has a 13-block mall, costing more than $73 million, under construction on 16th Street, Denver's main downtown shopping street. The Partnership is interested in trying to make this mall work and felt that the present zoning of 16th Street is inadequate for protecting light and air and preserving historic buildings and the unique character of the area. Hence, the creation of this advisory committee on a proposed new zoning district.

A suggested draft had been put together that included the creation of a bulk plane (lines drawn at an established angle from the center of the mall and extending over the properties on each side) to control heights and establish setbacks, requirements that new structures have retail uses on the ground floor, and even suggested the introduction of the use of transfer of development rights (explained in a later chapter) to aid in encouraging the preservation of historic structures. Not more than 10 minutes into the meeting to discuss these proposals, a high-ranking official of the Zoning Department informed those present that "the city" would never agree to the bulk plane idea since the developers in the area would not agree to it, and "the city" certainly didn't want to drive away any of those who were bringing in all those "ratables." Never mind what a concrete and steel-walled canyon would do to the mall, or what long-range effect it would have on the character of downtown, or what costs will be to future citizens due to the loss of quality—and perhaps failure—of the mall. (It should also be noted that 85 to 90 percent of the development downtown is being done by Canadian firms with Canadian money.)

This attitude, prevalent in many cities, as lacking in concern for the future as it is, is unfortunate, particularly in this period of cutback in federal aid to cities. This is a time when municipal officials, concerned primarily—if not only—with a four-year term and a tax-payer rebellion, are entirely too willing to take the easy way out and give in to demands made on behalf of any proposal coming down the pike. Unless we can find a way to resist this, the losers will be not only those of us in the general public of the here and now, but also our children and those who come after us. Ownership of land carries with it the obligation of recognizing that development must provide a benefit to both public and private interests, and, while it may retain the right to private profit from its development or sale, it does not carry the right to exploit or be subsidized at public expense.

In the Beginning—There Is Land Use

We should now have begun to understand why the use of land is so vitally important to all of us and why it is time to reexamine our philosophy about land ownership. In my classes, I try to stress that importance by asking my students to try to think of a single basic source for the economy that is not dependent on land use. Usually, some wiseacre will throw in sex, or someone will come up with fishing, but eventually we will agree that the first has to have a place to happen and that even if it takes place on a ship, that ship must have a place to land. It is then but a step to agreeing that the source of all economics in a capitalistic society derives directly from the use of some piece of land. We have now gone so far in this country as to allow the use of land to become one of the major means for individuals to make money and gain power.

Paradoxically, we are now beginning to realize also that land use is what makes our city, our living environment, what it is, and we have seen in the previous discussion how important this is. Just what the role of government can or should be in influencing land use depends upon our philosophy regarding land ownership. We have drifted a long way from that philosophy of the Indians and early settlers, and, without any advocacy of socialism, communism, or autocratic control, I am dedicated to the thesis that it is time for us to move the pendulum swing that followed the opening up of the West back a bit to a better balance between private interest and community interest in land use. For this to be done, we must develop a better understanding of the zoning process and how it can be made a much more effective tool for community good than it has been in the past.

Before getting into the details of that zoning process, I would like to go back to the proposition that I made that land use—the pieces put together—is what makes a community. The question then is How many kinds of land uses are there? Most of us would start to list residential, commercial, industrial, etc. That is not what I mean by the question, however. Rather, the important matter is how many types of causes of land use there are. It is my contention that there are only two, and, if we understand the importance of that, we have gone a long way toward understanding the essential aspects of both good planning and good zoning. By examining any community structure, we find that land use is the result solely of public and private development of land. The public sector locates roads, parks, educational facilities, open space, municipal buildings, and so on. We, as citizens, through our elected representatives, provide the framework that causes and supports the private development of land. We also provide the facilities for governmental administration, education, and whatever cultural activities a given community will have.

This element of community structure is, or at least should be, the easiest with which to work. It takes only a reasonable amount of intelligence and a little foresight for the public sector to plan the lifeline network of a support system and public land use. In most situations, this is far less controversial than planning for and directing private development. A neighborhood lacking in park and recreational facilities can unite easily behind the idea of including these in a master plan and in seeing that funds are available for implementation. Let water pressure drop or water quality deteriorate, and it is not difficult to gain support for taking action to improve the water system. The recognition of this was the reason that early twentieth-century plans in this country were primarily physical depictions of proposals for streets, parks, schools, and other public endeavors. You could prepare a glorious map of many hues suggesting a grandiose scheme of civic improvements with a minimum of opposition as long as they were just proposals and as long as you showed only vague ideas for private land use. Achieving any resemblance between these patterns and private development was another matter.

There Are Two Sides to Every Coin

Again, going back to the idea of changing philosophy regarding land ownership and community interest, as the 1900s moved on, many people came to realize that there was more to community building than that provided by the public. It became increasingly clear that the second source of land-use generation, private investment, far outweighed that of public investment in its impact on the shape of community form. This is where we are today and why it is vital that we change our philosophy regarding private land ownership and to accept equitable, well-founded, well-administered zoning as the means of protecting a community interest—an interest that is ever-growing as more and more of us crowd together in less space, with fewer resources.

This is not to say that I advocate domination by a few over many. I am decidedly opposed to leaving the establishment of development policies, the formulation of land-use controls, and the sole determination of zoning application and administration to a political machine or power structure. Nor does a philosophy that recognizes the land as having the aspect of being a community asset as well as a private "commodity" mean the loss of freedom for a reasonable use or a fair profit for the individual. In fact, I will argue that careful and reasonable application of that philosophy will result in the furtherance of sound values and an increased market potential.

There Is Some Good News—And Some Bad News

Fortunately, in spite of human frailities, a great deal of zoning implementation has been well done and effective. Denver's Colorado neighbor to the west, Boulder, for example, is cited in numerous articles and publications for its commitment to a well-directed growth pattern for the future. The city of Littleton, Colorado, through its well-staffed, efficient Community Development Department and the support of the City Manager and Council, have expertly utilized the zoning process to give meaning to its comprehensive planning. On the other hand, my experiences along the East Coast, in Albuquerque, and now in Denver, suggest that there are places where zoning exists in name because of public demand, but in actuality it functions according to the "water faucet" principle—to be turned on or off at will when necessary for political or special interest purposes. During my time in Albuquerque, in spite of any opposition, if one of the two dozen or so wealthy exploiters who were card-carrying members of the power structure wanted a zone change to allow further exploitation of the city, they got it—to hell with any relationship to community interest or future problems created.

This same situation appears to exist today in the city and county of Denver. It is ironic that Denver has a past in which great pride can be taken because of the leadership and vision applied to its formative years as a city. During the early decades of this century, decisions were made and action taken by leaders like Mayor Robert W. Speer to develop a framework of public facilities, based upon long-range planning by such people as Frederick Law Olmsted, C. Mulford Robinson, and S. R. DeBoer. From these came magnificent parkways, parks and recreation facilities, the Civic Plaza, and outstanding cultural facilities such as the Museum of Natural History in City Park, as well as a sensible pattern of land development and a high degree of civic pride.

Today, Denver has a zoning ordinance that is outmoded and ineffectual. Its language is so confusing and contradictory that, if it had purposefully been written to make it impossible for anyone to understand and interpret, the writers could not have done a better job. A strong opinion exists that the attitude of the administration is that zoning is intended only as a means of allowing what will further its interest and the maintenance of its political power. Anything else can take its chances of qualifying under the confusing ordinances and the personal interpretation of that ordinance by the Zoning Department, a power unto itself. Zoning variances are usually granted upon request, unless there is a sufficient turnout of neighbors voicing objection to make doing

so a political liability. Nor do I place the primary blame for this sad state of affairs entirely on the administration. It reflects what is true in every place that has a similar situation. We are all at fault when we abdicate our responsibility for the present and the future to the professional politicians—often those least qualified to assume that responsibility.

These thoughts emphasize what I have been suggesting and do advocate: a change in philosophy about land ownership back to a recognition of the role of community interest as well as private interest. My position is that to have this work successfully, to maintain that fine balance between equitable application and abuse, requires our individual and collective citizen involvement. It involves people understanding that good zoning doesn't just happen, it is worked for, developed, and nurtured by concerned citizen participation in the process. It comes, or will come, when all of us accept the idea and turn it into a dedicated conviction that true values—community and individual—depend on a carefully conceived, impartially administered communitywide zoning policy. It means being interested not only when it affects us personally in our own back yard. Only in this way can community interest be justified in having something to say about private land use through zoning.

And in the Beginning, God Said . . .

Just when we began to move away from the wholly laisse-faire approach to private ownership is somewhat uncertain. As I indicated in the chapter "The Relationship of Zoning to Planning" in my book *The Citizen's Guide to Planning*, early regulations of private land use were predominantly those based on nuisance regulations prohibiting a use deemed inimical to the public health. This included local ordinances limiting the height of residential structures in order to improve tenement housing safety conditions, eliminating or forbidding objectional uses such as tanneries and slaughterhouses, and relegating other questionable use to specified areas. Mel Scott in his informative book on the historic development of planning, *American City Planning Since 1890*, indicates that Modesto, California, has been credited with creating the first zoning ordinance in 1885. Through ordinance action, the city restricted public laundries and wash houses "to a section situated on the west or 'wrong' side of the tracks."

Commenting further on the situation regarding land-use controls at
the turn of the century and the evolution of early zoning, Scott has
the following to say:

> The use of private land in American cities was almost everywhere con-
> trolled only in the most piecemeal fashion until, on December 28, 1909,
> Los Angeles adopted an ordinance creating seven industrial districts (later
> increased to 27) and two weeks afterward established almost all the rest
> of the city as a residential district. Within the latter, businesses were per-
> mitted, subject to certain conditions, as "residential exceptions."
> Municipal authorities actually ejected a number of small businesses from
> the residential district, but even more drastic was another attempt to pro-
> tect residential amenities. After an outlying area, in which a brick in-
> dustry was situated, had been annexed to the city, another ordinance
> was enacted prohibiting brickyards in residential districts. The owner,
> of course, fought the municipality's effort to put him out of business,
> carrying his case (Hadacheck v. Sebastian) all the way to the United States
> Supreme Court and losing in 1915 in a sweeping decision which stated
> that the city had not acted arbitrarily in the exercise of its police power.
> But the Los Angeles ordinances were less well known to other American
> cities than the zoning regulations of German municipalities. It was these
> laws which planning enthusiasts presently began citing as inspiration for
> cities struggling to find ways to combat the deterioration of residential
> areas and the congestion of population.[1]

After this 1915 decision, zoning ordinances grew in number, as did
the variety of provisions inserted and techniques used. Challenges
abounded, and delivered opinions as to legality varied from state to
state. Just a little more than 20 years before I went to New Jersey as
a young, newly degreed planner, that state's Supreme Court was
rendering adverse decisions on the constitutionality of zoning, primarily
due to a lack of a specific authorization provision in the state constitution and the lack of any state enabling act.

And Then There Was Light!

Two events of great importance to the future of zoning assisted in changing that in New Jersey as well as stabilizing the zoning concept in courts
across the nation. The first of these was the proposal in 1913 by a commission headed by Edward M. Bassett that the entire city of New York
be zoned. Following months of study by a newly created Commission
on Building Districts and Restrictions, an act of the state legislature

1. Mel Scott, *American City Planning Since 1980*, page 76.

amended the city charter to allow the Board of Estimate the authority to zone the city, and, after much opposition on the part of businesses, the first so-called "comprehensive" zoning ordinance was adopted. This term was used as a result of the incorporation—for the first time—of regulations pertaining to the use of land, the height, and the area or bulk of buildings into one ordinance for an entire city. While the ordinance was somewhat confusing and later revealed many shortcomings, it broadened the concept of zoning and encouraged its further acceptance and use in other places.

The second event, the *Hadacheck* case, was even more significant in making zoning a governmental tool for controlling land use and establishing the principle of community interest in the private ownership and development of land. After the 1915 hearing of *Hadacheck* by the U.S. Supreme Court, no real challenge to the constitutionality of the concept came before that body for a number of years. Numerous cases had reached the highest state tribunals, and, by the mid-1920s, some nine states had favorable rulings on the question as it pertained to municipalities in their jurisdiction. Three states, including New Jersey, continued to receive adverse legal decisions. In short, the future of zoning and the legality of its use as a part of the police power of government was unclear and uncertain, although 400 to 500 local zoning ordinances were in existence.

The village of Euclid, Ohio, had zoned for residential use only a portion of its area along a main arterial highway adjacent to commercial and industrial land within neighboring Cleveland's city limits. The Ambler Realty Company owned land within this residential zone and sought permission to use it for commercial and industrial purposes. When the village held firm in its zoning and denied the request for change, Ambler filed suit, claiming that such action resulted in a loss of value to their land and was in effect a taking of property without compensation.

The U.S. District Court in Ohio agreed with Ambler and issued an injunction against the enforcement of the ordinance, holding that the village's action was a violation of the Fourteenth Amendment of the Constitution of the United States. Undaunted, the village carried its case to the U.S. Supreme Court, which agreed to hear it. Following the last minute appearance of a brilliant Cincinnati attorney, Alfred Bettman, in an amicus curiae role on behalf of the National Conference of City Planning and other groups (an occurrence permitted only by Chief Justice Taft agreeing to allow the case to be reopened) the landmark decision sustaining the constitutionality of zoning under the federal Constitution was rendered on November 22, 1926 (*Village of Euclid v. Ambler Realty Co.*, 272 U.S. 375, 47 Sup. St. 114, 71 L.Ed. 303). In a carefully worded opinion, Justice Sutherland left no doubt as to the right of the village to utilize the police power embodied in zoning to determine its own desired land-use pattern. A portion of that opinion, still the foundation of the legal basis for zoning after more than 50 years, is germane to my contentions regarding community interest in the private use of land. It reads as follows:

> Point is raised by the appellees that the village of Euclid was a mere suburb of Cleveland, and that the industrial development of the latter had extended to the village, and that in the obvious course of things would soon absorb the entire area for industrial enterprise, and that the effect of the ordinance was to divert such natural development or expansion elsewhere, to the consequent loss of increased values to the owners of land within the village. But this village, though physically a suburb of Cleveland, is a separate municipality, with powers of its own and authority to govern itself as it sees fit within the organic laws of its creation and the state and federal constitutions. The will of its people determines, not that industrial development shall cease at its boundaries, but that such development shall proceed between fixed lines. If therefore it is proper exercise of the police power to regulate industrial establishments to localities separated from residential sections, it is not easy to find sufficient reason for denying the power because its effect would be to divert an industrial flow from a course which would result in injury to the residential public to another course where such injury would be obviated. This should not exclude the possibility of cases where the general interest so far outweighs the interest of the municipality that the latter should not be allowed to stand in its way.

Although pointing out that broader regional considerations cannot be overlooked, the Court established the right of a municipality to regulate development within its boundaries, to make determinations affecting private land based upon a public interest, and to use its inherent governmental police power in so doing. Today, with a far more complex society, potential shortages of resources, air pollution, overextended public services, and the rapid dimunition of our most precious *asset*—land—we need more than ever to recognize the wisdom of the logic in 1926 of our highest court and lay to rest, once and for all, the fable of the exploiters about land being a "precious commodity."

3

Fundamental Principles of Zoning

In order to understand zoning as a governmental process, it is first necessary to refresh our memories on some of the things taught us in civics classes, before such subjects became passe in elementary education. The government of the U.S. is based on a constitution that vests the sovereign power of governing in a federation of states. All power and authority, in theory, flows from these states. The federal government is given the right to do anything not expressly denied it by the states. The framers of the Constitution saw the action of the government in Washington as being limited to that which is necessary to hold the federation together and of national consequence, such as defense. Municipalities—counties, cities, towns, villages—on the other hand, are creatures of the states totally. They do not exist without state creation and approval and can do nothing for which the authority has not been provided by the state. The granting of that authority by any state legislature is by approval of a home-rule charter or the passage of an enabling act specifying just what local government can (or cannot) do.

The Lord Giveth and the Lord Taketh Away

Running through all this is the legal concept that government holds two powers of vital importance to you and me, especially to our land ownership. The first of these is the power of eminent domain. Through this authority, government has the ability to acquire private land for a legitimate public purpose as long as "just" compensation is paid to the private owner. If we do not want to sell our land and are not willing to negotiate, government, under the law of eminent domain, has the authority of "condemnation" and can then take the property after paying the price set by a condemnation court. This is an important aspect of governmental power with relation to the public sector's portion of community building. It is used to acquire land for roads, parks, public buildings, rights of way for public service lines, etc. The effectuation of proposals for public facilities on a master plan could not be carried out in most cases without the power of eminent domain. Unfortunately, in my opinion, we have permitted this power to be expanded almost to the point of abuse by extending it to quasi-governmental agencies such as authorities and special districts and to quasi-public agencies such as utilities.

A full discussion of eminent domain, its use and misuse, is not germane to the focus of this book. Rather we should turn to the second of the inherent powers of government, that of police power. In discussing this with my classes, I invariably tell them that they must understand that this means more than the ability of a government to put a uniform, a badge, and a gun on a person and allow that person to arrest someone for a law violation. Police power is the broadest authority granted to government in this country, and it affects our lives in a great variety of ways. It is the power of government to restrict and regulate all private action for the common good. It is the basic authority for all codes and ordinances enacted by local government. Without the theory of police power, there could be no traffic control, animal regulations, health codes, parking restrictions, building standards, etc., enacted into laws by government.

Any such enactment, regardless of whether it restricts and regulates private personal action or private use of land, need only to be founded on the principle that it is in the best interest of the public health, safety, and general welfare. As distinct from eminent domain, the resulting loss of what we may consider to be a freedom of choice or action does not require that we be compensated in any way. All such regulation may be challenged in courts, but, in most state constitutions, a specific provision instructs judges to favor local units of government with the presumption of having acted properly. The burden of proof is on the challenger, and the contested action only has to stand the test of being reasonable and in the best interest of the public.

It is under the police power that we find the basis for the enactment of all regulations relating to guiding the development of private land. This includes building codes, plumbing codes, subdivision controls, land development ordinances, and zoning. As was indicated earlier, zoning in its direct effect on each individual owning land has received the most attention, is almost always controversial, and has been the subject of most court challenges. In the majority of cases, the question raised, now that the Supreme Court has found the concept to be constitutional, is over the legal question of whether a specific zoning action is an undue denial of property rights or, as is so often charged, "the taking of property without just compensation." A good attorney taking the case of someone challenging zoning action will usually include a scattergun blast of charges in the complaint filed just to be sure of not missing any opportunity. This will include phrases such as the action violates the state and federal constitution (especially the Fourteenth Amendment), is a taking of property without due process, is a denial of right, is unreasonable, arbitrary, capricious, and confiscatory. Our lawyer friends are good at throwing around these kinds of things, as well as writing laws and ordinances in language not easily understood by others.

When God Created the World— First Came the Plan

A well-prepared municipality can usually defend its zoning successfully provided it has acted in a reasonable fashion. Underlying any good defense is the assumption that the action was taken in accordance with its comprehensive planning and is founded on and justified by careful planning studies. The question of which came first—planning or zoning—used to be as prevalent as the chicken or the egg question. This is no longer so. Today, any thinking community that doesn't have zoning first undertakes the development of a master plan and then bases its zoning on the principles and objectives of that plan. Likewise, any progressive community with zoning makes certain that there is such a plan supporting it and that any zoning changes are founded on conditions set forth and substantiated by a continuing planning process. This is not just good sense; it is fast becoming a requisite of judges hearing zoning cases in sustaining municipal zoning action. Having zoning coordinated with a good planning base is the best way possible to overcome any charge of being arbitrary and unreasonable—the most serious test zoning must withstand.

Planning provides the goals and objectives for community direction, the reason for the taking of public action to assure that community betterment will be the result of both public and private endeavors. Without legal effectuation tools, planning would accomplish little. The best plan in the world is not going to change any jurisdiction without the follow-up of codes and ordinances based on those objectives of the plan that affect private development, combined with a firm policy on the part of elected officials to see that the proposals of the plan are carried forward. Zoning is the primary implementing tool of the planning process as it relates to private land and development. Just as planning should be comprehensive and strive to fit together the individual pieces of development into a coordinated total picture, so should zoning.

Planning is meaningless without a "planning attitude" on the part of officials and the means to carry it out. Similarly, zoning is not a panacea for curing all local ills or preventing future problems by itself. Neither one will be effective without the other. Zoning is but one of the legal tools necessary for any area to make planning worthwhile. The total package in the local government's arsenal includes carefully thought-out, long-range comprehensive planning, a clearly written zoning ordinance, a subdivision control ordinance, and a five- or six-year projected capital improvements program. Only by understanding the value of all of these and making certain that each relates to the other can we expect to see constructive results.

A Good Place to Start Is with a Definition

Having talked about the authority of government to regulate private land use through zoning and how it should fit into the planning function, we turn next to the meaning of zoning and what it can and cannot do. Many people know the word zoning but have never examined a zoning ordinance or what is in it and just what it means, or should mean, to guiding growth and development. As usual, I believe that you should start a learning process with a good definition. The best one I have found is an old one that I used in the original edition of this book and in the section on zoning in *The Citizen's Guide to Planning*. Since the principles of good zoning have continued to be the same over the years, and I have not found a better definition of the zoning process, here it is again. It was originally in a book called *Local Planning Administration* and reads as follows:

> Zoning consists of dividing the community into districts or zones and regulating within such districts the use of land and the use, heights, and area of buildings for the purpose of conserving and promoting the health, safety, morals, convenience, and general welfare of the people of the com-

munity. Zoning is the instrument for giving effect to that part of the comprehensive city plan or master plan which is concerned with the private uses of and the private developments on, privately owned land— as distinguished from that part which is concerned with public uses and facilities. The zoning map or zoning plan along with the regulations pertaining thereto are thus a part of the master plan—in essence the comprehensive land-use plan of the community—while the enactment of the zoning ordinance and its administration are the legislative and administrative acts or processes for giving effect to or carrying out this part of the comprehensive plan.[2]

This serves to emphasize what I have said in the first two chapters, as well as beginning to explain the idea of how zoning functions. The concept of there being several districts, with differing regulations and different uses allowed and regulated, again stresses the importance of having a good factual base. That base should come from a comprehensive plan. If we know that we live in a residential district where only single-family homes are permitted and that other areas have apartments, businesses, and industries, we begin to get a clearer concept of zoning districts. These districts and their regulations, while seeking to improve standards of development and encourage harmonious compatibility of uses, must relate to the predominance of uses already in existence at the time of the adoption of the ordinance. This is why rural areas and smaller towns should establish planning standards and adopt zoning regulations while there is the opportunity to determine the pattern of development in advance of it occurring. In older communities and large cities, zoning can still accomplish a great deal, but it is much more difficult to change development patterns and correct mistakes of the past.

While private landowners resist zoning and shout about it infringing on their rights, the jurists who hear zoning cases, as illustrated by the extract from Justice Sutherland's opinion in the *Euclid* case, have long recognized how essential zoning is to collective society in any form. One of the best statements on this was made several years ago by a former justice of the New Jersey Supreme Court when he said:

Zoning is the modern response to the individual and collective needs of community life, the living together of unrelated, interdependent people, a society growing more complex as it expands. Although a concept of comparatively recent origin, zoning has its roots in basic societal necessities and pressures that from the very beginning of social life demand the accommodations of individual interests to the common good and

2. J. H. Beuscher and others, *Local Planning Administration* (3rd ed.), edited by Mary McLean (Chicago: The International City Managers' Association, 1959), page 403.

welfare, for the alleviation of the intricacies and complications of living
under the same environment by the dictates of natural law by the power
of natural law that cannot be other than it is, the primary duty of man
to his neighbors to contribute to the general well-being for the relief of
compulsions and restraints of man-made circumstances.[3]

Justice Heher has laid the foundation of the principle of "the accommodations of individual interests to the common good and welfare"
far better than I, and in language understood and supported by jurists
all across the country. What he was saying is that the fundamental
precept behind zoning is that it has become necessary in our increasingly
complex society for the balance of the scale weighing private rights pertaining to land use on the one side and community interest on the other
if we are to begin to shift in favor of the latter. During his lifetime,
Justice Heher wrote many of the farsighted and progressive zoning
opinions rendered by the New Jersey Supreme Court, all of which
reflected the soundness of this principle—with but one exception.

You Can't Win Them All

That one exception was in an opinion he wrote, unanimously supported
by the other justices on the court, declaring a zoning ordinance prepared
by my planning consulting firm to be unconstitutional. As early as 25
years ago, some of us in planning were urging our client communities
to abandon rigid, traditional zoning classifications and instead reduce
the number of zones or districts but, based upon an analysis of their
impact, allow certain more intense uses in specified areas. In 1958, I
recommended just such an ordinance to Chesterfield Township, a
semirural farming community in New Jersey. There was to be only one
zone—residential/agricultural—and all other uses were to be subjected
to submittal of a special application, public discussion and hearing, and
an analysis of their impact on the immediate neighborhood, the
surrounding area, and the entire community. The Chesterfield officials,
including their 82-year-old township attorney, liked the idea and
adopted the ordinance. Unfortunately, one landowner who didn't like
the prospect of zoning took the action to court. Following a favorable
opinion supporting the municipality from the lower court, the New
Jersey Supreme Court by-passed the appellate court and certified the

---

3. From an address before the 1956 Convention of the New Jersey League of Municipalities
   by the Honorable Harry Heher, then Associate Justice of the New Jersey Supreme Court.

case for their hearing. From this came Justice Heher's "bad" opinion.

The above is said somewhat facetiously, since, at the time, the provisions of the ordinance were radically innovative with little established legal precedent for their support. Mentioning it here does serve to point out that the fundamentals of zoning do change and how much they have changed over the intervening years. The underlying principles of that ordinance are the basis today of such new techniques as planned unit development (PUD), performance zoning, and growth management plans, all of which have been and are being sanctioned by courts in many states. I am happy to report that before Justice Heher retired he, too, had written several opinions sustaining that concept.

My, How That Kid Has Grown

Over the more than 60 years of zoning's existence, there have been numerous changes in the techniques as well as in basic thinking about its fundamental purpose. From the negative, nuisance regulation of the early ordinances, zoning has grown into a vital and positive tool for guiding community development. It is recognized as an adjunct to comprehensive community planning—meaning that zoning is related to a careful comprehensive consideration of all development problems within the municipality. Zoning, therefore, has become an arm of planning and a tool for carrying out plans for the future growth and development of the community. This is a far cry from its original use.

No longer among those who understand zoning do we find much negative thinking regarding its potential. Instead, it is readily accepted by those who adopt ordinances and those who interpret them that zoning can do more than simply prevent something. It can help to implement the development policy of the community. A zoning ordinance that simply locks in place the mistakes of the past is inadequate. A zoning ordinance that looks to the future development is desirable. Unless we do progress with new and positive techniques, we will not continue to develop zoning into a more effective tool for guiding our communities' growth.

In understanding the fundamentals of zoning we cannot, however, underestimate or fail to understand the vast amount of negativism that still exists in the minds of many people about it. Most of this is based upon the fixed notion, contrary to the idea of there being a vested community interest in private development, that any zoning takes away the "inalienable rights" that go with land ownership. The interesting thing is that well-founded, well-administered zoning provides a right that we as individuals otherwise would not have—the right of protection of our investment in our property and in our community. Nowhere has this been stated better than in a speech in 1953 by another jurist, New Jersey Superior Court Judge Donald M. Waesche, when he said:

> Lawful restraints upon the conduct or acts of persons are not intended as infringements upon liberty, but instead they are intended as a protection of freedom, and to the quiet and peaceful enjoyment of property. Such restraints are in the common interest and promote the general welfare. Zoning ordinances, therefore, provide the only means by which the right to the full enjoyment of property use can be protected against the prejudicial influence of other uses which do not constitute a nuisance. Consequently, valid zoning gives to a property owner a right which did not exist before, that is, the right to prevent a use which is forbidden by the ordinance. In other words, valid zoning ordinances create valuable property rights that did not exist prior to their adoption.

Thus, while the exercise of the police power of government in any form may restrict personal exploitation, it is the only way in which this right of self-protection can be made legally available to the individual. The key word in the quotation above is "valid." Zoning is only valid if it is based upon carefully developed principles and objectives of planning, has involved individuals acting collectively and has their support, and is administered impartially and equitably. Our refusal or unwillingness to accept a responsibility for this involvement leads to zoning abuse and the success of those who want to destroy its effectiveness or who, because of emotional opposition, want to prevent it from happening or get rid of it where it exists.

This opposition comes in two forms. The first is the most dangerous. It comes from those whose only interest is a self-interest that is frequently not obvious and is always veiled by expressing high-sounding motivations. Included among those fitting this category are the business people who see all growth only as representing future buyers of automobiles, appliances, and furniture and zoning as a threat to this potential new market. This motivation is never expressed, however, but rather the public arguments presented are idealistic or highly emotional. Their pitch usually is that this is just more government, it will prevent the creation of new jobs for the poor unemployed, and that old, tired bromide—it is un-American. Joining in these arguments, but with slightly different veiled self-interests, will be a small cadre of short-sighted representatives of the real estate fraternity, the construction industry, the professions, and landowners who bought land cheap at a tax sale and have held on, waiting for the right time to get the most out of it. Underlying all this, but never expressed, is the same theme of, "We don't care what the problems are or what uncontrolled growth will cost the rest of you and the community, we want to be sure we get ours." As such people in most cases are influential in the political arena and part of the power structure of the community, this type of opposition is hard to fight. To do so successfully means getting others with like interests and in similar power positions who are not so myopic and self-centered involved in supportive roles. The support of neighborhood organizations and neighborhood leaders also is an effective way to counteract the influence of submerged self-interest.

Ignorance, in This Case, Is Not Bliss

The other type of opposition, far more numerous and far more effective unless overcome, is that from a generally uninformed or misinformed citizenry—the everyday voter and taxpayer. They know little about zoning and don't understand what they do know. Opinions they already may have frequently are based upon rumors, some of which were started by those falling in the classification of the first type of opposition mentioned above. Fortunately, the bulk of those in the lack of knowledge group are somewhat open-minded and willing to learn, or if they have formed an opinion, that opinion can be changed by well-presented facts. I still have enough faith in the general public to believe that there are only a few who are like one of the two women depicted in a cartoon as part of the audience listening to a speaker. In the caption she was quoted as saying to the other woman, "I wish she wouldn't confuse me with the facts, my mind is all made up."

Regardless of whether it is a question of getting that first zoning ordinance, amending or strengthening an old one, or making certain that good administration of an existing ordinance takes place, there will be opposition. Whether we know anything about it or not, zoning is too personal, too much out in the forefront of governmental regulations for there not to be. In view of this, before going on with the technical details involved in a zoning ordinance, I think it well-advised to look further at some of the standard and well-worn objections into which municipal officials and good zoning advocates may run. Ten stances of opposition of the sort most commonly encountered, especially at public hearings, and some statements with which to counter these are presented for your consideration

Zoning is unconstitutional   The most frequently stated opposition is that zoning is illegal and unconstitutional. This is still advanced as an argument despite the fact that zoning has been in effect in this country as a legal exercise of governmental authority for more than 60 years. During this time, the courts and jurists of every state have found zoning constitutional. The U.S. Supreme Court has upheld zoning as an appropriate function of municipal government. At the present time, over 10,000 municipalities in the nation have adopted zoning, and many more are doing so with each passing day.

It is a well-established fact that zoning, if properly done, is legal and constitutional. We pride ourselves in this country on the fact that the Constitution of the United States is a flexible and changeable document that can adjust to meet social needs. And the needs of our country have changed. With the population explosion and land becoming increasingly scarce, the necessity of zoning to protect the public welfare is unquestionable. Not only have the courts recognized this in upholding the constitutionality of zoning, but any thinking citizen can readily see that, as people are crowded together in less and less space, there is the necessity for some kind of direction and regulation in order for each one to be assured of fair treatment and protection from any abuse by neighbors.

Zoning is undemocratic   This objection takes many forms, and its effectiveness depends largely upon the oratorical skill of the person presenting the argument. "Undemocratic" is a term that is very broad and can be used in a variety of ways to attempt to substantiate arguments against zoning. When it is fully examined, however, it seems impossible for anyone to argue that zoning is undemocratic. In fact, it is one of the most democratic processes that we have available to us as citizens today. The zoning ordinance, from its very inception, brings into play the idea of citizen interest. It is one of the few ordinances adopted by a municipality that must originate by either a zoning commission or a planning commission comprised of citizens, some of whom do not hold elective office. It must be subjected to constant exposure to public ideas and desires. Further, it must be subjected to a public hearing, at which time every party and interest is afforded an opportunity to be heard. There is a constant give-and-take in the evolution of a zoning ordinance.

Frequently this opposition can be refuted by simply asking the questioner to explain how an ordinance can possibly be undemocratic when it is adopted in a democratic manner, its basic purpose is to establish standards so that each person will know in advance just what he or she can and cannot do, and it assures the maximum amount of protection for private property and its investment.

We must protect the "little people"   It harms the little people—the young folk, the veteran. This might be termed the flag-waving argument which would have it that, if this zoning ordinance is adopted, the young people who cannot afford expensive mansions will have no chance for a small lot and a little house. If this does not carry the evening, the flag is hoisted still higher with the reference to the veteran who fought in Vietnam (or in some other notable conflict) for the freedom of this country and who is not going to permit these dictatorial measures to deprive him of the freedom for which he fought.

Zoning is probably the greatest protection of the little folk—the young people and the veteran—that can be provided by government today. Let us suppose, for example, that there is such a thing as the little person who cannot afford to locate unless he or she is going to be able to do so on a small lot and in a relatively small home. What will happen to their investment—a much more important factor to them than it is to someone in better economic condition—if they have no protection as to what will happen on the property next door? Suppose, for example, that these so-called little people borrow to the hilt in order to afford their place. Then suppose they wake up some morning to find a junkyard or some other type of objectionable land use suddenly being located next door or directly across the street. What happens to their investment? The answer is obvious: their investment could be wiped out. The same argument applies in connection with the young people.

As far as the veteran is concerned, if he fought for this country, he was fighting for the right of all of us to determine how we will be governed and to adopt rules and regulations under which we will all agree to live. This is exactly what zoning does, and the veteran who is sincerely interested in his country can readily understand this.

Zoning takes away independence   This variation is worthy of separate mention because the objectors will contend that certain privileges and independence of judgment will be denied the individual.

In point of fact, zoning does limit privileges and independence, but the privileges and independence that are limited are those of being able to do as you please without regard to the effect on the rest of the society.

No regulation can be adopted as a part of the police power without limiting and restricting privileges and independence. When the municipality adopts an ordinance requiring that dogs be licensed and kept on your own property, it is limiting your privileges and independence, particularly if you consider that you have the right to let your dog roam indiscriminately. When a community enacts traffic regulations and locates stop lights and stop signs, some people may feel that this limits privilege and independence. Indeed it does, and zoning is exactly the same sort of thing. It is a measure adopted to protect the public health and safety, and it will, if properly done, assure the maximum privilege and independence. The lack of zoning gives the unconscionable and immoral individual a special right that is not available to the average citizen who exercises restraint on personal actions. If there is any serious restriction of privileges and independence through zoning, it is upon that person whose private actions would be detrimental to the general welfare of the community as a whole.

Other codes and ordinances do the same thing   Some people insist that a building code or a health code can accomplish all desirable features of zoning, without the limitation and restriction on private property rights. It is obvious that this is not the case. A building code deals with the regulation of construction and the quality of materials going into structures. It does not direct the development of land or control the use of land. The health ordinance relates to the protection of public health and is primarily directed toward the prevention and correction of nuisances. In this case, little action can be taken until after a nuisance has occurred. It is then too late as far as zoning is concerned. Once a use or a particular structure has been placed on the land, it acquires a vested right and cannot be torn down or corrected.

While building codes, sanitary codes, plumbing codes, and housing codes serve a definite beneficial purpose to a municipality, they cannot replace the zoning ordinance, nor can they accomplish what zoning can. But far too many municipalities do labor under the illusion that they can prevent undesirable development without zoning.

One incident in my experience occurred in a rural municipality where a number of people were successful in opposing the adoption of a needed ordinance on the basis of this particular "code" argument. Before many months had elapsed, the municipality was faced with the prospect of having a rather large junkyard located in it. In spite of an elaborate search of all of the codes and ordinances in effect, no way could be found to prevent this detrimental and economically depressing use from occurring, and the community is stuck with it to this day.

The only purpose is to keep people out   A stirring plea is frequently made that zoning will be utilized simply to stop development and to keep out people who will have children and thus add to the tax burden of the municipality for education. While it is true that some municipalities have unreasonably sought to utilize the zoning provisions to prevent development and keep rural communities for themselves only, this is the exception rather than the rule.

Where it does occur, a well-drawn complaint taken to the court can readily set aside such unreasonable and arbitrary action. On the other hand, zoning is a great and good friend of the children of a municipality, just as it has been indicated that it is a friend of the so-called little person. We have a moral responsibility to our children to assure them that the communities we build will be the best-organized, most efficient, and most economically sound communities possible.

Zoning leads to more politics   It is argued that zoning leads to bigger government and more politics, but there is really very little need to enlarge governmental functions. When there is a land-use regulatory ordinance, the politics of special privileges and favors prosper less than in a community where such a measure has not been adopted.

Zoning has built into its process the protection of public disclosure and public expression, which also helps to prevent political maneuvering and the build-up of government bureaucracies. In communities where zoning is properly used and where it functions correctly, it assures the average citizen of the maximum amount of protection against political favoritism and governmental boondoggling.

It will change our countryside   This argument is found most frequently in rural communities where growth has not yet been felt in the same measure as it has in more built-up areas. When zoning is considered, some of the misinformed then put forward the argument that the adoption of the ordinance will open the floodgates and permit all types of development to come in and will, in fact, encourage it to do so. But, if the floodgates were to be unloosed and development did come pouring in, without zoning there would be absolutely nothing to assure that it would be done properly.

In an urbanizing countryside, our land will change whether we like it or not. With the population growth we are facing, we are bound to have development. More and more areas will be taken over by urbanized growth. It has been estimated that, in a very short period of time, 85 percent of the total population of this country will be located in an urbanized area. It is certainly true that, even where growth is less rapid than it is now on the eastern and western seaboards, no community is static; no community can remain long without some kind of change. Therefore, our countryside is definitely going to be changed by any development. The only way we can assure ourselves that this growth will be according to a pattern that makes sense for all of us is through zoning.

We don't understand it   Some opponents of zoning say, "We don't understand it, and we do not have enough information about it." This may be a perfectly honest statement of fact. It is always possible that communication between the drafters of a zoning ordinance and the general public may have broken down. If this is the case, some public education and information program is suggested. It could, however, be opposition of a more invidious sort. A person, or persons, opposed to the ordinance for selfish reasons may be deliberately playing on a normal anxiety about something new by planting rumors designed to turn that anxiety into fear.

I once witnessed a hearing where an audience of 230 people was absolutely convinced by a prevailing rumor that, if the proposed zoning ordinance were to be adopted, they would not be able to change the color of their houses without obtaining a permit from the municipal building. The rumor mill is a favorite tool of both the malcontent and the self-seeker. If, prior to a hearing, there are rumors being circulated, it would be a good thing to track them down as quickly as possible. Also plan to have some recognized and informed leaders ready to speak in favor of the ordinance.

Zoning is the cause of the high cost of housing   This is the "hot" item in the antizoning arsenal these days. There is a great concern about the effect of inflation on the rising cost of everything, especially housing. One of the objectives of most federal programs over the past 40 or so years has been to provide decent, affordable housing for as many of our people as possible. At the time of this writing, the phrase "affordable housing" is bandied about by just about everyone while the *average* price of a single-family home is rapidly approaching $80,000. The idea of finding a way to reduce the price of housing to the point where more people can afford their "dream" home is an admirable one, but finding a way to bring this about is difficult and, at the moment, seemingly impossible. In any inflationary time, the reduction of those things contributing to higher costs is a complex problem. There are many factors involved, not the least of which is greed.

In the urgency to find a scapegoat to blame for the increasing prices of dwelling units and the decreasing amount of affordable housing, the exploiters have seized this golden opportunity to accomplish two things that would be to their advantage. They see this time as an excellent opportunity to destroy sensible regulations relating to housing quality and to direct attention away from themselves as contributing in any way to inflated prices. The hue and cry of the speculators and entrepreneurs is now that the real culprits are local governments and their regulations pertaining to land and building development—especially zoning. This has an emotionally popular, but extremely dangerous, appeal. It provides the opportunity for all zoning haters to get together and mount an attack that can be formidable.

Reasonable thought of any duration immediately shows the fallacy of placing the blame on local standards and regulatory measures. There are cases where outmoded or overly restrictive codes and ordinances with built-in time delays make a contribution to costs. However, it is sheer idiocy to single out the local control system in a broad shotgun approach and attempt to make it primarily responsible for rising housing costs or to propose its elimination as being the best way to reduce these costs. These very regulations came about because past experience has shown that, left to their own devices, a great part of the building and construction industry would cut every corner of quality they could find and leave the picking up of the pieces and the cost of doing so to the buyer of housing and the general public. Even under the present standards, few major private housing developments occur without it being necessary for them to be subsidized from public funds in providing improvements to the service and utility infrastructure.

Let's assume that we did away with such things as zoning and subdivision controls or drastically reduced their requirements. This might mean that the initial cost of housing could be lessened slightly to the purchaser of a new home. It would also mean the possibility of unpaved or poorly paved streets, inadequate drainage, little, if any, landscaping, poor traffic circulation, no open space, and little attention paid to grouping of units and overall design. Who pays for correcting any mistakes made? The homeowner, who pays more than it would have cost originally to meet adequate standards—costs that could have been placed in a long-term mortgage—and who is assisted by you and me as the taxpaying public. Of course, we may be able to pass these costs on to future generations so we don't have to worry about it, that is, if we don't give a damn about future generations.

Looking at it another way, we can draw an analogy to planning that dream house. We put in all the things we want: basement, fireplace, lots of closets, den, family room, and a spiffy kitchen. Eagerly we call in our builder and ask for a price estimate. After going over it, the builder quotes us a price $20,000 more than we expected. Just like we are being told that we can save a lot of money by cutting out the standards of quality in community development, we are told that if we cut out a few frills in our house plans perhaps the price could be reduced. We decide to be austere and drastic. We cut out the fireplace, the den, several closets, and tone the snazzy kitchen way down—all things that made it a quality home. The builder does a quick refiguring and congratulates us; we have reduced the price, or, as we are told, we have *saved* $2,500. We also have given up things that would have made it a lasting, worthwhile investment. So it is with municipal regulations affecting land development.

One last kicker. If you hear the argument that zoning and land development controls should be done away with to reduce housing costs, just say that this might be worth considering provided all profits on any building construction are legally limited to no more than 10 percent. This will place an effective damper on the conversation.

The Best Defense Is a Good Offense

These are but a few of the arguments that will be encountered when a new zoning ordinance is being considered and, in many cases, even when good administration of an existing ordinance is practiced or a major amendment strengthening it is proposed. All possible objections cannot be listed, but it is useful to examine these, the most common and prevalent ones here, so that those interested in good zoning or making zoning work better could anticipate some of the thinking that will need to be combatted. Over the past 30 years, I have run into all of these, some cleverly and intelligently presented and some simply emotionally and militantly put forth. In 95 percent of these cases, it has been easy to identify the prime motivation of self-interest. I also have found that it doesn't pay to try to hang a tag of self-interest on those objecting in the hope that public disclosure will either silence them or win others over. Frequently, this will work the other way in generating sympathy or solidifying a coalition of those with like interest and motivation. It is far better to have as many people as possible involved who previously have been indoctrinated in the fundamental principles of zoning and who understand its value and necessity for the future.

Zoning is, and will continue to be, a controversial matter. Any legislative act that must impose restrictions on private action in order to be effective for the common good is going to be. Especially is this so with one that has such direct effect upon economics and the profit potential of an individual. On the other side of the coin, we have seen that anyone interested in seeing a community develop in accord with good planning principles and their own investment in the composite picture will support what is necessary to achieve those results. Such a person will see through these arguments put forth against zoning, be able to recognize hidden motivations where they exist, and, with missionary zeal, convey to others the fundamental principles of valid zoning. Like everything else in our political system, if enough of us believe strongly in something and collectively support it, it will happen.

4

The Process of Developing
Zoning Regulations

In talking about the process of developing or improving zoning regulations, it is necessary for a full understanding to go back to the beginning. We have noted that all counties, cities, towns, and villages (any local governments) are creatures of the state. Of equal importance is remembering that the ability to utilize the fundamental police power of government and enact a zoning ordinance must be passed on to municipal and county governments by the state. It follows, therefore, that the first step in this process is the passage of an act by the state legislature enabling municipalities under its jurisdiction to prepare and adopt zoning ordinances. This is referred to as the state's zoning enabling act, and what it says is of utmost importance to the success and effectiveness of local zoning.

Even a Good Foundation Needs
to Be Checked Now and Then

One of the major difficulties in the past has been the failure of state legislatures to revise and update statutes pertaining to zoning as conditions change. In Chapter 2, it was pointed out that the first acceptance of a form of zoning as a tool to regulate land use began in the early part of this century, grew after the enactment of the comprehensive zoning ordinance adopted by New York City, and mushroomed after the decision in the *Euclid* case. Another event contributing to the growth of the popularity of zoning occurred between 1921 and 1924. For a description of this and its importance, we turn again to *American City Planning Since 1890*:

> In 1921, Herbert Hoover, who could have been Harding's Secretary
> of the Interior but chose instead to be his Secretary of Commerce, became

so impressed with the importance of zoning that he appointed a special advisory committee to draft a model or standard state zoning enabling act under which municipalities could adopt zoning regulations. To the committee he named as chairman Edward M. Bassett, whom many called the father of zoning. Serving with him were Irving B. Hiett, former president of the American Association of Real Estate Boards, and such well-known members of the National City Planning Institute as Frederick Law Olmsted, Nelson P. Lewis, J. Horace McFarland, Lawrence Veiller, Morris Knowles, and John Ihlder.

Within a year the committee had a preliminary draft of its proposed standard act ready to circulate in mimeographed form; and by February, 1924, the Government Printing Office was issuing a final version with a foreword by Hoover. "The discovery that it is practical by city zoning to carry out reasonably neighborly agreements as to the use of land has made an almost instant appeal to the American people," the Secretary wrote.[4] He noted that, when his advisory committee began its labors in September, 1921, only 48 cities and towns, with fewer than 11,000,000 inhabitants, had adopted zoning ordinances. By the end of 1923, he was happy to report, zoning was in effect in 218 municipalities, with more than 22,000,000 residents, and new zones were being added to the list each month.[5] Most satisfactory of all, within a year of the issuance of the final draft of the standard act, 11 states had passed enabling legislation modeled either wholly or partly after it, and four other states were considering similar acts.

The danger of attempting zoning without the sanction of the state legislature was nowhere better illustrated than in St. Louis. In 1918 that city was the second in the nation to adopt a comprehensive zoning ordinance, but it did so under a city charter provision giving the board of aldermen authority "to prescribe limits within which business, occupations, and practices liable to be nuisances or detrimental to the . . . general welfare . . . may lawfully be established," rather than under a specific grant of power from the state legislature.[6] Five years later the Missouri Supreme Court, in a five-to-four decision, invalidated the ordinance because the city had used the police power to zone without having the proper authorization from the legislature. The overthrow of the ordinance was followed by a two-year hiatus in zoning in which approximately $10,000,000 was spent for buildings whose uses violated the districts established by the original ordinance. The large, older residential areas west of Grand Avenue were invaded by apartment houses; older residents fled; renters moved in who did not maintain the properties well; and entire neighborhoods deteriorated.[7]

As Scott has pointed out, the guideline model that states could use in setting parameters, to follow if they so chose, was important from

4. Herbert Hoover, "Foreword," U.S. Department of Commerce, Advisory Committee on Zoning, A Standard State Zoning Enabling Act (Washington, 1924), p. iv.

5. Ibid.

6. Quoted by Edward M. Bassett, "Present Attitude of the Courts Toward Zoning," Proceedings of Fifteenth National Conference on City Planning, pp. 128-129.

7. Scott, American City Planning Since 1890, pp. 193-194.

two aspects. It first encouraged additional state enabling action and thus an increase in local zoning and, second, provided a prototype for states wishing to avoid the unfortunate situation in which St. Louis found itself. As is the case in most suggested models, there also is a negative side of the coin. No model has ever been prepared that can fit perfectly the particular and peculiar situations of each and every state. Using the suggestions for general guidance and direction, the unique problems and needs of disparate areas must be worked into the final legislation by those most familiar with them—the legislators and their legal advisors in each state. In many cases, this did not happen. The model simply was adopted and enacted.

Not only did this mean that in the period after 1925 many states were passing enabling acts not especially suited to the needs of their municipalities, but also it has meant that such a situation exists in some states to this day. Due to the controversial nature of governmental regulation of private use of land, state legislators have not eagerly moved to modernize and revise zoning enabling acts, even when changing conditions demand it and the fundamental policies of the zoning process have been constantly changing. For example, I could hand you a copy of the Bassett committee's model, pick up a copy of the Colorado (or the New Mexico) zoning enabling act, start reading from it, and you could follow me almost word for word. This means that in the last quarter of the century, with over 50 years intervening, local governments in such states are still hamstrung in trying to deal with today's problems of community development with ideas devised in the first quarter of this century. There are those who suggest that this might be a modern parallel of Nero fiddling while Rome burns. Those interested in the future would be well advised to see how their state has responded to the need for providing modern tools and broad authority to the local communities with which they can work effectively.

If It's Your Responsibility—
Then You Can't Blame Me

One other point should be noted regarding a state's role in achieving a sensible pattern of land use, even though we have honored for years the concept that land-use regulation is the prerogative of local counties and municipalities. It is my contention that state legislators have a direct responsibility to the residents of the entire state for the preservation of precious assets, protection of resources, and seeing that areas, problems, and events with a regional or statewide impact or influence are dealt with from a broader perspective than that of a single municipality or even a county. This can only be done if there is strong leadership in state legislatures that results in the adoption of state land-use planning and policy that is backed up by a seriously intended state land-use act.

One of the greatest problems in this area is having legislation passed that is referred to as a "land-use act" but that is such in name only. There are several axioms of mine to which I refer as "Smith's Law of Politics." While I won't list them all here, I will tell you that the first one is that the prime credo of the run-of-the-mill politician is, "Wait 'em out! We've got more time and more patience than they do." This, of course, works well when there is a highly controversial issue supported by a lot of folks, but opposed by a few of the "good old boys" and the special interests. Naturally, the answer is to postpone any action and, if necessary, keep on postponing until the general public loses interest and things quiet down. Down the line in these laws of politics, I would say in about fifth position, is another oldie but goodie. It says, "If there is a public clamor for legislation to do something constructive that is contrary to what special interests want and it can't be postponed, go ahead and enact some sort of legislation, put a title on it that implies it deals with the issue, but be sure you give it no teeth." In this way, any time anyone or any group gets agitated about anything related to the title given the act, it is very easy to say that there is already a statute on the books covering that subject and there is no need for anything else to be done.

While I have yet to see a state legislature that was not adept at applying this Smith law, the grand prize winner has to be the one in Colorado. This one seems to be able to work adroitly within this law on just about any issue, whether it be conservation of resources, state planning, the mineral severance tax, regional coordination, or land-use planning. The outstanding example of this embodies two areas related to land use. After several years of effort by a large number of people and many organizations concerned about the future of Colorado, especially a sensible approach to land use, the legislature reluctantly created a state land-use commission and later passed House Bill 1041 that was referred to as the "State Land-Use Law." The commission and the law both still exist. The first has no authority left, having what little it did have in its beginning gradually stripped away each year at the insistence of the mining, ranching, oil, and development interests. Any legislator approached about a stand on future state land use, however, will immediately tell you that we have a land-use commission, they really haven't done very much, and she or he only wishes they would do more. Shades of Orwell's double-speak of 1984.

Even worse is poor old House Bill 1041. This was originally intended by the groups proposing it to encourage local planning throughout the state, especially the counties, and to provide the state with a role to play in determining critical areas of state concern having a regional or broader impact. Any similarity between what was first proposed and what was passed was strictly a coincidental oversight. Again, year by year, even the faint possibilities of improving planning and zoning for good land-use practices that slipped through in the statute have been eroded away by weakening amendments sought by the same bunch of "enlightened and concerned" interests who succeeded in making the land-use commission totally ineffectual. In both of these cases, having something on the statute books purporting to be concerned with land use is worse than having no law under that title at all. Such a situation is a subterfuge to the public and a crutch for legislators not wanting to deal realistically with problems of the future. In the meantime, the ravishing of the Colorado landscape and environment continues at a rapidly accelerating pace.

You Can't Build a House Without Tools

Thus we see that the idea of successful local land-use controls—local zoning—is not only dependent upon modernized, meaningful state zoning enabling acts but also is only part of a bigger picture of coordinated development. No community can do a good job with zoning without the proper kind of state authority. No single community can correct or avoid regional problems. No group of municipalities, counties, or cities can solve problems of statewide consequence. It is, again, the old jigsaw puzzle idea of putting the pieces together to obtain the whole with the whole necessarily working to make the pieces relate and keeping it all together. A good first step in putting a zoning ordinance together at the county or municipal level is to be sure that state zoning statutes are well written and that any other legislation pertaining to land-use control is what it is supposed to be, not just a figment of the imagination reflected only when the politicians find it useful.

Foremost among the needs for coordinated land-use practice is that of a clearly stated, well-supported state (and I, personally, say even national) land-use policy. The enunciation of policy that provides a sense of direction is essential in doing local planning and zoning. Without countywide, statewide, nationwide policy, the individual local efforts are just that—individual. Unless there is a pulling together, these, in many cases, are contradictory and destructively competitive. We are in a period of time when the mood of the country has been read as one of wanting to get government—big government—off our backs. While, like many other ideas in theory, this is an admirable objective, it will be a serious mistake if we permit this thesis to detract further from the desirable goal of coordination of land development and preservation of resources through well-defined national and state policies into which local action can fit.

Looking at this from a state viewpoint and assuming we have not matured enough to effect a national land-use policy (the late Senator Hubert Humphrey tried for years to get this considered seriously to no avail), two observations are worthy of note. The first is that state legislators for years have been the ones most willing to abdicate responsibility to the federal government on major problems such as air pollution, water, open space, welfare, transportation, and a host of other issues. Now that most of these state representatives seem supportive of the withdrawal of federal controls and financial aid, the question that should be foremost in our minds is whether or not the people representing us are willing and able to accept the responsibility for dealing with these as problems of state government. Regrettably we will find that the answer is a resounding No in many cases. This does not portend a bright prospect for those who look beyond today with a concern for the future.

The second observation is that state legislative willingness to permit local governments full responsibility for land-use regulation through zoning under the banner of "local control must be preserved" may well be a myth which the time has come to debunk. This is not to argue that zoning powers be taken away from the local level. I have come to believe, however, that a total hands-off attitude about matters relating to land-use regulation by state representatives is a mistake and is based more on a desire to escape having to deal with a controversial matter than it is on the commitment to the high-sounding motivation of being a dedicated supporter of local prerogatives. If this latter is so true about land use, why is it not equally true about local budgets, taxing, and spending?

As I have indicated, there is a role for the states to play in land-use direction and, I believe, in zoning. It is ridiculous, inefficient, uneconomical, and destructive for some 28 municipal and five county governments in the Denver metropolitan area to all go their own way in controlling land use and land development, fighting each other over tax ratables, and scattering shopping centers, office parks, and industry willy-nilly over the landscape. Granted, there is a Regional Council of Governments comprised of elected officials from these same units of government. It has no authority to cause anything to happen that they were not willing to do in their individual jurisdictions before they got together to tacitly comply with federal requirements for regional coordination in parcelling out federal funds. The megalopolis building up from Fort Collins to Pueblo along Colorado's Front Range is of state concern, it is a state problem, as is the New Jersey, New York, Illinois, California, Georgia, or Florida metropolitan morass. To this extent, it is time the banner of local control—that is no more than a gutless excuse for inaction for state legislatures, with but few exceptions such as Minnesota—be lowered, if not all the way, at least to half-mast.

Take Part "A" and Attach to Part "2"

Having laid that framework for the importance of adequate state legislation, we come back now to the local perspective. Accepting things as they are—the theory of inviolate local control—simply means that each of us has to recognize that our communities are going to be what we make them or permit them to become. We can have zoning that does the job it should do provided enough of us understand what that job is and are involved. With the heavy burden of this responsibility, there are many important roles that must be carried out at the local level for this to happen. Even though you may live in a community that has had zoning for years, in order to understand these roles and the steps that must be taken, it is best to illustrate the part each plays in all zoning—new ordinance or amendment— by looking at them from the standpoint of any place considering zoning for the first time.

Let us assume that we have a case community which at present does not have a zoning ordinance. Let us assume next that some proposal for the use of land in the community has been made about which there are strong pro and con feelings. Finally, let us assume that a group of residents in the community have met together, informally, and have come to the tentative decision that they probably should have a zoning ordinance to guide appropriate decision making with respect both to this present proposal and to others they anticipate in the near future.

How would this group proceed? What questions would they need to ask? What materials would they need to gather? What help can they expect from state and local officials?

Step 1—Talk about it   I have tried to emphasize most strongly that it is very important for there to be a widespread interest and concern for sound local zoning. From the very first, therefore, there should be extensive conversations about the possibilities. These conversations, however, should not be a case of the blind leading the blind. They should be informed conversations, which means that some individuals are going to have to take the responsibility to do some studying themselves and perhaps to arrange for some resource people to come into the community to talk about it.

There is considerable merit to this idea. Inviting people who have had close working experience with zoning is one positive way to inaugurate the learning process. It should be obvious, however, that such invitations should be selective. It is one thing to invite someone whose experience has been broad—who has seen the whole process of zoning at work, who has observed or participated in many aspects of zoning— and quite another thing to invite someone whose total experience has been as participant in just one piece of litigation resulting from a zoning decision.

As a general rule in this connection, I would suggest that a zoning or planning official, or a consultant with considerable experience in zoning, would be a most likely candidate for some initial conversations. I also would suggest the high possibility that there may be a state government service that could help. Many of the states have offices with professional staff people whose job portfolios include experience with precisely this kind of local advisory assistance. Also, most states have some type of a statewide association of planning and zoning officials. They usually have at least one annual meeting and probably would be pleased to have a group of people from any community meet with them to discuss the possibilities of both planning and zoning. The most important thing in all this is to engage in full conversations about the essential purposes of zoning with as many people as possible. By so doing, you will have gone a long way toward building up a solid base of understanding, which will be most important for the whole future of zoning.

Step 2—Organize a citizens advisory committee   Citizens advisory groups have been used throughout the country in many different ways and on many subjects. Zoning is one area that is particularly adaptable to their utilization in view of its direct effect upon each individual. There is, of course, no general and universally applicable rule about this. Each community must determine for itself whether or not a citizens advisory group organized on a formal basis will be helpful to the zoning process. The theory, however, is extremely sound and one to be encouraged.

The more people who can be brought into the initial stages of the consideration, the greater the understanding of the ordinance. Many places find the use of the citizens advisory committee an extremely effective one. Several have actually used the organization as a team of investigators and data collectors. In some instances, the general advisory committee has been divided into subcommittees. The subcommittees operate under the headings of land use, traffic-circulation, economics, or other categories that seem appropriate. The subcommittees are assigned specific tasks of gathering data and investigating available information that can be put together and turned over to the official zoning or planning commission authorized to prepare the ordinance.

The citizens advisory group should certainly not be a rubber-stamp agency for the zoning or planning commission. At the same time, it should not consider itself to be an autonomous body and attempt to shoot off in a direction contrary to that of the parent organization. Experience also has shown that the effectiveness or ineffectiveness of a citizens advisory group is often dependent upon the caliber of the chairperson named. If he or she is intelligent and dynamic, the work of the advisory group will probably be effective and beneficial.

It is to be noted that, while the use of the citizens advisory committee is a recommended one, it should be approached with care and used only if a program has been worked out so that the group can feel it is accomplishing something and that the general bounds within which it should operate can be made clear. Do not create a citizens advisory committee just for the sake of having one. Do create one if the attitude of the community is future-oriented and if the intent of approaching the matter in a carefully thought-out program is the underlying policy to be followed.

Step 3—Name an official group for preparatory work   If one exists and is duly authorized to perform the work, the planning commission is the agency authorized by state legislation to conduct the studies and to prepare the initial draft of the zoning text and the zoning district map. If there is no planning commission, there still is the need for the governing body of the community to name a commission to function in this capacity. The members of this commission become, then, the technicians for the preliminary development of the zoning ordinance. (See Figure 1 on page 55.)

They can, of course, obtain professional assistance and use the services of a consultant if they so desire and if adequate funds have been made available. They can call on the municipal attorney for legal advice or, again, if adequate funds are available, they can engage an attorney to advise them on this particular matter. Their basic job is to be certain that the zoning ordinance is related to proper and appropriate planning principles and planning standards for their community. If they have already had prepared for them a comprehensive development plan, this becomes a much easier matter. If such is not in existence, they must be sure that adequate studies are made that can be used, not only for zoning, but for future planning activity.

They should also consider themselves playing the role of liaison between the elected officials and the citizenry. This includes the problem

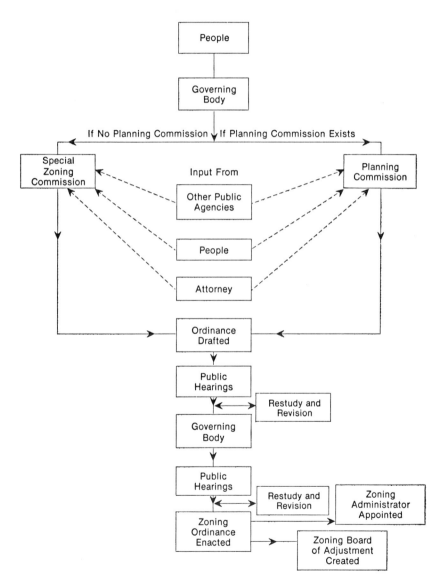

Figure 1. Flow chart: Steps in zoning ordinance adoption

of providing adequate public information, as well as expressing a cross-section of opinions from the public to the governing officials. They should not consider themselves as zoning experts necessarily; nor should they consider themselves clairvoyant and overly authoritative. They are, in fact, a group of citizens appointed to do a job of planning and zoning for the future of their municipality. Their responsibility is an important one and should be so treated by each member of the commission. As the ordinance progresses, they should inform the governing body, as well as the public in general, of what is going on. They may, from time to time, want to conduct neighborhood meetings to obtain ideas from the citizens as well as to inform them. The role, then, is that of a technical advisory board to the governing body—doing a technical job and making recommendations to the elected officials who have been delegated the authority of passing legislation for the community.

Step 4—Make public the findings   The next step in the process is to make public the findings and recommendations of the commission and to allow all of the people to see for themselves just what is being considered. This may be done in a number of ways, including holding informal discussion meetings, organizing neighborhood group discussions, or conducting mass meetings during the formulation of the ordinance.

Regardless of whether these are held (and it is extremely desirable for them to be), the next *official* step is the *required public hearing* on the matter under consideration. In most states, the agency charged with the organization of a zoning ordinance is also charged with the responsibility of submitting the ordinance officially to the public and then enabling the people to express themselves at a formal public hearing. The public hearing is extremely important, and one which is improperly conducted can be most detrimental. The purpose of the public hearing is not to encourage debate or argument, but is, instead, just what is implied by its name—that of giving the public an opportunity to be heard. It is such an important part of the zoning process that further discussion of the public hearing and the conduct of such a meeting will be included in a later chapter. Assume now that the hypothetical commission has gotten through its public hearing, heard certain objections, and has found that the ordinance seems to be basically sound. They then meet to review the suggestions and comments made by the public and to put the ordinance and map into final shape before submitting it to the governing body. Once this has been done, it is then turned over to the elected officials for their action.

Step 5—Adoption of ordinance While legal advice is desirable all through the process and probably has been made available during the organizational work of the commission, it is at this point especially that the municipal attorney or an attorney specializing in zoning comes into an extremely important role. In order for the governing body to take action, the ordinance must be put into proper legal form. The attorney takes the recommended ordinance of the zoning commission and studies it, reworking it wherever necessary to adapt it to the proper form to be used within the particular community. It is then submitted to the governing body as an ordinance. In most states, the elected officials introduce the ordinance on first reading and vote upon it. The first vote is simply on the question of introduction and whether or not it will be given further consideration. In all probability, it will be a favorable vote if zoning has gone this far. Once the passage on first reading has been concluded, the governing body is required to print the ordinance in a newspaper of general circulation within the municipality. This will include the printing of the zone district map as well as the text and any other material necessary to properly present the ordinance. A further public hearing is then scheduled before the ordinance can be subjected to second or third final readings and official passage. After the official public hearing by the governing body, if a favorable vote is then given, the zoning ordinance becomes law. Immediately following passage of the ordinance, the mayor or the governing body must appoint the zoning board of appeals or board of adjustment, which is usually comprised of five citizens of the municipality. The ordinance itself spells out their administrative duties and function. In addition, their operation is explained in state zoning enabling legislation and in published booklets and pamphlets that draw upon the various court decisions and judicial interpretations of zoning boards' functions. With the passage of the zoning ordinance and the creation of the zoning board of adjustment, the municipality is in the zoning business.

In outlining the five steps above, it will be apparent that there are many critical roles to be performed. The whole process, in fact, is not unlike an orchestration. If all the parts are not played, and played well, the product will be a discordant cacophony. I would like, therefore, to quickly review these roles with you.

The Citizen's Role   It is obvious that the citizen is deeply involved throughout the zoning process. The effect of a zoning ordinance is a far-reaching one, both in the private and public lives of people in the community. If zoning is to be properly done and to prove a benefit, people within the community must recognize their responsibility and must be involved. This responsibility is defined in a number of ways. First, there is the individual responsibility for seeing that a community understands the benefit of zoning and, where an ordinance is lacking, that one is considered and adopted. This responsibility means more than just having an individual feeling that someone should do something about the problem. It carries with it the necessity for being informed and for instituting action. In many cases, if a zoning ordinance is to be adopted, it will require that there be a number of thinking civic leaders who are informed in order to overcome the rumors and misconceptions that will be rampant. The concerned person, therefore, should be able to exercise that degree of intelligence which will permit the reaching of an objective conclusion without being influenced by emotionally charged objections. Anyone starting out with the idea of encouraging a zoning ordinance should be prepared for frustrations and discouragement. The responsibility, however, is inclusive enough that such discouragement should not be permitted to dissuade or to influence the recognition of the importance of this governmental function.

Once the psychological hurdle of the first introduction of zoning has been overcome, responsibility then carries forward into the investigation and studies leading to the preparation and adoption of the ordinance. Many communities are sold on the idea of introducing zoning and fail to recognize the importance of thorough and careful studies in order to form the base of the ordinance. Due to the newness of zoning in many areas, only a few people understand how technically involved and complicated it is. The uninformed may believe that a good zoning ordinance is being presented to them when in fact it has been prepared in a very short time simply by pasting together phrases taken from ordinances adopted in other communities. Unless this zoning is related by careful study to the particular municipality for which it is intended, not only will it be defective, it will be extremely difficult to sustain legally. A zone district map that is prepared without the advantage of detailed information as to lot and parcel sizes and existing development is simply an arbitrary map, replete with opportunities for criticism as well as inequitable treatment of individual properties. Similarly, the creation of the zone districts in such a way as to recognize as a legitimate use each noncompatible use in a predominantly residential area will be ineffective and hard to administer. It is the responsibility of all interested parties to understand the necessity of careful study in order to have an adequately prepared ordinance and to insist that such consideration be given before the people are told that they are being afforded the protection of good zoning.

The individual also has a responsibility at an early stage of the process to see that neighbors are well-informed, not only in connection with the ordinance under consideration, but also with the factual data and information that will enable anyone to make a determination as to the quality of zoning. This responsibility continues after adoption and passage into the administration of the ordinance. One of the basic precepts of sound zoning is equitable and fair treatment for all, with a total absence of discrimination or the granting of special privileges. The surest possible way to erode a zoning ordinance is to have someone with knowledge of discretionary treatment or a violation of the ordinance who, because of not wanting to get involved in any trouble, ignores the matter and does nothing. It is almost impossible for the administrator of the zoning ordinance to cover all possibilities of violation and to be aware of everything that goes on in a community. Each of us has a direct responsibility to call any violation to the attention of the proper authorities and to insist that the rules of the game are properly observed by all. Only in this way can zoning be a fair and reasonable process of government. Since there is sometimes the unfortunate tendency in some of our communities to reward the politically faithful with jobs, there is the possibility that the persons selected as zoning officers are lacking in the necessary qualifications. There is also the possibility that, due to political involvement, the enforcement officer may fail to take notice of an existing problem. The concerned citizen, therefore, has the responsibility of insisting that personnel selected to administer the ordinance are qualified and that they administer the ordinance impartially and diligently.

Finally, we should consider the individual's responsibility in the community that has had an ordinance in effect for some time. Here, the responsibility may be even greater than in the case of developing a new ordinance. Unfortunately, many governing bodies feel that, because a zoning ordinance has been around for 25 years, it is automatically an excellent ordinance and has no need for comprehensive amendment or revision. A careful investigation will probably disclose that the ordinance has been amended many times and that the zoning board of appeals or adjustment has granted numerous variances, many of which have struck at the very heart of the original intent and purpose expressed in the ordinance. It becomes almost impossible for the concerned individual to become informed about all provisions contained in the ordinance and on the zoning map. A trip to the municipal building in order to do so becomes a frustrating and discouraging affair, with individuals passing the buck from one to the other. Even if the ordinance text is available, any number of amendment sheets must be attached to the original document in order to tell the entire story over the years. Zoning theories and techniques have also changed, and many of the original ordinances were founded on less than adequate information and study. Modern standards and techniques may be entirely missing from the ordinance.

As concerned citizens, our responsibility is clear where a community has an older ordinance. First, we should be certain of the vintage as well as the general provisions of the ordinance. We should further be sufficiently informed in order to be able to evaluate just how adequate and effective the conditions and terms of the ordinance are. Where there is the least bit of inadequacy or failure on the part of the document or the process, responsibility calls for insisting that something be done about it. We also should be aware that zoning amendments are being made from time to time and that, on an almost regular basis, variances are being granted to the ordinance by the zoning board of appeals or adjustment.

Whether these occur in our immediate neighborhood or are far removed in another part of the community, they have a direct effect upon us and our investment within the community. We have the responsibility, therefore, of making certain, not only that the ordinance is properly amended and revised to be brought up-to-date, but that any amendments that are made are constructive and are related to proper planning and zoning principles. At the same time, we should not hesitate to express our opinions and solicit others to do likewise regarding the many variances that are considered by the board. Too many people take the attitude that an appearance before a zoning board regarding a requested variance is simply asking for trouble and something to be avoided. If we are to fully accept our responsibility as members of our society, we must be informed and take a stand that is expressed to the appropriate authorities. Only in this way will zoning do the job it is supposed to do.

This leads us to the point of discussing the collective community attitude in approaching zoning. While it is inconceivable that any group of people can be of one opinion completely, it is often found that many people are concerned and would like to be able to express themselves better regarding such vital matters, and they are looking for leadership and direction. The attitude of individual citizens regarding their responsibility, taken collectively, will then determine the attitude of the community. Where this is questioning and yet constructive, it will be helpful. Where it is based upon a sincere concern regarding the future and the development that will take place, it will assure a better end product and, in turn, a better environment for all. What is really needed is a community attitude of caring about what is going to happen. Zoning for zoning's sake, or an ordinance passed primarily to offset pressure that has built up in the community, will not be beneficial or effective.

The Governing Body

It is obvious that the governing body has the most vital role to play in zoning adoption. Its first job is to have adopted policies pertaining to future growth and development upon which the zoning can be based. It also must be the agency that initiates official action if an ordinance is ever to be considered. Once it has accepted the fact that zoning is a desirable process and has created the zoning commission or authorized its planning commission to undertake study and investigation, the role of the governing body is a relatively inactive one during the initial stages of preparation. This does not mean that the individual members of the

DOESN'T COMMISSIONER GURKIN OWN PROPERTY OVER HERE ?

council or commission, or whatever form is used in a community, should boycott or stay aloof from the zoning preparation process. It does mean that they actually assume the role of a board of directors; they have asked some other body to conduct an investigation for them and report to them.

They should, during the early stages of zoning consideration, discuss the matter with as many people as possible within the community. Above all else, they should attempt to keep as objective a viewpoint as possible, not being overly influenced by their own emotions or those of others. They should make certain that the members of all agencies dealing with the question are the leaders of the community and the most competent and concerned individuals possible. During the stages of organization, they should be informed as to the activity of the zoning commission and should read and study the preliminary reports or other material made available to them.

Of course, they assume a far more direct role in the adoption of the ordinance when the initial document is readied and turned over to them. They must also work very closely with their municipal attorney and be sure that they are obtaining proper legal advice, as well as making this available to the zoning commission.

The Attorney

We have already indicated that the attorney plays a vital role in the formulation of a zoning ordinance, as well as in its passage. Many attorneys are specialists in zoning while others are not. Because someone is municipal attorney does not necessarily imply expertise in all aspects of municipal law, including zoning. The really competent municipal attorney will recognize her or his own limitations and insist that the governing body provide adequate funds so that experts may be used when needed.

During the early stages of preparation, the attorney should be available for a general discussion with the agency authorized to prepare the ordinance. This person should be in a position to give the general legal principles that will guide them. As the work progresses, he or she should be available for review and comment, being very careful not to present opinions as being infallible or as being the direct word from the supreme court of the particular state in which the community is located. The attorney should give legal advice but not make judicial decisions. When the ordinance is ready, the attorney should sit with the zoning commission or planning board during the public hearing, making certain that legal questions are answered and that the hearing is properly conducted. Following this, the job is to put the ordinance in its final appropriate legal form for submission to the governing body and eventual adoption. The attorney should also be available to advise the governing body while they are considering it and, again, to assist them in conducting the required public hearing before final passage.

Professionals

It has been pointed out that the preparation of the zoning ordinance is a fairly involved and technical matter. It is, therefore, desirable to take advantage of professional services and assistance. This assistance may be available from public agency staffs within the area or from private consultants. Regardless of the source, it should be professionally competent.

In many cases, governing bodies or zoning commissions that embark upon the zoning process ask a professional consulting firm to come in and prepare the investigation and study for them, submitting a recommended ordinance text and map for consideration by the appropriate agency. This does not mean that this is done in a vacuum with the consulting firm having no contact with the local agency. Instead, it simply means that professional, technical know-how is brought into play in an advisory capacity to the agency charged with the zoning ordinance preparation. The technician serves as staff for the official body as well as the entire official family of the community. In this way, the time-consuming process of studies and investigations can be taken care of without overly imposing on the volunteer citizens serving on local boards.

It is important, however, for local people to make certain that they are getting the best possible professional advice. Even though there may be a county or state agency that purports to be skilled in local planning and zoning work, the personnel in that agency may not be technically qualified. This does not mean that all public agency planners are unqualified; but many governmental agencies within the past few years have been unable or unwilling to find individuals sufficiently trained to really be considered competent planners and zoners. In order to preserve a political position, unqualified and untrained personnel are often employed and given a planning or zoning title. The local community should not hesitate to question the qualifications of personnel made available to them. Sometimes a so-called zoning advisory service offered by a higher level of government on a no-cost basis is worth exactly what it costs.

Qualifications and professional background of individuals can be readily checked, and should be. Good zoning is such a vital aspect of the future that not making certain that any advice given, whether from a private consultant or a public agency representative, is based upon knowledge and experience that has been proven, is asking for serious trouble and may shortchange that future. It is equally important that any outside expert show the ability to work with the people and the problems of the community involved and not seek to impose ideas that were used elsewhere with uncompromising zeal. With the increasing popularity of zoning, many people are trying to become classified as zoning and/or land-use experts. This applies not only to those offering to give advice in the preparation of zoning ordinances, but also to those who appear as expert witnesses in zoning litigation. True experts in zoning have had a number of years in the planning and zoning battle arena. In all probability, they have been schooled and trained in city or regional planning and have had experience working with local governments and grass roots citizens organizations in zoning formulation. I have yet to see a really qualified zoning expert, lawyers included, who did not have some kind of planning training or, at least, had bothered to give themselves that background and had developed a genuine "planning attitude." The smart community will not be misled by self-styled experts and will be extremely cautious regarding anyone who is not a member of a recognized professional planning organization or who is not willing unhesitantly to produce a list of clients and previous experience in the zoning field.

5

The Nuts and Bolts
of a Zoning Ordinance

From exploring the reasons for zoning, its importance, and its enactment or modification, we turn now to the specifics of the ordinance itself. To do so, we will be looking at what kind of background data the agency responsible for the study and initial preparation will need, as well as the elements of the ordinance itself. Much of zoning is technical, and the ordinance is a legal document. This book will not attempt to cover either of these aspects in great detail. The focus here will be on what a zoning ordinance is, how it is organized, and what terms are most frequently used. No single book on zoning can make a person into an expert, and it is not the intent here to try to do so. Rather, the material discussed in this and other chapters should provide enough knowledge of the process so that those interested can take an active part in this very important aspect of community affairs. If a broad understanding can be imparted, it will serve as a means for the citizen to evaluate zoning action taken in any community.

Policy Points the Way

In developing a zoning ordinance, it is important to start the process with a clearly written policy statement. The minute you mention policy in local government, you must think immediately of the elected officials. They are the policy makers! No commission, committee, or board serving in appointive capacities can set governmental policy. Appointed agencies and public staff can advise and recommend that policy be adopted or changed, but, until it is adopted by those elected to office, there is no meaningful policy statement. It is equally true that any policy statement adopted by these elected officials will be successful in direct proportion to the support they give to seeing that the policies are carried out.

Nowhere is this need for enunciated and supported policy more essential than in zoning. In essence, every statement in a zoning ordinance and every symbol on a zoning map is nothing more than implementation of policy. Unfortunately, far too many governing bodies operate without any sense of overall direction and policy. Any community that has not made a concerted effort to determine where it is going and where it wants to go with that effort reflected in a clearly stated policy position should stay out of zoning.

There are many examples that illustrate the importance of such policy. Consider the suburban community that is now comprised predominantly of single-family residences but is lying directly in the path of intensifying urbanization. Should more space be zoned to provide for apartments and industry? Should the community try to remain low density? If so, is this feasible? What about the smaller, more rural community that finds itself falling heavily under the influence of a major mining development located outside of its jurisdiction? Should pressures dictate what will happen, or should the community set its own policy to try to preserve its good features and perhaps even some of its unique characteristics? Crested Butte, Colorado, threatened with a gigantic endeavor of the Amax Corporation, is just such a place at the time of this writing. To give credit to the people of Crested Butte, their mayor, and other elected officials, they have staunchly let it be known that they are going to set their own policy for development.

People Working Together Can Determine Future Patterns

While economic pressures and outside forces beyond the control of the people within a community will have an influence on what development an area may be facing, the final decision as to type and character is one that can and should be made by the local citizens and their elected officials. Even in some of our more densely populated and built-up regions, there is room for a community that is chiefly a one-family residential area. But the community must analyze its situation and be willing to pay the cost necessary to support a low-density development pattern. If the community is in a desirable area, there will be pressures by economic forces to have the law of supply and demand determine its future character, rather than having the present inhabitants do so.

One of my classes has been assigned a project in a community facing somewhat similar problems. Edgewater, Colorado, nestled in the midst of the metropolitan area just west of the city of Denver, is an incorporated enclave of 440 acres with a population of 5,714, bordered on the east by a major arterial highway. Despite this location, it has remained predominantly a single-family, residential city inhabited by blue- and white-collar workers. Recognizing outside pressures and the need for some self-determination, Edgewater's progressive and future-oriented mayor, backed by her council, has asked the University of Colorado to help them find out where they are, what their prospects are, where they should try to go, and what kind of policy they need to get there.

This is a nice lead-in to making the point that zoning policy is best determined through the planning process. Planning studies and the development of a comprehensive plan for future growth should be— but is not, by legislative act, in most states—a prerequisite to zoning. Some states are changing their statutes to require this, and more and more judges who hear zoning cases are clearly indicating that their upholding of municipal zoning action has been influenced by the planning studies upon which that action was based. (To be sure that the wrong conclusion is not drawn about Edgewater, let me say that they have had a planning commission for years and had a consulting firm prepare a comprehensive master plan for them in 1965 that has served them well, but they recognize the need for reexamining and updating their policy as well as their plan.)

Now, Let's Act It Out

Perhaps the best way to get into more of the details of putting a zoning ordinance together would be to assume that you have just been appointed to a zoning study commission in a small town that has no zoning and, unfortunately, no planning commission or master plan. As a serious, dedicated member, naturally you ask yourself, what do we do first? Having read what has already been said, you look for some sense of direction by trying to find out about policy. We will assume that the elected officials are farsighted and will work with you and the other citizens to develop such a statement. If this is not the case, the first job for you and the other commission members will be to come up with a series of policy recommendations to consider for adoption by the mayor and the council. First, you probably will have to conduct a community attitude survey to get the residents' ideas on what they would like to see changed and what they like about their town now. You will also probably need to hold several brainstorming sessions of the commission and several open public meetings, as well.

Once some idea of policy has been established, by whatever method used to obtain it, the commission moves on to the next step. You need to gather, in written and mapped or graphic form, as much information about the community as you can, and study it thoroughly. The tendency of people who have lived in a place a long time is to think they know everything worth knowing about the town. My experience has shown that, regardless of how long someone has lived in a place and how well they think they know it, a carefully documented study invariably turns up a great deal of important information that astonishes them. You are also going to need materials and information to support your recommendations, to show other people why you did what you did. Time spent in gathering data and effectively presenting it in written and graphic form will pay dividends in achieving understanding and support.

The Basic Ingredients

Just what should be studied? The easy answer would be to say everything—the more the better. However, there are practical limitations to attempting this, and there is the possibility of a procedural danger. Some zoning commissions get carried away with data collection and research and lose sight of the primary elements of community structure upon which zoning should be based. For some people, information-gathering and study can become the excuse for not coming to grips with decision making and the formulation of specific recommendations.

None of this contradicts the statement made about the need for study or implies that there are not essentials that must be given careful and detailed attention. In essence, the required studies and investigations closely parallel those going into the development of a good comprehensive master plan. They should be concerned with the physical, social, economic, and environmental fabric of the community. No attempt will be made to cover all of the technical aspects of these studies, but the following categories of investigation and study are indispensable.

Natural Features   After the agency responsible for the preparation of the zoning ordinance has provided itself with an appropriate map or maps for displaying information and for organizing the zone districts, the natural features of the community should be carefully investigated. This includes topography, drainage, soil condition, and availability of mineral resources, as well as the beauty of the natural features that should be preserved. These are important to zoning because the use of land and density of population will have a serious effect upon them and vice versa. Natural features often influence the lot size for residential development. They can also have a major effect upon the location of industrial as well as business and commercial zones. A great deal of material regarding these matters can be obtained from already published sources; however, there still may be the necessity of original research and investigation within the community in order to be sure you have the necessary information.

Population/People   This is perhaps the most important element of any community study. In theory, all action of representative government should be based on a careful consideration of how best to serve the people of that jurisdiction. In attempting to do so through planning and zoning, attention must be paid to their numbers, characteristics, needs, and desires. The purpose of zoning, whether preceded by a master plan or not, is to set the development pattern for the future for the existing population as well as those yet to come. Basic information about past trends and the numbers and characteristics of the present inhabitants can be obtained from the U.S. Census Bureau's publications and from special studies frequently available from state, regional, or county planning agencies. Projections for the future also may be obtainable from these agencies or from utility companies and chambers of commerce. All such projections should be carefully evaluated in terms of what you know about your individual community. Be sure to remember to look at the regional trends around you. External forces may have as much, if not more, bearing on the problems you may be called on to face than internal factors.

Zoning that works is zoning that is supported by those it will affect. There is an aphorism in planning that applies as well to zoning: "You don't plan *for* people, you plan *with* them." Involving as many people as possible, making them feel a part of the process, and learning what they think about their city, town, or village is fundamental to success in zoning. A good way to start this is to devise your own community attitude survey. Include questions that give everyone the chance to indicate what they like about the "home town," what they don't like, what they would like to see happen, and their priorities for getting what they feel is needed. You also can do a lot to get community involvement by organizing a volunteer corps to conduct such a survey on a door-to-door, personalized basis.

Land Use and Existing Development   Study should then be made of all of the present development within the community. This is frequently referred to as a land-use study in that it involves the investigation of the existing utilization of land. Such a study is usually done both in map and statistical form and indicates how each parcel of land within the community is used. Included also should be full information on the size of lots, the average setback and yard dimensions presently in existence, and as much other information as possible on physical development. This survey is extremely important in that it becomes the basis for the zone district map and should be used in the preparation of a future land-use plan prior to making zoning district recommendations.

Traffic and Circulation   Many people do not recognize the fact that traffic and circulation have a direct relationship to zoning and are an appropriate consideration in the formulation of the ordinance. Because of this relationship, it is important to have a thorough investigation and study of these elements prior to forming conclusions about zoning patterns. The question has long been debated about whether land-use planning or transportation-facilities planning has the greater effect on shaping the physical environment and which should come first. We only need to look at the influence of the federal interstate highway system and what it did to contribute to urban sprawl to see the importance of traffic and circulation to zoning.

Municipal Facilities and Services   Another essential study is one dealing with the existence and adequacy of municipal facilities and services. It should include schools, parks and playgrounds, water supply systems, sewer systems, and other phases of general municipal housekeeping services. Where adequate facilities do not exist or where they are inadequate to take care of expansion, consideration must be given to establishing the type of development and the densities that will permit the community to absorb the growth reasonably and feasibly, without overtaxing and overburdening its existing capacities.

Too little attention is paid to the idea of the carrying capacity of the existing infrastructure of a community. There is such a capacity for every facility or service, both now and in the affordable future. Think about the last major development that occurred in your town. Did anybody really worry about what it would do to the ability to provide water, sewage disposal, garbage collection, police and fire protection, street maintenance, and adequate schools for the kids, or did everybody just get caught up in the rat race for ratables? With the rush toward cutting back or eliminating federal funding programs and passing the responsibility for financing problem solutions to states and local governments, these matters become of even greater concern for all of us.

Economics   During the first half of this century, the courts of this nation were hesitant to recognize economics as a legitimate basis for developing zoning requirements. Within recent years, there has been a tendency to permit the inclusion of economic considerations as one of the allowable fundamentals in making zoning determinations. It is an extremely important and vital factor. No community can properly zone for itself unless it has carefully considered its fiscal and economic condition, both existing and projected for the future. Good zoning will relate land utilization and development to a sound economic program for the municipality. At the same time, the establishment of use districts within the zoning ordinance can, to a large measure, determine the economic base. It follows logically that a thorough knowledge of the general economics of the area should be part of the study used in preparing the zoning ordinance.

Environmental Concerns   In spite of recent political trends, what we are doing to our environment is an inescapably important matter. If you live in an area with unique natural beauty, a village sitting near a fragile ecological location, or a city already beset with a high degree of air pollution, you should turn a deaf ear to anyone trying to tell you that environmental considerations, whatever they may be, have no place in zoning. There are only two threats to natural environments other than nature itself—people and land development. I certainly don't advocate doing away with either, but I strongly argue for the use of zoning, the only legal tool available, to guide and direct the action and location of people and to mitigate the effects of land development on something so important to us collectively. A good hard look at environmental factors should be included in the zoning study package.

The Completed Production   Assuming now that you and the other members of the zoning commission have gathered data, gotten other people involved, collected opinions, and completed your initial studies, it is time to move into the preparation of the recommended zoning ordinance. In case it has not become clear, when a reference is made to the "zoning ordinance," it should be understood that this includes a written text and a map or maps depicting zone district boundaries and identifying the district classifications. These are the items that must be passed into law by the elected officials at the enactment stage. Both have equal status as legal documents; both affect and control the development and use of land. They should be as clear and easy for everyone to understand as is possible.

The text is the bible of the use and area requirements. It provides the do's and don'ts of land planning and development and, by necessity, is rather involved and complicated, although frequently the influence of the legal profession makes it more so than necessary. It consists, in its final form, of numerous pages setting forth the requirements of the ordinance. This ultimate presentation for public information of both the ordinance text and the zoning map takes many forms and varies from community to community. It may be printed in its entirety in a newspaper of general circulation (something that is required by state legislation before adoption) and extra copies of tear sheets from the paper made available to the public as requested, or it may be printed in booklet form. In larger cities, it is incorporated as part of a codified set of municipal ordinances with the complete set or the zoning ordinance alone available in loose-leaf ring binders for ease of updating.

Since it deals with a subject that affects more people directly than any other legislative enactment, copies of the ordinance should be available to those who are interested. These can usually be obtained from the municipal offices and probably from the municipal clerk. A number of communities print the ordinance text and then charge a nominal fee in order to offset the cost and to assure that those who ask for copies will be genuinely interested in it. Regardless of how it is reproduced, it is a public document and should be readily accessible for public study.

Outline of Typical Ordinance

The text is divided into articles and sections. Each deals with a different function of zoning and has a particular purpose in the ordinance. The articles and sections are numbered for easy reference with varying kinds of numbering systems used in different parts of the country. The important thing is that the numbering system be consistent throughout a particular ordinance. Listed below is a simplified outline of the usual main divisions of the zoning ordinance. A further breakdown could also be made. For example, Section 602.4 could be broken down into subsections 602.41, 602.42, and so forth.

I. Title
II. Purpose
  Section 201—General purpose
  Section 202—Establishment of zones and purposes thereof
  Section 203—Zoning map
  Section 204—Zone boundaries
III. Definitions
  Section 301—Words and phrases
  Section 302—Specific words and phrases defined
IV. Permitted Uses
  Section 401—Permitted uses defined
  Section 402—Table of permitted uses
V. Dimensional Requirements
  Section 501—Requirements for each zone
  Section 502—Special requirements in each zone
VI. General Regulations
  Section 601—Regulations applying to all zones
  Section 602—Regulations applying to specific zones
    Section 602.1—Agricultural
    Section 602.2—Residential
    Section 602.3—Commercial
    Section 602.4—Industrial
VII. Special Regulations
  Section 701—Off-street parking and unloading
  Section 702—Signs
VIII. Nonconforming Uses
IX. Administration
  Section 901—Enforcement
  Section 902—Zoning permit
  Section 903—Certificate of occupancy
  Section 904—Records
  Section 905—Zoning board of adjustment
X. Interpretation

For our purpose here, we will not go into the details of all that must be covered under each of the above divisions. Suggested model ordinances and approaches for handling almost any king of zoning situation that may arise can be obtained from the American Planning Association and the American Law Institute, as well as from other sources of reference listed with the agencies in Appendix B. Having noted that, a word of caution is necessary, however. Do not copy and adopt model ordinances or any suggested general wording prepared solely as something to serve as a guide for giving you a sense of direction. Make certain that the enacted provisions, while perhaps following the ideas suggested by knowledgeable people in the zoning field, have been drafted to meet the problems and needs unique to your community. In other words, don't use the cut and paste technique of zoning ordinance preparation.

Two items included in the above outline deserve special comment in any general discussion of the makeup of a zoning text in view of the importance they carry in defending against any legal challenge. The first is the article relating to purpose. Too many ordinance drafters treat this lightly, thus requiring a court to interpret the intent of a local governing body or leaving the interpretation to the imagination of the judge. On several occasions, I have witnessed a section of regulations of great importance to the direction a community wanted to take struck down by a court on the basis of not being able to determine the intent and purpose of the legislative body in its adoption. Do not skimp on spelling this out in your recommended ordinance. It is wise to include even the major points of the community's land development policy statement, to which I referred earlier as an indication of the basis upon which zoning has been founded.

Say What You Mean and Say It Clearly

The second part of the outline that I feel merits special attention concerns definitions. Here, too, the principal reason is the vital role these can play in any legal challenge. This is one place that model ordinances or suggested wording from other sources can be very helpful. In most instances, definitions found in these models will have been tested over the years in other places and will have been found capable of withstanding that test. There is no guarantee that all judges in your state will be inclined (or in some cases, sufficiently well-read and informed) to accept a precedent from somewhere else, but it does strengthen the argument when you can show that your language is not totally innovative. As just one example of what I mean, the definition of the word *family* has probably been challenged as often as any other single word used in a zoning ordinance. Even after several major court cases, the definition of general acceptance to withstand judicial review is still debated, but the point here is the need for concern about carefully defining just what you do want a word or phrase to mean in your ordinance. No *Alice in Wonderland* talk of "they are my words and they mean what I say they mean" will do here.

The following example emphasizes this. A city in New Jersey was ordered by a court to permit the complete restoration of a manufacturing plant that was an inharmonious, nonconforming use in a residential district. It has been totally destroyed by fire and the entire building had crumbled except for the main smokestack. The reason given by the court—the lack of a clear definition of what constituted partial destruction. In the text of the ordinance relating to nonconforming uses, the city had stated that such uses could be restored in the event of partial destruction "by act of God or natural causes," but had failed to define what was meant by partial destruction. The judge ruled that, lacking any other indication of the intent of local officials, since the smokestack had been part of the entire structure and it had been left intact, the destruction was therefore partial, and the owners were entitled to the opportunity for full restoration. Need more be said about the importance of carefully worded definitions and the value of expert advice in drafting them?

Different Folks Do It Differently

To supplement the simplified outline of an ordinance text given here, copies of the tables of contents of the ordinances of Denver and Albuquerque as well as the first page of the ordinance of the latter have been included in pages 76—80. You have not had to read between the lines to know by now that I don't hold Denver's ordinance in high regard. Nevertheless, they did not abandon good practice and understandable wording until after the table of contents, and, as it shows another idea of what should be covered in a zoning ordinance text, it is reasonably safe to include it. The Albuquerque text page does not follow my recommendation for a broad and encompassing statement of purpose, but it does serve to illustrate the standard one found in the 1928 U.S. Department of Commerce suggested model, as well as most ordinances across the country. This page also provides some idea of Albuquerque's approach to definitions.

Denver Zoning Ordinance

Table of Contents

Albuquerque Zoning Ordinance

Table of Contents

Albuquerque Zoning Ordinance

Commission Ordinance No. 2726

An ordinance adopting comperhensive zoning regulations for the city of Albuquerque, adopting a zone map, repealing commission Ordinance No. 1493, as amended, and declaring an emergency.

Be it ordained by the governing body, the city commission, of the city of Albuquerque:

SECTION 1.   Title

This ordinance shall be known as the Comprehensive Zoning Ordinance of the city of Albuquerque.

SECTION 2.   Purpose

This ordinance is intended to promote the general health, safety, morals, convenience, and welfare of the people of the city of Albuquerque, and these regulations are necessary to provide adequate open spaces for light and air; to avoid undue concentration of population; to secure safety from fire, panic, and other dangers; to lessen congestion in the streets and public ways; to control and abate the unsightly use of buildings or land; to facilitate adequate provisions for community utilities, such as transportation, water, sewer, schools, parks, and other public requirements; to encourage the most appropriate use of land; and to conserve and stabilize the value of property.

SECTION 3.   Application of the zoning ordinance

The zones and boundaries of zones as established and shown on that map attached to and made a part of Ordinance No. 1493, effective March 27, 1959, and all subsequent amendments thereto, are incorporated herein and designated as the Official Zone Map of the city of Albuquerque. All property, except that controlled by an adopted Neighborhood Development Plan and that property owned or controlled by the federal government, the state of New Mexico, the county of Bernalillo, and the city of Albuquerque and their subdivision or agencies, is governed according to the zone in which it is located. Any use not designated a permissive or conditional use in a zone is specifically prohibited from that zone, except as otherwise provided herein.

SECTION 4.   Definitions

Words used in the present tense include the future tense, and words used in the future tense include the present tense; the singular number includes the plural number, and the plural number includes the singular number. Words not defined herein but which are defined in the Building Code of the city of Albuquerque are to be construed as defined therein. The following definitions apply:

Apartment means one or more structures containing two or more dwelling units each.

Automobile dismantling yard means a yard in which is conducted the dismantling of automobiles and the selling of automobile parts, and the storage of inoperative automobiles awaiting dismantling or removal, provided there is no hammering, mechanical cutting, grinding, or blasting.

Bath means a space containing a wash basin and water closet. Rooms referred to locally as one-half or three-quarter baths are one bath for the purpose of this ordinance.

Boarding or lodging house means a dwelling containing one or more but not more than five guest rooms where lodging is provided, with or without meals, for compensation.

Boat means a vehicle for traveling in or on water, not exceeding 30 feet in body length, 8 feet in width, or 11 feet in overall height. Height includes the trailer, if the boat is mounted on a trailer. A vehicle meeting the above definition except for size is not deemed incidental to a dwelling unit.

Building, accessory, means a building detached from and subordinate to the main building and located on the same lot or parcel of land with the main building, the use of which is appropriate, subordinate, and customarily incidental to that of the main building or main use of the land.

Clear sight triangle means an area of unobstructed vision at street intersections defined by right-of-way lines of two streets and by a line between two points on the two right-of-way lines 25 feet from the intersection, three to eight feet above the gutter line.

Conditional uses means those uses enumerated as conditional uses in the various zones. Such uses require individual approval on a given parcel of land.

Contiguous means separated only by an alley.

Drive-in restaurant means an establishment where food or beverages are sold and consumed on the premises outside a structure.

The Zoning Map

The second essential element of zoning is the zoning map. This may have a number of different titles in various places. It may be called the building zone map, the zoning district map, or just zoning map. Regardless of its title, it is the map or maps of the entire community, or the area for which the zoning ordinance is adopted, showing the boundaries of the area, the streets, and the boundaries of the various zones or zoning districts. Depending upon the complexity of the community, the map may include other things such as individual parcels or tracts of land, natural stream courses or other natural features, and certain other identifying elements. It should not, however, be so detailed that it is hard to interpret.

The scale of the map will vary depending upon the area to be covered. If the community is small and compact, the zoning map can usually be printed on one sheet. If the area under consideration is extremely large, it may be necessary to provide a number of sheets in order to cover the entire territory. Where this is done, the entire collection of maps is referred to as the zone atlas. A location key sheet or map index covering the entire area is provided, with grids to identify which sheet contains the location of any parcel. Examples of this method (Figures 2, 3, and 4), taken from the Albuquerque Zone Atlas, are found on pages 81, 82, and 83. An illustration of a single zone map for an entire city (Figure 5) is shown on page 84.

The principle to be followed is that the scale of the original drawing of the map should be such that locations within the area can be readily recognized and the zone district boundaries clearly identified. Zones or zoning districts are shown either by numbers or letters, together with an identifying pattern. One map, for example, might use cross-hatch patterns to indicate the different districts. Another map could use a plastic overlay to indicate by shades or tones the permitted uses in the various districts.

The zone district boundary lines should, wherever possible, follow lot lines and should avoid the center line of streets or roads. The reason for this is the underlying principle of zoning which states that like

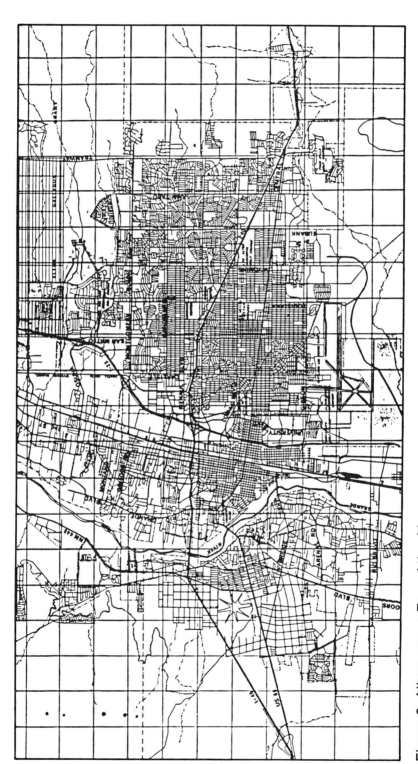

Figure 2. Albuquerque Zone Atlas Map

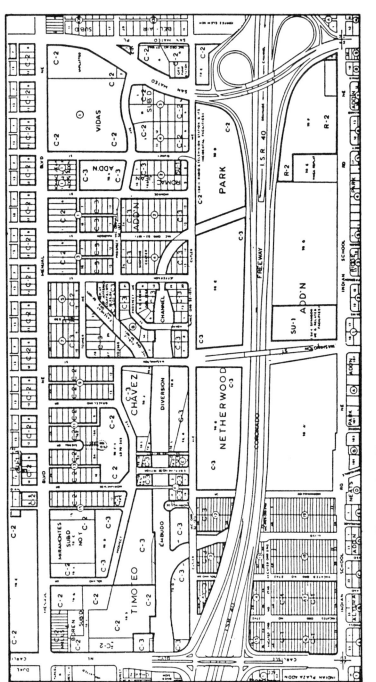

Figure 3. Albuquerque Zone Atlas Sheet

Figure 4. Albuquerque Zone Atlas Sheet

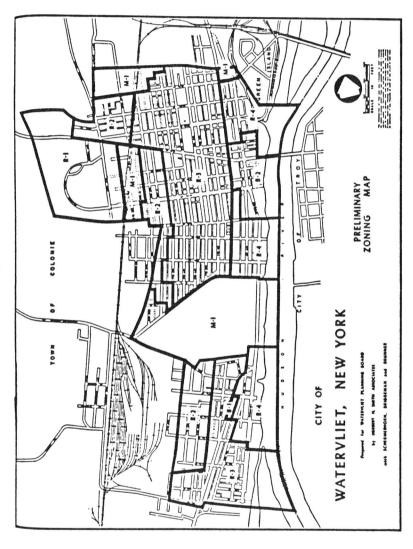

Figure 5. Watervliet, N.Y., Zoning Map

properties should be given like consideration. In other words, if a piece of property on one side of the street is appropriate in a business zone, in all probability the property on the other side of the street and immediately adjacent thereto is also appropriate for business zoning. While this is a general rule-of-thumb, it obviously cannot be applied in every case, and there will be occasions when the center line of streets or roads will have to be used as the boundary. The divided limited access highway is an example of where this may be necessary and, in some cases, even desirable. It is also a good idea wherever possible to locate a zoning district boundary in connection with some identifiable natural feature such as a river, stream, or heavily wooded, sloping area.

The zoning map should be accurately drawn, and, wherever possible, show the distances from major intersections and from streets of the boundary lines between the districts. Not only does the zoning officer have to attempt to interpret the location of the zone boundaries, but the interested individual should also be able to tell whether his or her property lies in one district or the other. This can best be done if dimensions are given. There should also be a clear legend describing any symbols that are used to indicate either the zones or districts or the boundary lines. This legend will usually be on the map in the vicinity of the title and will state the number of districts or zones into which the municipality has been divided and show the symbols used for each one.

The Schedule of Requirements

A third element that may be found in some zoning ordinances is the schedule of requirements. Originally, all of the standards and requirements were placed in the written text. However, a number of years ago, the technique was developed of extracting from the text as much as possible of the statistical or numerical requirements and placing them in a simplified schedule. Such a schedule lists the various districts and then, indicates, in columns, the dimensional requirements for each district. For example, it will state that a particular district has as permitted uses one-family houses and will then describe the precise dimensional requirements for lot area, setback from the street, front yard, side yard, or rear yard, as well as the maximum height of the building, minimum floor area, and any other dimensions relating to the particular zone. It may also include, in schedule form, certain other requirements for that zone if these are simple enough to be explained in a very few words or to be indicated numerically. Again, the schedule should not become so complicated that it becomes confusing. A copy of a sample schedule (Table 1) is included on page 87.

Graphic Illustration of Requirements

A fourth element that can be very helpful in understanding zoning dimensional requirements but is not frequently found in zoning ordinances is the graphic depiction of the requirements pertaining to the location of the building on a lot in any zone. A relatively new technique that has been incorporated in some of the more recent ordinances, it clearly indicates *exactly* how the requirements would affect the building of a structure on a lot. It is used, for example, to show how a one-family house can be located on a typical lot. The illustration would simply show the variety of lots that can be developed in conformity with the zoning ordinance and, then, by perspective drawing using a hypothetical structure, show the appropriate setbacks from the lot boundaries as well as the limitations of height or any other requirements that might apply to a typical building in that zone. It is a very valuable tool if done carefully. It is practical, however, only in a community that has personnel adequately trained to produce the drawing in the first place and then to interpret it during the administration of the ordinance.

Regardless of the method used to describe the zone district boundaries, the illustrative explanation of zone requirements must be adopted together with the text in order for these elements to be legally a part of the zoning ordinance. The most common practice is to have the text itself state that the map and the schedule, as well as other graphic material, are incorporated as a part of the ordinance and are just as legally binding as the text. It goes without saying that care should be exercised to make certain that there is no conflict between the written text and the graphic presentations, either on the map or in the form of a schedule.

We have now examined the basic technical elements of zoning. One or more of these must be present in order for the zoning process to be undertaken. While all of them are desirable and helpful, it is not necessary that anything other than a zoning ordinance text be adopted. The zone boundaries and district lines can actually be described ver-

Schedule of Area, Yard, Building (Bulk), and Unit Requirements*
(A Part of Article 5)

Zone Category	Permitted Uses	Minimum Lot Size Area (sq. ft.)	Width (ft.)	Minimum Yard Requirements** Principal Building — Front (ft.)	Rear (ft.)	One Side (ft.)	Both Sides (ft.)	Per Cent of Maximum Lot Coverage of Buildings	Minimum Floor Area of Building Coverage (sq. ft.)	Max Height Principal Building Stories	Principal Building Feet	Accessory Building Feet	Minimum Area for Each Dwelling Unit (sq. ft.)	Special Permit Uses***
R-1-22	One-family dwellings, public and quasi-public uses	22,500	150	35	35	10	20	30	1,200	2½	35	15	1,200	Residential cluster development
R-1-15	One-family dwellings, public and quasi-public uses	15,000	120	35	30	10	20	30	1,000	2½	35	15	1,000	——
R-1-10	One-family dwellings, public and quasi-public uses	10,000	100	35	25	10	20	30	800	2½	35	15	800	——
R-2	Same as R-1 zones, two-family dwellings	10,000	100	35	25	10	20	30	800	2½	35	15	800	Town Houses, Garden Apartments
R-3	Same as R-1 zones, two-family dwellings	10,000	100	35	25	10	20	30	800	2½	35	15	800	Town Houses, Garden Apartments, Rooming and Boarding Houses, Fraternity and Sorority Houses, Conversions
C-1	Retail and Service Shops, Business and Professional Offices	10,000	100	25	20	10	15	60	1,000	2	30	15	–	Public Garages, Gasoline
C-2	Shopping Centers	44,000	150	75	50	25	50	40	2,000	2	30	20	–	Filling Stations
C-2	Auto-Oriented Commercial Activity	10,000	100	30	25	10	20	40	1,000	2	30	15	–	Public Garages, Gasoline Filling Stations
C-3	Commercial, Professional, and Industrial Service Shops	10,000	100	25	20	10	15	60	1,000	2	30	15	–	Public Garages, Gasoline Filling Stations
I-1	Light Industry, Scientific, and Research Laboratories, Office Buildings	44,000	150	75	50	25	50	40	2,000	2	40	20	–	––

*   See text of this ordinance for additional requirements.
** For Accessory Buildings see Article 6, Sub-section 601.3-6.
*** Public Utility Installations may be allowed in all zones by Special Permit.

Table 1. Sample Zoning Ordinance Schedule

bally by what is referred to as a "metes and bounds" description. It is considered a cumbersome and complicated way of doing it, but, in dealing with a rural community or one that has not experienced a great deal of development, it may not be necessary to have a map, and simple boundary descriptions can be included within the text. A map is a desirable tool, however, and the inclusion of one will lead to a better understanding of enforcement and administration.

So Now You Have Zoning—So What?

When all the outlined steps have been taken by the zoning commission, the preliminary ordinance text and map prepared, and public hearings held, you are ready to submit your final recommendations to the governing body. Assuming you have performed your duties well and have gained strong public support, it could be that the governing body can introduce the ordinance on first reading, conduct the required public hearing, and pass it as a law with the minimum of objection and no major changes. Life being what it is and zoning being what it is, the probability of this being the case is very slim. Your commission may have held firm against a few objectors because its members weren't elected and planning to try for re-election. These objectors and others as yet not heard from will be out in force before those who must be voted into office. If you have kept the mayor and council informed all through the process, explained why you have recommended as you did, and sought their support on anticipated major issues, they, too, might stand firm.

It must be accepted, however, that they are the policy makers and as such must have the final say. On their own, or after comments and suggestions made at public hearings, they have the authority to change or modify your recommendations. They may do this by instructing the municipal attorney to redraft a change in language, delete portions from the ordinance enacted, or have boundary or classifications changed on the map, or they have the prerogative of referring the ordinance back to you as a commission, with instructions about what they want to see changed. There is probably no greater test of the strength of character of an elected municipal official than that embodied in having to vote on a zoning ordinance. The only other type of local action I have seen that even comes close concerns considering the adoption of a dog and cat licensing, spaying and neutering ordinance.

An ordinance is finally passed, and, if you were part of the ad hoc zoning commission and not a member of an existing planning commission, your official duties have been completed and your commission is dismissed. As an individual, you should consider that a major step has been taken but that the work of building a better community has only begun. There will be many battles yet to be fought, many efforts to coordinate good planning with zoning needed, and many implementing policies and procedures to be established and carefully observed. As will be seen in the next chapter, effective administration of a zoning ordinance is vital but often difficult to develop and maintain because inept administration can totally destroy all your efforts. As a concerned citizen, your responsibility, like the job of building an improved community through zoning, has not ceased with the ordinance passage. It has just begun.

6

Zoning Administration

At the time of writing this, the expression, "the bottom line is . . . "
was in great vogue in the U.S. Actually, I have grown to hate the expression, and yet, I find myself unable to conjure up anything that could
more emphatically make the point I want to make. Therefore, I am
going to come right out and say it. The bottom line in effective zoning
after the passage of a well-drafted ordinance is administration. To add
emphasis to this, I would take the position that, if a local community
cannot or will not provide effective, professional administration, it
should not consider getting involved with zoning.

Any local ordinance depends upon administration and enforcement
for its success, but nowhere is there more true than with zoning. I have
said that having a foundation of comprehensive planning, and the structure of a well-prepared ordinance based upon that planning, is the
desired formula for establishing the mechanism of community protection and improvement. Even when this approach has been taken, all
will go for naught unless the municipality is totally committed to the
most competent, efficient administration and effective enforcement
possible. Proper enforcement is an affair of the entire community—
the individual citizen as well as the elected official. If any one or any
group ignores, abuses and overlooks too many human frailties, the
ruination of the zoning process will not be long in coming. A number
of individuals and agencies play an important role in determining the
success or failure of zoning administration and enforcement; these include the zoning officer, the responsible attorney, the zoning board of
adjustment, and the governing body.

When one starts looking for the basic force underlying the community
attitude determining the policy of administration of any matter of local
government, it is not long before the governing body is singled out.
These are the people elected to represent us all. They are the ones who
set the framework for the tangible character of the community, even
though their leadership may be but a reflection of the desires and

concerns of the people they represent. In other words, they are the tone setters, and, in order to understand zoning administration, it is necessary that we start with their role and their responsibility.

Unless a governing body understands the zoning process and lends full support to the ordinance, it will be impossible to achieve sound zoning practices. Legislative authority cannot be delegated and must rest squarely on the shoulders of the elected officials. Therefore, if they are convinced that zoning is important enough to the community to have an ordinance adopted, they certainly should understand that administration and enforcement are going to have to be a constant, living part of the process.

Policy Makers or Policy Breakers?

Each person or agency charged with administration of zoning, in fact, acts for the municipal government and is therefore directly responsible to the governing body. This is true whether it is a large city with a full complement of professional and trained personnel or a small, rural municipality with part-time officials.

In spite of this truism, it is amazing to find a condition that develops from time to time among the officials of a community. This is the attitude that, once the governing body passes a zoning ordinance, and appoints a zoning officer and a zoning board, there is nothing else they can do in connection with the administration of the ordinance. Elected officials may feel that anyone connected with zoning administration is independent of them and that they have no control over enforcement or the policy and attitude behind it. While it is true that under the zoning enabling legislation in most states the zoning board of adjustment is considered to be a semiautonomous body of a quasi-judicial nature, the appointments are still made by the governing body, and, therefore, the policy of the community should directly reflect that of the elected officials. There is no way to escape this fact, and there is no reason to try.

Volumes could be written on the importance of the appointments made in conjunction with zoning administration and still inadequately tell the story. One of the flaws in our American political system is that elected officials—who are members, in most cases, of a political party— feel obligated to appoint other members of the same political party to administrative positions within a municipality regardless of qualifications. In a great many cases, appointments are made as political patronage. Even though the positions may be unsalaried, there seems to be a certain amount of prestige attached to them, and they are viewed as political plums to be awarded to the party faithful, whether or not the individuals are knowledgeable on the subject.

I have seen zoning officers and members of zoning boards of adjustment who were appointed solely because of their political connections and who, I am sure, have never even bothered to read the zoning ordinance they were called upon to administer. Needless to say, the results in such cases are usually disastrous, not only for the zoning process, but for the entire community development program. We as citizens have only ourselves to blame. By failing to express our opinions either at the polls or during the course of the year following the election, we have permitted these conditions to develop; we shrug them off, saying, "Oh well, that's politics." Such an attitude is severely destructive of the democratic process.

Planning Commissions Can
Do More Than Just Plan

At the same time that the governing body has an important role to play in zoning, so does the planning commission. It has already been stated that a planning commission can be the zoning commission responsible for originally drafting the ordinance. Where this situation exists, their function in connection with zoning does not cease once the ordinance has been drafted and adopted. Just as the governing body has a responsibility for setting the zoning administration tone, so does this commission in their day-to-day work. In its approval of subdivisions, in its keeping the master plan current, it is, in fact, establishing a planning and zoning climate within the community. The members of the planning commission can and should be watchdogs over the zoning ordinance and zoning policy.

If the zoning officer or the zoning board of adjustment finds that a provision of the zoning ordinance is impractical or unworkable, the planning commission should be brought into the picture to make a study and recommendations. The matter can be referred to the planning agency, and it, in turn, can relate the question to its effect upon the overall comprehensive development plan. In many states, before a zoning amendment can be made, regardless of where it is started, it must be referred to the planning commission to study and report on. Enabling acts that carry this provision usually state that the opinion rendered is recommendatory and not mandatory; but, on the other hand, they add that more than a simple majority is required to override the opinion of the planning commission.

The commission can also be used as an advisory body in many routine zoning matters. There is nothing to prevent the zoning board of adjustment from delaying a decision on a matter before them until they can submit it to a planning commission and ask for its advice or comments. In this way, the zoning process, which is the effectuating tool of land development, can be closely related to comprehensive planning. In many ordinances where newer techniques of zoning such as planned unit development are used, the planning commission is called upon to be one of the agencies reviewing the application and determining its effect upon the master plan before permission for such use is granted. Above all else, it should be well-remembered that the planning commission and the zoning board are partners in zoning administration. When these two bodies work closely together, a municipality can expect better administration of its zoning. Where there is a feeling of jealousy or petty bickering resulting from a fear of infringement into the authority of either individual agency, the results will be harmful and inefficient.

A Thankless But Important Role—Zoning Officer

The zoning officer's job is day-to-day interpretation and administration of the ordinance. When a zoning ordinance is passed, the procedure is established requiring anyone who wants to build or alter any structure in the municipality to obtain a zoning permit. The application for a permit is filed with the zoning officer who, in turn, inspects all plans and specifications to see if they conform with the ordinance. Since most communities require a building permit for all structures under an adopted building code, it is usual practice in smaller cities to find that the zoning officer is also the building inspector. In larger cities, of course, this is not feasible, and building permits are obtained from a separate department. In rural communities, where the zoning officer frequently is also the building inspector, as a part-time municipal employee, with specified office hours within the municipal building, he or she is sometimes rather difficult to find and is nearly always particularly hard-pressed for enough time to take care of both jobs adequately. With the increasing complexity of our urban society, the day is rapidly approaching where it will be necessary for all municipalities to have full-time competently trained employees to administer the various codes and ordinances.

Whether it be on a full or part-time basis, the zoning officer's task is to make certain that the zoning ordinance functions properly. This person is the direct contact with most of the citizens who are applying for permits or who are asking questions about the zoning ordinance. The zoning officer also reports to the governing body on the problems that arise and on the difficulties they may have in enforcement. This officer has to make sure that the requirements of the ordinance are observed. The job does not cease on a building after issuing a permit for it. As it goes into the construction stage, it must be inspected from time to time to see that the specifications and standards set forth in the plans filed are being observed. The zoning officer is the recipient of many complaints and questions from neighbors and citizens within the municipality. The officer must patiently explain the ordinance to constituents and be able to give them interpretation of it in language they can understand.

While having considerable authority, this individual must also remember that he or she is a public servant and must at all times be courteous and friendly. However, a good zoning officer cannot afford

to be too friendly. If they pass out special favors to friends or overlook violations of the ordinance from them, not only are they failing to discharge duties properly, but they are asking for a great deal of trouble. It is always hard not to acquiesce when asked to do a favor for a friend; but anyone accepting the job should recognize that there is a sworn duty to uphold and that each person much be treated alike, regardless of whether known by the officer or not.

An additional word of caution: the zoning officer cannot deviate from any requirement of the ordinance in their interpretation. Anyone holding this position must be thoroughly familiar with the terms and conditions set forth in the zoning ordinance and be able to explain them. In granting or denying of permits, they are bound to the wording exactly as it is stated. They cannot change anything, or decide to ignore a particular clause, or interpret that something was meant in the ordinance but not stated. If there is any question or if there is any reason for a special interpretation, it is the officer's responsibility to see that the applicant is advised that this matter must go before the zoning board of adjustment. The zoning officer will find that the duties and responsibilities of that office are usually carefully spelled out in the state zoning enabling acts and in the ordinance that has been adopted. Not only should he or she be familiar with these provisions but should also be familiar with the entire zoning enabling act and zoning ordinance.

The Right Person—The Better the Job

Since this person plays such a vital role in the zoning process, it is important to give consideration to the qualifications for the job. He or she should be intelligent and of good character. There is no reason that a qualified person might not be someone who has at some time or another been engaged in the building business; however, he or she certainly should not be active in such affairs when called upon to assume the job of zoning officer. No one should undertake to administer a zoning ordinance who has a direct or indirect interest in anything that takes place in the municipality in connection with building development. If there is any situation that could cast a shadow on the zoning officer, the appointing body should be very certain that the matter is cleared up before the appointment is made and the duties of the office assumed.

In some communities, these facts are overlooked. I have heard people say that having an individual in the building business within the community as a zoning officer is extremely desirable because of his or her familiarity with problems involved. Nothing could be more detrimental to the administration of the zoning ordinance and more unfair to the official. An individual in that position is at a disadvantage by having his or her actions subject to question by people who fear a conflict of interest. At the same time, there is also the potential of having a zoning officer who is less than honest, and who will take advantage of the position for his or her own economic benefit. This is regretable but it is certainly something to bear in mind.

A good zoning officer, therefore, is one who is familiar with the community, is dedicated to it and interested in seeing it improved, has a general knowledge of building construction, gets along with people, and likes to deal with them. This is a very tall order, and it is not easy to find such an individual. Efforts to do so, however, will be rewarded by the efficient administration that will result. The zoning officer is the key to proper zoning within a community. The governing body that approaches this problem conscientiously, takes its time in making its selection, and provides a sufficient salary to attract a competent person will, in the long run, be rewarded for its efforts and the entire community will benefit.

The tools of enforcement available to zoning officers are numerous. First and foremost, of course, is the zoning ordinance and zoning map. They should be able to explain both of these to any applicant or to anyone questioning them. It is extremely helpful if their office has printed copies available so that applicants for permits or other interested persons can have one for their information. Also, there will be a variety of administrative forms to work with if the job is being done well. This starts with the form necessary to apply for a zoning permit. The zoning permit is that document issued by the municipality which indicates that an applicant has stipulated or filed plans showing that what will be done is in compliance with the requirements of the ordinance and is entitled to go ahead with the proposed construction, as long as compliance continues. The administrative form used for the application for the zoning permit should be carefully worded so that it is not too complicated but, at the same time, has all of the necessary information.

The zoning officer will also have administrative forms dealing with various inspections. Once construction starts, periodic inspection trips will be made, and there should be cards or forms upon which to log these trips and make pertinent comments. All of this material should be carefully filed in the zoning office so that all information on a particular construction job is readily accessible. Once construction has been completed, most zoning ordinances then require the individual to obtain what is known as a certificate of occupancy—in some ordinances referred to as a certificate of compliance. This is a further check to make certain that the construction is in compliance before occupancy of the structure can take place. Therefore, after construction has been completed, the applicant has the responsibility to return to the zoning office and to indicate on appropriate administrative forms that the project is finished, complies with the zoning requirements, and is ready for final inspection. The zoning officer studies the information submitted, conducts final inspection, and, then, if everything is in order, issues a certificate of occupancy.

Now Where Do We Fit In?

This brings us back to the question of the responsibility of the citizen in enforcement and administration. I have already mentioned the desirability of perpetual vigilance and a determination to express opposition to any violation of the zoning ordinance regardless of whether or not it may be unpopular. This applies to elected officials, to the zoning officer, to members of the zoning board of adjustment, and to the individual citizen. It may be difficult to stand up in public and object to something a neighbor wants to do but you must remember that, if they are permitted to do something to the detriment of the community, then, it is, in effect, granting a special favor at the expense of others and setting a precedent that will allow additional changes to occur that will downgrade property values.

The citizen's role in enforcement is to recognize that each of the aspects have a bearing on the success or failure of the zoning ordinance. We have the responsibility of seeing that the governing body is careful in its selection of personnel. We clearly have the responsibility of seeing that these people perform in the manner in which they have sworn to perform. Most of all, we have the responsibility of seeing that we are familiar with the original intent and purpose of the objectives of our zoning program, that we understand the purpose of zoning, that we recognize the importance of equal and fair treatment for all, and that we, ourselves, expect no special favors.

Then There Are the Relief Grantors

For the next several pages, we turn our attention to one of the most vital aspects of the zoning process. While the zoning board of adjustment has been mentioned many times already, the role that it plays in zoning administration is of such consequence that it is important to devote detailed discussion to its function.

We will start with the statement that, as used here, the zoning board of appeals and board of adjustment are one and the same. The difference lies solely in the wording of legislation, which varies from state to state. Running through all of these legislative acts, however, is the notion that while the state has given the municipal or county unit the right to zone, it also recognizes that there will probably never be a perfect ordinance.

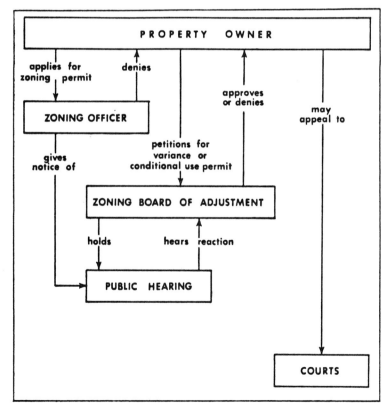

FIGURE 6. BOARD OF ADJUSTMENT
In a typical community, the Board plays a central decision-making role in the zoning process.

There will be situations that call for some adjustment to be made to the ordinance to provide a degree of flexibility. Not only is this flexibility desirable from the standpoint of having better zoning, but it may be absolutely essential to assure the community that each person will be able to utilize property in a reasonable manner. There will be unique situations in which the ordinance, if strictly applied, would be unfair or cause undue hardship. Recognizing this, the role of the zoning board has evolved and has become an established practice in the zoning process. Hence, part of the adoption of the zoning ordinance includes the creation of a zoning board, whether it is referred to as an appeals board or an adjustment board.

The Function of the Zoning Board

It is essential to avoid confusing this agency with the one previously referred to as the zoning commission. The zoning commission's function is to do the studies and make the recommendations for the original zoning ordinance. This is true whether this authority is delegated to an existing planning board or given to an especially created body that ceases to exist when its duties have been performed and the zoning ordinance adopted. The zoning commission is a creative agency while the zoning board is an interpretative agency. If you were to secure a copy of your state's zoning enabling act, it would describe how the zoning board is to be created, specify terms of office, and establish general standards for the conduct of business. Included would be a provision setting forth duties, powers, and authority. The best way to become familiar with the way a zoning board is created and how its members are appointed is to obtain a copy of this state zoning legislation. This usually can be done by contacting one of your local state representatives.

Regardless of which state you live in, as a result of the suggested model act of the 1920s mentioned earlier, you will find that the wording, setting forth how the board is created, and rules concerning appointments of its membership and their duties, will be similar to that included below. This was taken from the New Jersey act with with I was well acquainted some years ago, as follows:

40:55-36—Board of Adjustment; Appointment, Term, and Removal; Vacancies
The governing body or board of public works shall provide for the

appointment of a board of adjustment, which shall consist of five members who shall not hold any elective office or position under the municipality, each to be appointed for such term as the governing body or board of public works may prescribe and be removable for cause by the governing body or board of public works upon written charges and after public hearing. The governing body or board of public works shall provide for the filling of vacancies resulting from the unexpired term of any member. (As amended L. 1948, c.305)

40:55-37—Rules; Subpoenas

The board of adjustment shall adopt rules in accordance with the provisions of any ordinance adopted or in force pursuant to this article. The chairman, or in his absence, the acting chairman, shall have power to issue subpoenas for the attendance of witnesses and the production of records and may administer oaths and take testimony, and the provisions of the County and Municipal Investigations Law (1953) shall apply. (As amended L. 1953, c.37)

40:55-38—Meetings and Records

Meetings of the board shall be held at the call of the chairman and at such other times as the board may determine, and shall be open to the public. The board shall keep minutes of its proceedings showing the vote of each member upon each question, or, if absent or failing to vote indicating such fact, and shall keep records of its examinations and other official actions, all of which shall be immediately filed in the office of the board and be a public record.
(Source, L.1928, c.274)

40:55-39—Powers of Board of Adjustment

The board of adjustment shall have the power to:

A. Hear and decide appeals where it is alleged by the appellant that there is error in any order, requirement, decision or refusal made by an administrative official or agency based on or made in the enforcement of the zoning ordinance.

B. Hear and decide, in accordance with the provisions of any such ordinance, requests for special exceptions or for interpretation of the map or for decisions upon other special questions upon which such board is authorized by any such ordinance to pass.

C. Where by reason of exceptional narrowness, shallowness, or shape of a specific piece of property, or by reason of exceptional topographic conditions, or by reason of other extraordinary and exceptional situation or condition of such piece of property, the strict application of any regulation enacted under the act would result in peculiar and exceptional practical difficulties to, or exceptional and undue hardship upon the owner of such property, a variance from such strict application so as to relieve such difficulties or hardship; provided, however, that no variance shall be granted under this paragraph to allow a structure or use in a district restricted against such structure or use.

No Relief Impairing Zone Plan

No relief may be granted or action taken under the terms of this section unless such relief can be granted without substantial detriment to the

public good and will not substantially impair the intent and purpose of
the zone plan and zoning ordinance.
(As amended L. 194S. c.305)
(As amended L. 1949. c.242)
(As amended L. 1953. c.288)

The Games Some Politicians Play!

For legislative language, this provides a reasonably clear statement of
the powers of the board as intended by those who first conceived the
idea of a comprehensive zoning ordinance. These three functions are
those required for granting relief from a literal interpretation of the ordinance that would deny reasonable use of land and result in an undue
hardship. It is to be noted that the legislation prohibits the granting
of a variance relating to use.

I must be honest and confess I did not include here a section D that
had been tacked on to 40:50-39 of the New Jersey act at the insistence
of the politicians of that state. This omission was fully intentional. That
section is one of the worst things that ever happened to New Jersey
communities. What it did was to permit the zoning boards to hear appeals for use variances and to recommend approval to the governing
body upon the finding of "special reasons " The governing body could
then grant a permit for *any* use in *any* district by the passage of a simple resolution. As a consequence, over the years, the effectiveness of
most zoning in that state has been undermined by the creeping paralysis
frequently referred to as "spot zoning." It is my conviction that boards
of adjustment should be strictly prohibited from acting on or
recommending a variance that is related to use in any way. Changes
of use should result from amending a master plan of land use and the
subsequent zoning ordinance amendment passed by a governing body.

What and How to Appeal

In view of the key role played by this agency in good zoning administration, further explanatory comments about the duties and responsibilities
may prove helpful. First, it should be clear that it is just what the name
implies--an agency that can be appealed to for fair and equitable adjustment. As indicated in the New Jersey act, the initial need for his
can be the result of an administrative action by the zoning officer.

Upon applying for a permit, an applicant may be turned down by that officer because of the interpretation of a planned use. Where such a difference of opinion exists, the zoning officer should inform the applicant of the appeal process and the right to request a hearing by the zoning board. The board should not treat this matter lightly but should thoroughly research the issue calling on planning and zoning staff members for information and seeking well-founded legal advice before reaching decision. Zoning officers have been known to be wrong, and it is not the job of the board to quickly or arbitrarily support an administrative decision.

The second function involves a number of things, all of which should be spelled out in detail in the adopted ordinance. These include interpretation of the zoning map designations for district boundaries and graphic depiction of use categories, special exceptions, and any other matter that the governing body by specific ordinance language has deemed advisable for review by the board before the issuance of a permit. The special exception is the most complicated and difficult of these. This is one of the accepted ways to allow for certain uses that may be desirable, or even essential, in one or more zones but, because of their characteristics, should be allowed only under special conditions and after a clear demonstration that well-defined standards will be met. An example of this could be a community center, a church, or a private school. They may be beneficial to a single-family residential area, but, rather than allowing them as a permitted use, careful review of plans by the board ensures that they will relate well to the surrounding area. I would emphasize that this is not a matter of discretionary action by the board and that standards relating to such things as traffic, parking, open space, noise, and glare must be provided in the ordinance for guidance.

The third function—acting on requests for variances—is of such consequence that it will be discussed in detail in the next chapter.

Pick and Choose Carefully

Depending upon where you live and the enabling legislation of that state, the zoning board will be comprised of from three to probably not more than five people. Just who these people should be is an important question that is left up to local discretion. It is easier to point out the type of individual who should not be a member of the board than it is to describe the well-qualified member. No one should be appointed to the zoning board solely because of political connection or as a reward for political service. Just as is true with the zoning officer, no one should be on the board who has the possibility of a conflict of interest or whose personal business affairs could come under suspicion—for example, involved directly in a business endeavor that is dependent upon local construction.

It is frequently contended that such people as engineers, architects, real estate brokers, and builders are logical choices for members because of their knowledge and experience in the development field. This is certainly true, provided that they are not engaged in development activity within the municipality in which they serve. A person trained in architecture, for example, is well-prepared for zoning board duties as a result of background. If someone with this training can be found who is a local resident but who earns a livelihood through an enterprise located in some other commnity, appointment to the board would be appropriate.

On the other hand, a well-qualified architect who is designing houses for local subdividers or handling a lot of the construction activity of builders within the community, while certainly capable or rendering good decisions, and giving good advice—and may be perfectly capable of being objective—probably should not be asked to serve. There are any number of other professional backgrounds that can produce well-qualified, excellent members; these include law, planning, economics, and the social sciences, as well as representatives of the business and industrial community. Also, my experience has shown that women, whether they are professionals or not, perform better as zoning board members than men. However, I would add that, when all is said and done, the determining factor for all appointments should be the integrity and capability of the individual.

A general summary of the desirable characteristics of a zoning board member can be stated as follows: that person should:

1) Have a genuine interest in the community and be dedicated to serving the public;

2) Be intelligent enough to look objectively at a question and reach a decision on merit rather than on emotion;

3) Have enough time to devote to the duties and be willing to do so;

4) Be interested in broadening his or her own knowledge and be willing to study in order to learn;

5) Have an interest in the community as a resident or a property

owner but not have personal or financial involvement in the development taking place which would create a conflict of interest;

6) Be aware that practical politics play a role in everyday life but not be obligated to a political party—in other words, be a citizen of the community first and a member of a particular political organization second.

If these criteria are observed, it will make little difference as to the background of the individual appointed to the board. That person can be a doctor, lawyer, or Indian chief and still perform service to the community. A good appointee must recognize the role to be played and realize that there will be times when difficult decisions will have to be made. All members should be willing to make these decisions and to stand up for their convictions when called upon to do so.

We Are All on the Same Team

Once the makeup of the zoning board has been established and the members, in turn, understand their functions, the process of administering the zoning ordinance is underway. One of the more important questions will concern the proper relationship of the zoning board to the governing body and to the planning commission within the local jurisdiction. All three of these agencies should be on the same team and cooperate with each other in carrying out the development policy of the community. The planning commission has a vital role in determining direction for an area, and the zoning board contributes to carrying out planning policy. Both the planning commission and zoning board are established to serve the best interests of the municipality and to work with the elected officials.

At the same time, the relationship between the zoning board and the courts of the state is important. Members of the zoning board should recognize that they are considered to be a quasi-judicial body or an arm of the court. It is the court of the first resort for anyone concerned with proper administration or seeking adjustment relief under zoning law. Because of this, the zoning board must follow procedures that normally do not have to be followed by other administrative agencies within the community.

First of all, a careful record must be kept of all that goes on at the zoning board meeting. In some states, it is required that an actual court transcription be made of zoning board meetings, particularly when public hearing is involved. The courts are insisting, when they are called upon to review a zoning question, that the records be complete and that the entire case be presented before the board. The role of the court is to review the case and not to hear new testimony or accept new evidence.

It is important that the zoning board also have competent legal advice. In order for this advice to be impartial in all respects, it is probably desirable that the attorney giving it be appointed to serve the zoning board specifically and no other agency within the municipality. Some states are insisting upon this and are going so far as to say that even the municipal attorney should not advise the zoning board, since there may be a situation where the governing body will differ with the action of the zoning board and will want to ask its own attorney for advice on the matter. This is particularly true in New Jersey where zoning boards have the recommendatory function in connection with the so-called use variance, and the governing body then has the final decision. As zoning is basically a legal document, competent legal advice is a necessity for proper interpretation and to make certain that equitable decisions are reached. A word of caution: remember that even the appointment of the attorney to advise the zoning board should not be based upon political connections but on special skills in the legal aspects that relate to zoning.

Returning to coordination between planning commission, zoning board, and governing body, it should be mentioned that some states achieve this by the make-up of the organizations. In most enabling acts, membership on the planning commission is comprised, in part, of people serving the community in an elective capacity. In this way, a liaison is established between the elected officials and the planning commission. The planning or zoning legislation frequently says that a member of the zoning board may also be a member of the planning commission, this providing a bridge between the planning and zoning functions.

Unfortunately, as is true with so many other well-intended legislative provisions, the insertion of the human element frequently causes a problem. I have seen zoning boards of adjustment and planning commissions that are at loggerheads and literally do not speak to each other— this, in spite of the fact that they are both sworn to provide the kind of service to the community that will result in the greatest benefit possible.

Where a governing body clearly establishes development policy within the municipality, the planning commission follows the dictates of the responsibility assigned to it, and a zoning board recognizes itself to be quasi-judicial in nature and, called upon only to act on appeals, coordination should be assured. If this does not exist, the entire program is threatened and will suffer.

There's No Room for Battling over Turf

From time to time, the question will arise as to who should handle the evaluation of a zoning amendment or originate a change. There are some who say that it is logical for the zoning board to do so because its members work with these matters on a day-to-day basis. While it may sound very good on the surface, it is, of course, not good policy. The zoning board is an interpretative body called upon to make a determination on legislation that has been passed by another agency. Just as the courts are not expected to recommend legislation or to enact laws they must interpret, so the zoning board of adjustment should not be called upon to initiate zoning changes. In most of the state enabling acts, this point is made absolutely clear. Nevertheless, there are still those who, for one reason or the other, seem to misinterpret it. Foremost among these people are the members of the zoning board themselves.

The proper role of the zoning board in amendment and change should be indirect and advisory. A planning agency, either in originating or reviewing an amendment, should relate its decision on that amendment to knowledge of the comprehensive plan and the planning program of the community. If it is wise, it also will be interested in having a reaction from the zoning board, advising of any difficulty with the present ordinance.

The zoning board should call to the attention of both the governing body and the planning commission provisions in the ordinance that they are causing an undue number of requests for variances or provisions that are found to be impractical and unworkable. The planning agency should recognize that the knowledge gained by the members of the zoning board from day-to-day enforcement can add a great deal to an intelligent consideration of a major revision in other aspects. Those involved with planning should not hesitate to tap the zoning board members' experience and knowledge. The governing body should call upon the zoning board for recommendations; but the zoning board should certainly not take offense if it is not the one given the prerogative of drafting amendments or major revisions to the ordinance. Where there is a proper interrelationship and cooperation among these three agencies in a community, zoning policy will be greatly enhanced, and the end result will be much more effective.

7

Understanding the
Zoning Variance

Few people, including most members of zoning boards of adjustment, understand a zoning variance, why it has been built into the system, and how the justification for granting a variance should be determined. The greatest single cause for the failure of zoning to effectively guide land-use development so as to result in the betterment of our urban form has been the misuse of the variance technique—sometimes mistakenly or through ignorance and sometimes through purposeful and willful intent. Richard Babcock, a Chicago attorney noted for his zoning expertise, has been quoted as saying that 95 percent of all zoning variances granted in the United States are illegal. My experience in the field causes me to agree with this statement and, if I had any disagreement, it would be that I believe the percentage figure to be too conservative.

Regardless of whether this great number of variances would be found to be illegal if challenged and taken to court, few who understand the principles of good zoning would argue that the bulk of them would stand the scrutiny of justification based upon merit. The reasons for this are many. We have indicated one or two of the major ones in preceding chapters in the discussion of our political/profit society and the challenge of staffing a board of adjustment. Some other factors to consider include the unwillingness of both elected officials and appointed board members to learn what zoning is about, what the basis is for a legitimate variance, and how to avoid misconceptions of the duties of the board. In commenting on the latter, an even safer wager then backing Babcock's percentage figures would be the bet that 99.44 percent of all local officials involved in zoning adoption or administration have never read the zoning enabling act of their state, a good zoning text, or even their own zoning ordinance in its entirety. Even worse, they probably have never been exposed to a master plan or a planning study and certainly have not been troubled with the idea that good zoning practice is based on good planning principles.

The Continuing Saga—Of How Not to Do It

Again, Denver is a good illustration of how the lack of coordination between the zoning board and the planning function, careless board appointments, and a disinterest on the part of the administration and elected officials can lead to the failure to carry out desirable urban design principles and permit laissez-faire, haphazard development. I have indicated the unfortunate arrangement of the city's structure that allows a separate, independent zoning department. Over the years, this department has been permitted to be the authority on the intent of the ordinance, all amendments, and all variances. As such, it has become the power in shaping the pattern of development, both with the council and the mayor's office, and seems to do so with total disregard of planning and urban design principles. The director of the department shows little regard for planners or planning policies and has established himself as the final word on what the ordinance says, who can and cannot do what, and the way variance requests are handled.

To further add to this disjointed approach to planning implementation, Denver has a separate ordinance relating to the control of height of structures around the State Capitol/Civic Center complex and in areas where a pitiful attempt has been made to preserve one of the city's most valuable assets—the view of the Rocky Mountains. The zoning ordinance itself does not contain any height restrictions; the only controls, other than in these preservation areas, are the Federal Aviation Administration regulations. Those responsible for this separation from comprehensive zoning of one of the most important aspects of land-use control in their wisdom decreed that variances could be granted to the height limitations but by yet another independent agency, known as the "Board of Plan Enforcement Review and Variation"—a misnomer if there ever was one. The planning department and the planning function are totally ignored, but the zoning czar has a great deal to say about any variance requested, although the height ordinance is independent of zoning.

The point I want to emphasize in this chapter on zoning variances by these references is that the failure of citizens to understand the need for comprehensive planning, zoning's relation to it, and the vital aspect of all forms of administration to building a better community almost always will be found in any place where it is said that zoning has not or does not work. Zoning has been killed, where this has happened, by the failure of the elected officials, the policy makers, to have the intestinal fortitude to pass effective laws, to appoint capable people, and to insist on competent, objective, professional administration. They have allowed, instead, zoning boards to exist, even thrive, on a diet of improper and illegal variance granting. As is true in so many cases in our society, it is not the system that has failed, it is the people who have failed to make it work.

To change this situation, there is only one avenue available to us. We need to do a great deal more in the way of educating the general public in understanding the need for planning and the relationship of zoning and zoning administration to achieving any degree of success in community betterment.

All the elements of zoning discussed so far are vital, but it is my firm conviction that most important to understanding the principles and to making zoning work is the variance function. It is the key to whether a carefully formulated ordinance will be meaningful or not. The misconceived notion that "one little variance won't hurt" has been the seedling that, once planted, leads to the growth of the forest that obliterates a clear vision of the true purpose of land development controls through zoning.

Variance—Difference, Divergence, Discrepancy

If you want to be one of those working to improve things in your community, a good place to start is with the definition of variance. Even though I have said that use variances are expressly prohibited in most state legislative acts because there are exceptions and because my experience has been that many local boards ignore that prohibition, for the purpose of the discussion here they will be included, albeit reluctantly. The word "variance" is defined as:

> 1. The quality, state, or fact of varying or being variant; a changing or tendency to change. 2. Degree of change or difference; divergence; discrepancy.

Webster's *New World Dictionary* goes so far as to include,

> 3. Official permission to bypass regulations; specifically, permission to make nonconforming use of zoned property.

A quick reading of this might lead to the conclusion that Webster has recognized and sanctioned the "use of land" variance, but understanding the phrase "nonconforming use of zoned property" can correct that mistaken impression.

As is implied by the word, any structure or parcel of land located within a zoned community when an ordinance is passed or an amendment is adopted that does not comply in every detail with the terms of the requirements is nonconforming. A grocery store existing in a single-family neighborhood becomes a nonconforming use, entitled to continue operation indefinitely, when the area is zoned in accordance with the predominant use. So, too, does a house become a nonconforming use if the ordinance specifies side-yard requirements greater than the distances existing on that property at the time of adoption. Likewise, any lot having less area than that set forth as a minimum necessary for the creation of a legal lot, but already platted, assumes nonconforming status. It then follows that any variance granted creates a new "nonconforming use of zoned property." As nonconformance and any approved variance runs with the land—is transferrable from one owner to another—the seriousness of the consideration that should be given to approval of any variance request becomes obvious. If the approval pertains to use, legally or illegally sanctioned, it can result in a change of characteristics of an area that can lead to requests for other variances, deterioration of property values for the purpose of the zoned use, and, ultimately, the necessity of an amendment permitting more intensive uses. Indiscriminate variances, therefore, can be considered blockbusters in the worst sense of the term.

Under the provision existing in the New Jersey statutes allowing consideration of use variances, during my years of involvement there, I witnessed many examples of this practice and the horrendous results. In most states, the changing of use by the variance technique would be considered an inappropriate delegation of legislative authority, declared illegal by the courts, and referred to as "spot zoning." In New Jersey, at least at the time of my involvement, it was astounding how large that "spot" could become. I recall appearing as an expert witness on behalf of a citizen group that was protesting the granting of a variance that would allow a 17-acre shopping center to be imposed on a residential neighborhood, contrary to the existing single-family zoning of the property. There were no special use permit standards or any other kind of standards set forth in the ordinance to provide guidance to the zoning board. The proposed use, clearly large and dominant, would change the entire character of the area, alter the traffic volume and pattern, and have an impact on the total environment, yet the opportunity for planning review and better public scrutiny available through the amendment process had been bypassed. Happily, in this case, enough evidence was presented to convince the judge of this, and the matter was remanded to the governing body for proper consideration. The developer, not wanting to run the risk of examination of the project in terms of good planning principles, then quietly stole away, no doubt to find another community where citizens were not as concerned, organized, and determined.

Protection of Rights, or Granting of Special Privilege?

With that as an example of variance misuse, what then is the basis for zoning variances that should be branded on the minds of zoning board members and elected officials? First and foremost is the principle that variances do not have to be granted automatically each time one is requested and that the process should be used sparingly. The applicant must clearly show that, due to unique circumstances, literal enforcement of the terms of the ordinance would deny him or her the opportunity to use the land in the same way others in that zoning district can use their land. This could be because of some unusual topographic features—an irregular-shaped parcel or an undersized lot lying between already developed property—or any number of unique situations not fitting into the zoning model through no fault of the applicant. The purpose of a zoning variance is to provide fair treatment and equal opportunities to all and to see that individuals are not penalized because of circumstances beyond their control.

Instead, most boards of adjustment grant special privileges to applicants. They allow something to occur on one lot that all other landowners in like circumstances are not permitted to do by right, without a true showing that denial would deprive the owner of a legitimate use of property. If I want to add a room to my house, thus infringing on the open space requirements for the lot, and am given the variance I request to do so, everyone else in that zoning district should expect to be able to do the same thing—either by variance or, more preferably, by a well-conceived amendment. To do otherwise is to grant me a special favor, perhaps at the expense of the light and air of my neighbor and the aesthetics of the area. Many communities adopt the position that a variance is the preferred way to operate, under the misguided belief that it is easier to deal with individual problems than it is to say no and preserve the integrity of a zoning ordinance; after all, not everybody is going to want to ask to do something similar anyway. No wonder Babcock says that the majority of variances granted are illegal.

The discussion here has been about a single-family residential situation, but variances for apartments, businesses, and industry where proven legal hardship has not been the reason for approval can be even more devastating to sensible zoning. One more experience from my New Jersey days illustrates the point very well (although I also could relate some hair-raising examples from Albuquerque and Denver). It dramatically shows the damage a zoning board can do as a quasi-judicial body not subject to any review, except by the filing of a court suit challenging the action taken.

Doing the "Jersey Bounce"

My consulting firm had been engaged by a client community to prepare a comprehensive plan and a revised zoning ordinance. The plan showed the need for increasing the economic development and tax base of the locality. It was predominantly a bedroom community with few assets for attracting business development other than a highway that traversed its entire length. Not wanting to permit this rather heavily traveled arterial to be subject to strip commercial development, we proposed the creation of activity center nodes in carefully selected areas along the road. Written into the ordinance were some rather stringent standards relating to design and impact that any applicant would have to meet to receive a zoning permit. Soon after our plan and ordinance had been adopted by the local governing body, an application was filed for construction of a chain discount store that failed completely to meet the standards set forth. The zoning officer had no choice but to deny the permit, and the developers immediately filed a variance application with the board of adjustment.

Their appeal was based on a claim of "hardship" in meeting the requirements for off-street parking, setback, ingress and egress with the highway, landscaping, building size limitations, and a number of other controls. Their hardship, of course, was that they would have to spend more and could not make as much money out of the parcel if they had to comply. The usual scare-tactic argument was also given that, unless they got the variances requested, they would be forced to take their beautiful tax-generating, employment-producing operation to some other municipality along the highway.

In spite of the 18 months of preparation of the plan and ordinance, newspaper articles and educational material distributed, and numerous public hearings on the intent and policy behind the zoning standards, it was as if the members of the board of adjustment had lived in solitary confinement during that period. In addition, they were obviously hypnotized by the eloquent arguments of the attorneys for the appellant and, after some 15 minutes of deliberation, granted variance from seven of the more important provisions of the ordinance. Had this decision been allowed to stand and become one more on the list of illegal variances granted, the total character of the highway frontage would have changed from that envisioned by the plan, and the potential for attracting desirable development of quality would have been lost.

In this case, the governing body, while having no legal review authority over the zoning board's action, was comprised of members with a determination to protect their zoning policy and the courage to do so. They rallied the planning commission immediately and collectively informed the zoning board that its action was improper and destructive in terms of the basic zoning policy and that, if necessary, a suit would be brought against them by the governing board and the planning commission. The zoning board decided that discretion was the better part of valor, revoked its action, and the integrity of the ordinance was preserved. It would be impossible to guess the number of times that destructive action such as this has been taken by uninformed boards and has gone unchallenged and unchecked.

Know the Difference Between Good and Bad!

I have said quite a bit now about bad variances and the principles to be kept in mind in testing the validity of a legitimate variance request.

Good Variance

The top solid line—The standards applying to all, the granted rights they have.

The lower solid box—An individual lot that, because of peculiar and special conditions, cannot meet those standards and enjoy the same granted rights as others.

The dashed line—The elevation of the "hardship" lot to the same rights and privileges of others by an allowed variance

Bad Variance

The solid line—The standards applying to all, the granted rights they have

The dashed box—Granting special privilege by variance that allows something to be done that others do not have a permitted right to do, and it is not necessary to overcome a proven hardship in order for a reasonable use to be made of the land.

The primary difference is whether the decision justified relief or awarded a special privilege. Years ago, Gordon Whitnall, an old friend and one of the best experts on zoning we have had in this country, taught me a simple, diagrammatic way to illustrate the difference between legitimate and illegitimate variances—good and bad variances--and there is no better way to emphasize what I have been saying than to include it here.

This simple graphic should negate immediately the most common argument put forth by an applicant for a nonhardship variance and the most frequent rationalization practiced by zoning board members in granting bad variances that "this one little variance isn't going to do any harm."

Why is it so easy to explain the principle of the difference between good and bad variances, illustrate it in a simple diagram, and yet have thousands of improper ones granted each year? If zoning as originally adopted is supposedly based on planning principles, why are there so many variances granted, even if the bulk of them are well deserved and could withstand a legal challenge? The record will show, for example, that Cincinnati, Ohio, a city that prides itself on being one of the first in the country to have a comprehensive master plan and an elaborate planning program, granted 1,493 variances out of 1,940 requests in a 10-year period. Nor should the Queen City on the Ohio be singled out. In Cleveland, in eight years, out of 2,307 requests, 1,289 were acted on favorably. Philadelphia showed that it was the "City of Brotherly Love" by awarding 4,000 out of a total of 4,800 in a period of only four years. Skipping around the country, Austin, Texas, approved 240 out of 359 requests; Milwaukee, 121 out of 136; and Trenton, New Jersey, 100 out of 110—all in a one-year period. Surely the basic zoning could not have been that bad and that wrong!

A Modern Fairy Tale

The answer to the two questions posed in the previous paragraph is a simple one. It is human nature. I said earlier that being a member of a zoning board of adjustment and doing a good job is one of the toughest assignments in local government. If you don't believe that, put yourself in the place of Jane Justice and Dick Doright, who have accepted an appointment to their local zoning board in their hometown, population 12,301. Both have lived there all their lives, know almost everybody, and are active in church and in social affairs. Dick sells insurance, and most of his clients are people of influence in town—the movers and shakers. Jane is a young attorney, just starting out on her own, trying to establish her clientele among the "right" people.

The zoning ordinance has recently been adopted, based upon two years of study and development of a comprehensive plan. The future land-use plan contained therein recommended a single-family area in one part of town that, because of the lack of public sewers and the inability to finance them in the near future, had to rely on septic tanks. Building lots should have a minimum width of 125 feet and an overall area of not less that 18,000 square feet. This was supported by a thorough study of the soils of the area and endorsed by the state health department and the local health officer. As a consequence, the town council, after several public hearings and considerable wrangling from the usual number of townspeople opposing all zoning, had screwed up their courage, passed the recommended zoning ordinance, including the zoning for this single-family area.

What is the first case brought before the board and our friends, Jane and Dick? You guessed it! Marvin Moneybelt, president of the largest bank in town, president of the local country club, and heavy contributor to the political compaigns of the majority of the members of council, happens to own a lot in this unsewered area that measured 200 feet wide, street frontage, and 150 feet deep. Marvin had bought the lot for speculation and had planned to divide it into two lots for sale. He had known about the planning and zoning studies going on but did not see why a man of his importance and influence should be bothered with such trivia. Certainly, he did not have the time to waste in reading things like lot dimension and area requirements in a zoning ordinance.

Since the zoning officer did not bank at Marvin's bank, Marvin's first shock was being turned down when he proposed creating two lots measuring 100 feet X 150 feet. So now Marvin and his attorney George Glib are before the zoning board. George is 64 years old, the town's "leading" attorney, handles cases for many of the town pillars, most of whom are clients of Dick's and represent the kind of business coveted by Jane. In addition, George is a key member of the behind-the-scenes power group of six people in town and is often referred to as a "king-maker." His magnificent oratory and melifluous tones spell out the strong case he feels he has for Marvin—surely the board would not harbor any thought of turning down this simple request for a man who has done so much for the town. George concluded, using God, mother, and country and the usual cliche, "when everything else is considered, what harm can this one little variance do?" Not once, however, in his prolix presentation did he lay a legal foundation that would move Marvin's application out of the category of the bad variance.

The board went into executive session, deliberated, and reached a decision. What was that decision? What did our friends Dick and Jane do? If the decision was to approve Marvin's request, did anyone challenge it and subject it to court review? What would you have done if you had been Jane or Dick?

After All—To Err Is Human

This fable tells a lot about one of the major problems in our system that makes effective zoning difficult. There is a need for providing some flexibility in zoning and certainly for allowing relief from inequities, but have we devised the best way to do this and to avoid the kind of situation in which the board in this story was placed? Few are those who understand the philosophy that, unless the applicant has proven his or her case beyond all doubt as one necessary to overcome a hardship not self-imposed, they have no choice but to deny the request. Acting on this premise becomes doubly difficult when we add that few, if any, applicants have the least grasp of the legal aspects of a justifiable variance and thus, no understanding of why they can, and should, have their request denied.

We are all human, all have human frailties, and like to think of ourselves as compassionate human beings. A vivid example of the pull of compassion concerns an elderly widow living in her home of 50 years. She wants to stay there but finds that rising taxes and utility costs make it impossible. She could solve the problem by taking in boarders or converting her third floor into a rental apartment. The fact that her home is in a restrictive single-family zone can mean very little to her in her quest for a solution to her problem. To her, it is a hardship not to be able to do what she wants with her house. However, in the cold, hard, light of the legal considerations of good zoning and the protection of neighborhood character, community interest must be given more weight than emotion. There is no question that widows like this have our respect and concern, but a meaningful zoning policy requires biting the proverbial bullet. It is a difficult position to be in, and our friends Jane and Dick and others like them are not to be envied when called upon to decide matters like this.

There are many reasons for bad variances other than exerted influence, personal involvement, and emotion. Prime among these is the lack of interest you and I as citizens exhibit in good zoning administration, especially the operation of the zoning board in acting on variances. Few persons who have not been directly involved are aware of the existence of such an agency and the importance of the role it can play in shaping the community. Not many of us would think of attending one of its hearings, just to see what they do and how they do it. Unless a variance request is in our immediate neighborhood, would obviously have an effect on our property values, and we know that other neighbors are going to protest, we probably wouldn't attend the meeting to add our voices to the protest. The granting of a variance to a major bank in Denver, allowing them to encroach into the mountain view protection area with the height of a new building, should have been of grave concern to the almost 500,000 residents of the city, and yet it aroused only a piddling few. Granted, it was done in an aura of secrecy with no general advance publicity—a climate guaranteed to foster bad variances.

The Name of the Game Is Politics

There is no question that many bad variances result from bad politics. We must accept that zoning offers the opportunity, through misuse and improper discretionary decisions, to be a powerful tool for building political power and political machines. Appointments to zoning boards are sometimes based only on political considerations. A political appointee is expected "to play the game" and will be called upon by less-than-honorable office holders and powerful political figures to "take care of the right people." As has been seen by indictments and jail sentences in some cities, the worst of these abuses can lead to graft and corruption. Doing away with zoning, rather than correcting this potential wrong, would only invite greater abuse and provide additional opportunity for it to occur. But we will never have good government if good people are not participants as well as leaders.

Outmoded or overly complex state enabling legislation and confusing and unclear local zoning ordinances can cause bad zoning variances.

Where the ordinance wording is a mishmash of legal jargon, difficult to comprehend, and sometimes contradictory, good administration by a zoning officer or a zoning board will be less likely to occur and undesirable desisions will be more frequent. Both state legislators and local elected officials have a responsibility for seeing that the tools provided for all zoning administrative procedures are modern, well prepared, and easy for both the public and official representatives to understand.

Still another reason for bad variances is the absence of adequate rules of procedure for the board itself. Frequently, there is a lack of comprehension on the part of the members as to procedural questions and administrative requirements. This leads to failure to require proper and formal application and sufficient proof by the applicant seeking a variance. In some communities with which I have been involved, members of the zoning board who have served a number of years still did not know the proper parliamentary or legal proceedings that should be followed. This is another reason, perhaps, for the failure of the zoning board to be willing to recognize the importance of relating zoning variances to the principles of comprehensive planning. Some board members seem to feel that any indication of a need for help from comprehensive planning in evaluating a variance request would indicate the lack of knowledge on their part. Nothing could be further from the truth, and this very attitude reveals more than anything else their lack of understanding of the zoning process.

Some Guideposts Always Help

It should be stated that many of the critical comments made here regarding the functions of zoning boards are included for emphasis and are certainly not applicable in every case. In all fairness, it should be pointed out that there are any number of good zoning boards in this country. While there may be a question as to the results of the total board, there are a number of devoted, dedicated people who are doing their best to assure that sound zoning principles will be followed. Unfortunately, however, we have not as yet reached the point where all of our zoning administration is of the caliber necessary and desirable to protect our communities.

In an effort to help those who have been or may be asked to take on this important assignment, here is some advice for zoning board of adjustment members:

- Take the job seriously and to be well informed;
- Be conscientious and objective;
- Be fair but firm, and do what you think is right;
- Make certain that fair hearings are conducted and that each party in interest is given an opportunity to be heard;
- Study each matter carefully and render a judicious decision based upon well-documented information, findings, and conclusions;
- Protect the intent and purpose of the zoning ordinance and established zoning policy;
- Relate all requests and action taken to the effect on comprehensive planning and the principles of good planning;
- Protect the best interests of all property owners, whether they are the applicant, neighbors, or those who live on the other side of town;
- Avoid setting undesirable and destructive precedents;
- Remember that any action taken may be subject to review by the courts.

Next, I would like to suggest some guidelines for zoning board procedure and some checkpoints that may help in avoiding bad variances:

1. The first prerequisite is a good ordinance. A sound fundamental base must be laid for the zoning process if zoning administration is to be successful and properly done. A weak ordinance will mean weak administration and problems for the zoning board.

2. The zoning board itself must know its job, be carefully briefed on its authority and responsibility, and be properly organized. The chairman should be someone who is capable of conducting a meeting, not only of the board, but also of the public. The board should have adopted carefully prepared and clearly stated administrative procedures that set forth their rules of operation, and these should be adhered to. In conducting meetings, everyone must be treated fairly but firmly. There should be no special privileges or special favors granted to anyone, either in the amount of time allotted or in placement on the agenda. The rules of procedure should be studied by each member, and, as new members are added, it should be their first duty to read the zoning enabling statute, the zoning ordinance, and to become thoroughly familiar with the procedural organization of the board.

3. A properly functioning zoning board of adjustment makes certain that it has good legal advice available. In most cases, it is wisest to

have a special attorney assigned to the board because there is the question of a conflict of interest if the municipal attorney is assigned this role. A qualified attorney should be assigned specifically to the board, and sufficient funds should be allocated so that adequate time can be made available to take advantage of this expertise. Not all attorneys are necessarily well-versed in zoning law. Just as you would not ask a corporation counsel for a opinion on a divorce suit, neither can you expect the average attorney to be able to walk into the zoning arena and be a zoning expert. There are a number of attorneys who are specialists in the zoning field, and you should insist that your board has available to it the best possible legal advice. A good attorney is invaluable in advising on the routine decisions of the board, in keeping the municipality out of the courts, and, when it is necessary to go to court, in presenting a strong case.

4. It is the job of the applicant to prove that the strict application of the ordinance will not be a fair and equitable treatment. The burden of the presentation is on the applicant, and, in this type of consideration, the ordinance is presumed to be equitable for all until it is proven otherwise. An applicant who comes in with a filled-out application but without a proper case, showing that the provisions of the ordinance as written create an inequitable situation, should not be granted a variance. The applicant who has the best possible case and who does not present the facts to the board likewise should not have a variance granted. It is not up to the zoning board to present the case for the individual, nor is its job to see how to find a way to do what has been requested and, in turn, to get around the law.

5. In presenting proof, it must be shown that the provisions of the ordinance as they are written cannot be fairly applied to the property. This is particularly true where there is any provision allowing a variance for use or permitting a use not otherwise included in the zoning district. Often, a variance has been granted for a use not permitted in a zone without adequate information to indicate that strict enforcement of the ordinance as written would result in substantial harm to the applicant's property. Each member of the zoning board should always measure the application with the question, Has this person shown me that he or she cannot do what our ordinance requires and still receive protection of the right to utilize property? In about 99 cases out of 100, the applicant could live within the law and still have fair and reasonable treatment.

6. Any time a variance is being considered, the members of the zoning

board should be convinced from the facts before them and from their knowledge of the community and its planning that the granting of the variance will in no way be detrimental to the zone plan and ordinance or to the comprehensive development of the community. In almost all state enabling acts, there is the provision that a variance can be granted only upon a finding that there will be no detriment to the surrounding property or to the overall community. Some zoning boards are reasonably careful regarding immediately adjacent property but fail to take into account that, if any variance or exception granted would be detrimental to *any* part of the municipality, they are duty bound to turn it down. At the same time, they must be careful to make certain that they have enough facts at their disposal to indicate the detrimental nature of the proposed use. It cannot be simply a matter of opinion.

7. Finally, while it may seem an overgeneralization, the members of a zoning board should post a sign in large letters that reads, "An Application *Can* Be Denied." They should remember that they can say no, regardless of how well known an applicant is or how emotionally appealing the proposal may be. By doing so, they will maintain the integrity of the zoning, probably have the gratitude of the thinking people of the community, and do a great deal to wipe out bad variances.

Perhaps We Should Dare to Be Different

Having discussed the present method of handling variances and zoning boards in general, I am compelled to suggest that, while I have defended zoning as a workable tool for shaping desirable development, I question whether the method we now use to process variance appeals is the best system for protecting good zoning policy. Unfortunately, state legislatures have been more than reluctant to consider modernization or any change in zoning board procedure or a better way to cope with the variance problem. Few state enabling acts have been greatly altered from the 1922 Department of Commerce suggested model. Where there have been attempts at updating or modernizing, the functions of the zoning board have remained much the same as before and the opportunity for politically inspired variances religiously protected. For example, New Jersey comprehensively revised its land-use laws in 1975, passed amendments in 1979 and 1980, but retained the same variance procedure except to make a use variance easier to grant. Since most of the members of the Colordo legislature are opposed to all land-use controls—and, if they thought they could get away with it, would repeal all zoning and planning laws—they certainly are not considering modernizing them. This in a state that has more need for such laws than almost any other, due to the present impact from energy-related development.

Nevertheless, change should be considered and should take place not just in Colorado, but nationwide. I would suggest four possibilities for revising the variance procedure:

1. *Create a "Public Defender" system.* The great bulk of zoning variances are granted on the basis of a one-sided case presentation or with the odds heavily stacked against citizen groups or individuals who might object. Applicants applying for a variance of major consequence, especially where it may relate to use, usually are corporations or well-financed developers with seemingly unlimited resources for case preparation and presentation. They march in a troop of professionals and experts with charts, slides, and fancy, colored drawings. A parade of witnesses testify how important the proposal is to the future of the community, the taxes it will produce, and that the variance will have no adverse effect upon the area or the intent and purpose of any adopted plan or the zoning ordinance. In most instances, they have done their homework well and propagandized the neighborhood in order to convince any objectors not to appear. Or the application may be for an area largely undeveloped, with the nearby land all owned by others awaiting their turns at the variance table. The difficulty comes from the inadequacy of the representation of the community interests before the hearing body.

The individual and most citizen groups do not have the money to hire experts and to go with an attorney before a zoning board to argue against a particular variance. They may not be familiar with or understand the procedure they will be facing. The zoning board, while it is supposed to represent the public interest in its consideration, is not, in most communities, equipped to send out its own team of investigators and researchers to uncover information that might present a different story. The planning commission, while it may be concerned, probably is not in the position to deal with the specific question of an individual lot. It, too, through the lack of funds and perhaps even the lack of knowledge of the fact that the application has been filed, cannot be expected to send a team out to obtain technical data and information to present at the hearing.

My argument is that we have a decided weakness in the zoning process, particularly since courts are now insistent that the case before them shall be the case that was heard by the zoning board and that no additional information or evidence can be added. This means that, unless a full case is presented *for the public* at the zoning board level, the court will not have facts presented on behalf of the public to consider when called upon to review the matter. If we are going to progress in the zoning field and if everyone, including the general public, is to be treated equitably, it behooves us to find some way for all facets of the situation to be explored and made part of the record. Unless this is done at the zoning board level, it may never be done.

A number of our courts are recognizing this and are remanding cases to zoning boards with instructions that there be full disclosure, not only of the information submitted on behalf of the applicant but also of information that might come from such sources as a governing body, a planning commission, or technicians employed by the municipality. I remember vividly sitting on a witness stand as an expert witness while two attorneys argued over my right to be there since I had not appeared before the zoning board of adjustment. In this case, no one in opposition to the applicant had appeared before the board. It had heard only one side of the picture, yet it was in no position to go out and do its own investigation. They were average, ordinary citizens, but they were expected to stack a professionally presented technical case against their own knowledge and to reach a Solomon-like decision.

I feel that we need to correct this situation and that in every case where a major item of concern is involved in a zoning variance (perhaps this could be limited to any variance, exception, or permit dealing with a use rather than area requirements), there should be a provision made for the presentation of the case for the public. Perhaps what is needed is a public zoning attorney, just as in some states we find a public defender in dealing with criminal matters.

2. *Abolish the Board of Adjustment.* There has been some experimentation, primarily in home-rule municipalities, with abandoning the zoning board idea and creating a paid, professional hearing officer. This is only being mentioned here and will be discussed further in Chapter 11.

3. *Give neighborhood organizations a voice.* Many people think that the hope for the future of more effective government lies in a greater role in decision making being assigned to the neighborhood level. Zoning amendments and variances would seem to be a logical place for this to occur. Legislative authority must remain in the hands of elected officials and cannot be delegated, but there are at least two ways in

which neighborhoods could be given an official voice in all zoning decisions pertaining to use and major bulk changes.

The first would be to create a formal system whereby the governmental structure recognizes organized neighborhood groups or associations. When a proposal arises for change in use or bulk beyond an established measurement of intensification—to distinguish between a major or minor change—the neighborhood would be authorized to conduct an official hearing and then vote on its recommendations. These would be forwarded to the zoning board or governing body, depending upon the legislation of the state, with a two-thirds vote required to overrule the neighborhood recommendations.

Another way would be more drastic. This is to establish an elected "zoning council" in each officially established neighborhood with the authority to make final decisions on those changes affecting use and substantial bulk. Admittedly, this system would have some potential for spreading the possibility of collusion and abusive misuse, but, with the decisions still subject to court review, I doubt that it would create a situation any worse than that which now exists in many places. A strong plus is that it would create a greater incentive for people to become more familiar with the zoning process and what is going on in their neighborhoods.

4. *Establish a zoning "jury" panel.* I believe this suggestion holds the greatest potential for correcting a lot of the present evils and doing some constructive good. We certainly are not getting qualified zoning experts on zoning boards now, and we have not found a way to get the general public informed and involved in this most important aspect of shaping our future physical form. One way to improve the situation would be to abolish all zoning boards and go to a zoning jury system.

Just as we are all subject to being called for civil and criminal jury duty, so would we be for zoning duty. Periodically, a jury panel would be picked from the same list used for other juries, and, as the need arose, a zoning jury of 12 citizens would be picked by lot from those on the panel subject to call. They would hear only cases related to use or major bulk changes requested by private interests, whether through amendment or variance. All other matters normally handled by zoning boards would be processed through a hearing examiner. The decision of the jury could be legislated as being final, or, it could be merely a recommendation to the governing body requiring a two-thirds or three-fourths vote to overrule.

Think of what such a system would do to the wheelers and dealers who now adroitly manipulate the present process. They would not know who would be hearing their case until the jury was picked. They would have great difficulty in gaining favorable action except on the merits of the case. Not only would the public have more knowledge of what was to be heard through the increased publicity that would result, they would have a greater opportunity to be heard without previously determined, sometimes stacked, decisions having been made. Knowing that they might be called upon to hear a case, more people would be interested in finding out just what zoning is all about and how it works—a plus that alone would be worth any increased effort or expense that might result.

Without doubt such a proposal would not be popular with professional politicians and would be bitterly resisted by them, but, who knows, maybe it's an idea whose time has (*should*) come!

8

Zoning Hearings and the Citizen's Role

Regardless of what action is taken in conjunction with a zoning ordinance, a public hearing is involved to inform the public and to allow public expression. This holds true whether it is an ordinance adoption, amendment, special permit consideration, or variance. Depending upon the matter under consideration, the state statutes, and the wording of the local ordinance, those hearings are held by the planning (zoning) commission, the governing body, or the zoning board of adjustment. Least understood is the role of the zoning board, although we should all be aware of the hearing process required by other similar agencies. Because of the need to understand this role, I am going to outline the steps resulting in an appeal for a variance that would lead ultimately to a public hearing by that body and comment on how it is conducted.

The Case of the Expanding Dining Room

Let's make the assumption that you own a home located in a one-family residential zone where there is a requirement for a 75-foot minimum lot width, with total side yards of not less than 20 feet, no one of which shall be less than seven feet. You built your house so that one side yard measured eight feet and the structure extended 50 feet across the lot width, leaving 17 feet for the side yard. You decide that your house would be greatly enhanced by expanding your dining room, located next to the larger side yard, but, to allow for that big, beautiful set of antique dining room furniture willed you by your rich aunt, you need to extend the room out six feet. That leaves 11 feet on that side, plus the eight on the other side for a total of 19—one foot short of the minimum open side yard total required.

You have your plans drawn knowing that you must obtain a building permit, but, not being too familiar with the zoning ordinance, you do not know about the zoning permit. You go into the local municipal building. You find that you must locate the building inspector, who turns out also to be the zoning officer. When told that you would like to obtain a building permit, you are asked what you have in mind and whether you have any plans. You show the zoning officer the plans you have had prepared, and they are checked against the zoning ordinance map. After some study, the officer informs you that what you have planned to do is not permitted by the zoning ordinance. He has no alternative because, where there is any deviation from the legal requirements of the ordinance, the person responsible for administration must deny you the zoning permit. They do not have discretion in this matter. At the same time, they would (or should) inform you of the procedure to be followed in case you want to carry the matter further. In other words, while they must deny you the permit, you do have the right, if you feel that you are justified in doing so, of appealing to the zoning board and asking them to grant you "relief" in this particular case. We will assume that you are interested in going further (although I make no comment on your having a legally justifiable hardship case). You, in turn, are instructed by the zoning officer as to what you must do.

First, you must fill out an application for a variance. The application form requires a great deal of information about what you have in mind, under what part of the ordinance you are filing an appeal, and why a variance is necessary for you to be treated fairly. When this is completed, you attach a set of your building plans and pay a filing fee, filing the application with the municipal clerk or some other appointed officer in the municipal building. The zoning board of adjustment will be notified and, in due course, its clerk will place your item on its agenda. You will be notified as to the date and told of your responsibility of informing your neighbors of your appeal and the time and place of the public hearing. This may require that you serve a written notice on everyone within a certain distance of the property affected, publish a notice in the newspaper, send a notice by registered mail to the last known owner of the properties in your vicinity, or post a sign in your yard giving notice that a zoning appeal has been filed for that property. At any rate, your appeal is now in the works. At the hearing, all of your neighbors have the right to appear and object (or even support you), stating their reasons therefor. You have the right to present your case and the argument as to why you should be allowed to do what you want to do. In order to file an appeal, therefore, you need a reason for so doing, a set of plans to indicate what you intend to do, a denial by the zoning officer, and the completion of the proper application forms.

Since zoning is becoming more complicated, it is probably desirable for you to consider engaging a lawyer if you are going to file an appeal. An attorney is extremely valuable in the preparation and the presentation of your case and making certain that your legal rights are protected. Some zoning boards are more insistent than others that an interested citizen be represented by legal counsel. It is not absolutely essential since you have the right to state your own case and to try to argue your own cause. It is particularly desirable, however, in case you have to appeal the decision of the zoning board to the court of the next highest jurisdiction. Regardless of the approach you choose, it is your job to present the case before the zoning board. They are there to listen and to receive from you as much information as possible as to why you think that your request is a justifiable one meriting their favorable action. You may decide to go to some expense and present maps and graphic material as well as expert testimony, or you may simply want to present the facts as you know them.

The Fact Is—Only Facts Count

The decision of the board must be based upon information that can be supported and is accurately and carefully presented. They are not, or at least they should not be, interested in emotional arguments or extraneous statements regarding the reasons you think you ought to be entitled to do what you would like to do. The question is primarily whether you are denied the right to do something because of a peculiar circumstance or an unusual situation. If, in attempting to prove this, you decide to present an elaborate case, you will probably have more reason to be represented by an attorney who, in turn, will perhaps suggest that you use the services of an expert in real estate, engineering, or planning and zoning.

The same opportunity for factual presentation applies to individuals who are not the applicant but oppose or are interested in a particular application. They have every right to speak and to submit information for the consideration of the board. Again, facts are what the members of the board should be interested in, not an emotional statement from someone who just happens to be opposed to something.

Regrettably, many zoning boards seem unable to distinguish between information that is germane to the issue and arguments based on personal ideas, convictions, or simple desires. It sometimes seems that a skilled orator with the ability to stir souls is far more successful in obtaining zoning variances or in effective opposition than is someone who presents the proper facts briefly and concisely.

On Attending a Public Hearing

In theory, before government enacts a measure that affects our lives, we are given an opportunity to review and discuss it and then to present our views to officials, elected or appointed. This is the public hearing technique, and it is extremely important in zoning. Throughout the entire process, one of the key provisions is for the public to have the opportunity to be heard. This is not put in enabling legislation simply to provide an exercise or to provide a meaningless forum. It is intended to indicate the importance of public understanding and support, as well as the necessity of having an expression given, both for and against, to those reponsible for framing the ordinance and for its administration. This is representative of the democratic process that can prevail where zoning is carefully administered. The hearing process has been designed to provide a check and balance system in the adoption of or varying from legislation that directly concerns us. It is our responsibility to be aware of the system, to take advantage of it, and to understand how it should work and when it is not working properly.

After an ordinance has been adopted and is in effect, the zoning board must establish the proceedings for scheduling and conducting the public hearings for which it is responsible. A date must be established and notice properly served. The zoning board must arrange a meeting room, making certain that it is large enough to take care of whatever size crowd might want to attend. A stenographer or secretary must be engaged to record the proceedings, and information to be considered by the zoning board must be assembled and made ready for display at the meeting.

It is important that the chairperson of the zoning board conduct the meeting in an orderly and businesslike fashion. It is important for the public attending the meeting, as well as for the officials participating, to recognize what information is pertinent and what can be valuable in assuring a judicious decision on the question. Many times public hearings are turned into political battlegrounds, and prospective candidates or those interested in future political offices seize upon the opportunity to be heard by an assembled group. While this probably cannot be avoided, it certainly should be kept to a minimum by the action of the chair.

The chairperson of the zoning board plays the key role in the proceedings. The success or failure of the meeting will be largely dependent upon performing this role properly. That person should be firm but courteous, polite but sincere, efficient but friendly. He or she should be informed on the subject matter and keep in mind that, although this is a public hearing and not a public meeting, the primary purpose is to provide an opportunity for the public to be heard. The chairperson should keep the meeting well in hand at all times and should set the pattern that will be followed throughout the proceedings.

The first job should be to inform those present about how the meeting will be conducted, its purpose, and any rules and regulations that will prevail. It is usually the responsibility of the chairperson in a zoning hearing to swear in the stenographer and any witnesses who may appear. Note that, since this is a quasi-judicial hearing, all witnesses should be under oath. It is also the chairperson's responsibility to recognize people who will be heard and to insist that the decorum of the meeting be maintained. If the meeting is allowed to get out of hand, the chairperson will find that it is quite difficult to bring back under control.

Where Would We Wander Without . . . Lawyers?

Legal counsel plays an important part in the public hearing. There may be an attorney to advise the board itself, as well as attorneys representing both applicants and objectors. The official legal adviser of the board provides legal direction and advice but not curbstone legal opinions. Attorneys cannot be expected to have at their fingertips all of the case citations and all of the law references necessary for rendering sound legal advice, and board members should avoid placing their legal adviser on the spot by expecting an immediate opinion. A matter of importance requiring legal investigation should be held in abeyance to give sufficient time for the research necessary to allow a well-thought-out opinion. No attorney advising the board can present an applicant's—or objector's—case before the board.

Attorneys representing either applicants or objectors have the role of representing a client. They are there because they have been engaged to see that their client's interests are properly protected. An attorney for an applicant will try to present the applicant's case in the best possible light. Neither the attorney for the applicant nor for any of the objectors should become involved in personalities or attempt to influence the board by strong-arm tactics.

The board is a group of lay persons who expect members of the legal profession, regardless of what they are trying to accomplish, to give them the benefit of their legal training and advice based upon carefully thought-out considerations and experience. A zoning hearing, while of a quasi-judicial nature, is not a court of law and certainly is not a trial court where a jury can be impressed by histrionics and soul-stirring oratory. Attorneys have a high degree of moral responsibility to see that hearings are conducted properly and that they help to set the tone by their exemplary, professional conduct.

At some variance public hearings, experts may be presented as witnesses before the board either by an applicant or by objectors. These may be specialists in engineering, real estate, or in planning and zoning. As experts, they are entitled to present information and to express opinions based on conclusions drawn from that information and their study. Their role is to provide a background of technical knowledge and data that can help the zoning board reach a considered opinion in their final decision. Any expert presented to the board should be well qualified, and any person interested in the hearing should make certain that no one is accepted as an expert witness by the chair of the board who has not presented proper credentials or experience records.

Like the attorneys, these experts are being engaged to perform a function and will attempt to present their client's case in the best possible light. It is the responsibility of the attorneys for the applicant, the opposition, and the board to ask questions that will draw from any expert answers that will be informative and helpful to the board. In some cases, the procedure of the board will permit questioning of the expert from those in attendance. Where this is permitted, expert witnesses should be treated with courtesy and consideration, regardless of their views. Little will be accomplished by belittling or making derogatory remarks about an expert's presentation or opinions. It is the zoning board's job to weigh the value of expert testimony and to be able to recognize improperly founded opinions.

The Rest of the Team Should Play, Too

Because no board is going to be stronger than its weakest link, good boards are made by the careful selection of appointees by the policy makers. An example of how important it is that all members take their responsibilities seriously is the simple matter of attendance and participation in all meetings, especially public hearings. A fundamental principle in this is that a quorum must be present at all official hearings and that only those members who have participated fully and heard all the testimony or read a verbatim transcript are entitled to cast a vote in making a decision. I have known judges to rule against municipalities when infractions of this principle were pointed out to them in a motion for summary judgment.

In addition to commitment, all members have a responsibility to see that both sides are clearly presented. They have a duty to the public not present, as well as those in attendance. Should a chairperson be negligent in any of that position's duties, they have the responsibility to see that any errors are corrected. They should ask questions, listen carefully, and make their own notes, in addition to having the transcript to review. They are acting in the capacity of judges and evaluators of the evidence. The action they take is important to the entire community and its future and may be subject to an appeal to the appropriate court.

Having explored the variance process and public hearings in general, I would like to suggest a summary of points by which anyone might evaluate the conduct of such hearings and the decisions rendered in any community. It might be an interesting exercise to drop in on one meeting of the board in your town, if you haven't done so lately, and see how it passes this test.

1. Before scheduling any public hearing, the responsible agency should have carefully examined the application or issue and should have its own house in order. Members of any board or agency should not be permitted to sit in a public hearing unless they can attest to the fact that they have studied the zoning ordinance, reviewed the master plan, and are otherwise thoroughly aware of the case up for discussion.

2. The chairperson of the meeting should make a statement at the very outset concerning how the hearing will proceed and clearly indicate that decorum and order will prevail. It should be stressed that the agency conducting the meeting will not engage in lengthy discussions or debates with anyone. The purpose of holding the hearing is

to listen to the views of the citizens of the community and then to evaluate the entire matter at a later date.

3. A secretary or stenographer should be present to take careful notes, and, if possible, verbatim reporting should be provided. This not only ensures an accurate record, it helps to keep speechmaking to a minimum and the language above reproach. Courts in many states now are requiring that this be done.

4. The subject under consideration should have been made public sometime prior to the meeting, and there should be no necessity for any lengthy restatement of the application during this meeting. Witnesses should be sworn, instructed to give full name and address, and asked to state their views as briefly and quickly as possible. Usually, it is better to give all of those speaking for a particular proposal an opportunity to speak first and then all those opposed.

5. At the conclusion of each statement, the chair should thank the witness politely, assure the person that his or her views will be considered, and then immediately move on to the next person. No cross-examination or prolonged argumentative questioning of the board should be permitted.

6. Upon the conclusion of the statements of the public, the chair should again thank all for their interest and attendance, assure them that their views will be studied carefully, and that the entire matter will be given full consideration. Each member of the hearing body should be afforded the opportunity to—and should be expected to—review the transcript of the hearing before rendering a decision. The written word is frequently subject to a different interpretation than the spoken word.

7. Those conducting the hearing should be aware that there are many things to be considered other than the expression of personal views. A public hearing should supplement the data-gathering, analysis, and discussions that have preceded the hearing, but at no time should the public hearing supplant this qualitative analysis. Above all else, the board should remember that it is appointed or elected to represent not only the 50 or 60 people present at the hearing, but the other 10,000 or 12,000 citizens of the community who did not bother to come out and express themselves publicly.

The Citizen Code of Conduct

What should be the role of the interested individual in these hearings? Here, too, a code of conduct probably would be extremely desirable.

I have become very disturbed recently by the behavior of some people in public hearings. It is understandable when participants become so emotionally involved in matters relating to their own property values that they may briefly lose their sense of perspective, but dignity and courtesy should prevail. While we cannot expect in a book dealing with the question of zoning to correct or improve the moral tone of our society, I cannot avoid commenting that the future of this country is extremely bleak if society has degenerated to the point where we cannot differ in opinions objectively without becoming involved in personalities and discourteous conduct.

Having said that, and recognizing that it will make little difference in human behavior, I would suggest some general guidelines that may help make the citizen's role in a hearing more effective.

1. Everyone with an interest in the community should take part in a public hearing, regardless of whether the matter affects one personally or whether one is for or against the question to be decided. The value of a public hearing is to have diverse points of view presented. Unfortunately, far too often only those opposed—usually opposed for a very personal or vested interest—take the time to participate in public meetings and public hearings. Therefore, as a concerned citizen, you should take part in public hearings whenever they deal with a subject that can affect the total community, as does zoning.

2. Immediately there follows the logical correlary that, if you are going to take part, you should be informed. This does not mean simply have a general knowledge of the subject matter, but informed to the point of having specific relevant data. You should have asked questions beforehand and gotten as much information as possible. If it is a zoning matter, information will have been available for some time before the hearing at the local municipal building or from the offices of the building inspector or the planning or zoning boards. Be sure that you have this information and that your conclusions, if you have already formed any, have not been based on rumor or misinformation.

3. If you are going to say anything, present facts. If the matter to be heard before the board is something in which you are personally interested and you want to express yourself, gather together information and be sure that all of it will be useful to the board. Present it concisely and clearly. Remember that hard facts will do a lot more for your particular cause than will opinions or an attempt to browbeat the members of the board into agreeing with your ideas.

4. Insist that the meeting be conducted correctly. To me, this is a responsibility of every citizen in the community. If you have the misfor-

tune of having a chairperson who is not conducting the meeting satisfactorily, do not hesitate to insist that he or she attempt to do so. Outside experts or those who have been called in to take part in the proceedings should be treated as you would treat guests in your own home, because they are, in fact, guests of your community, regardless of what point of view they express.

5. Don't be swayed by emotion. If someone has a case that is so weak that they must resort to this type of presentation, it behooves the individual to cut through the smoke screen of emotion and ascertain the apporpriate basis for the conclusion to be reached.

Remember too, that the board is not running a popularity poll. A zoning decision is not something that can be made on the basis of how many people are for or against any particular issue. Each person has rights—both from the standpoint or property ownership and as an individual—and they should be protected. Restrictions should be imposed only when warranted by the situation and when the community regulations are reasonable.

6. Be courteous at all times. It should not be necessary for any of us to have to be told that it is desirable for us to act in a courteous manner when we are participating in a community meeting or a public hearing. Unfortunately, it is necessary. You as an individual have a personal responsibility to remind others of this important rule of conduct and to insist that it be the prevailing atmosphere throughout the entire public hearing.

7. Be understanding of others, particularly the members of the board. In spite of some of the adverse comments that have been made regarding the ineptness and inefficiency of many boards of adjustment, the individuals who are board members also deserve consideration. They have at least indicated a willingness to serve their community. Many of the board members are dedicated and many boards are doing an extremely competent job. Their responsibility is a heavy one, and their duties are difficult and many times troublesome. Invariably, they are called upon to make a decision on matters of concern between neighbors. They are called upon to take sides, and the stand they take will probably be unpopular to a sizeable group of people in their community.

It has sometimes been said that the best member of a zoning board is the person who has no friends. This is an over-simplification but it indicates the difficult assignment given to a member of the zoning board. In order to do as good a job as possible, they need your support, your understanding, and certainly your recognition of the fact that they have tried to render the best possible decision for the benefit of the entire community.

Now for a Handy "How to Do It" Kit

Several years ago a reporter in Trenton, New Jersey, Mark N. Finston, was assigned by his editor to spend seemingly endless hours covering local zoning hearings. After several dozen of these—obviously ones where the above suggestions were not followed and some very bad decisions made—he wrote an article entitled, "So You Want to Win a Variance and Influence Your Township Board," that appeared in the *Trenton Times* and is presented below. Mr. Finston's talent is to be appreciated, but the article is almost too true to be funny.

Communications media are chock full of advice: advice to the lovelorn, advice on physical or mental health, advice to teenagers, parents, recipients of social security. You can even write in and get answers to such questions as "What is the second largest island in the world?" (Answer, New Guinea.) But nowhere do we find advice directed to the group of people, ever growing, who live in the "suburbs"—outside the big cities, in townships or boroughs, where government is close to home.

So, as a public service, we present a hitherto unpublished interview between a Typical Young Suburbanite, eager to get along with his committee, council, zoning board, planning board, or what have you, and an expert (who does not wish to be identified, for obvious reasons), who has been around a long time.

1. *Mr. Expert—you don't mind if I call you that, do you?—what's the best all-purpose argument I can use to get my way before various boards in my township?*
The best, by far, young man, is "children." This is the favorite ploy, and it always works. For example, suppose you own a liquor store and a potential competitor wants to build a store in a shopping center. At the hearing don't say: "I don't want the competition"—that's sort of un-American. Talk about children—how they're apt to stroll into liquor stores in shopping centers and be corrupted, how they're apt to see their daddies staggering out of the liquor store while they're shopping with their mommies in other portions of the center.

Or let's say you oppose your neighbor's plans to build a swimming pool—mention you're certain children will fall in it and drown, despite his planned eight-foot fence. I Once heard a well-known magistrate appear before a township committee asking the body to approve a zoning change that would allow a new housing development. His words should be committed to memory: "I could never say 'I'm here, and I don't want you here' to a 25-year-old rosy-cheeked boy with son in hand and a pregnant wife." There wasn't a dry eye in the house.

2. *That's very helpful, sir. Any other arguments?*
Yes. Talk about "morality." But be vague. Whisper if possible. For example, let's say someone wants to build a motel, and you want to oppose it. Speak quietly and earnestly: "Motels tend to lessen morality in a community." If you can bring in *childrens'* morality, so much better. It doesn't matter that everyone knows you're speaking nonsense. An official won't want to take the chance, however slight, that people will think he advocated immorality.

3. *I like your tactics. What sort of attitude should I adopt before the boards?*
It can best be phrased as "dignified begging." Never tell a board, "The law says you have to do this" or "The law says that you can't do that," even if that's what the law says. Local officials resent being told what they can and can't do, even if they know, which is frequently the case. If possible, say "I realize that I'm not required to ask your permission to do such-and-such, but I have so much confidence in you, I thought I'd ask anyway."

Don't use sarcasm to win an argument. Few will understand it. Those who do will think you're nasty, and that's the ball game right there, as they say in the sporting world.

4. *How about "group psychology?"*
Ah, I see you are an apt pupil. Whenever you appear, bring a group with you. Make it clear they, too, are voters. Let them applaud every sentence. Have them mumble such things as "That's true." "He's right." They should scrowl and mutter epithets at your opponent. The fellow your're against who has appeared with a lawyer, experts, and all sorts of documentary evidence, won't stand a chance.

5. Now, in regard to principles, like "conservative" or "liberal" . . . Forget them. All arguments should be based on your personal economic situation—"devaluation of my property," "loss of my business." Never voice an opinion on a subject that doesn't affect you personally (such as, "A curfew is discriminatory legislation and is probably unconstitutional") or you'll be looked upon as a busy-body. But don't be afraid of accusing your opponent of being only interested in the "profits" he can make. Making a profit is looked upon as slightly immoral, especially if your opponent is a large corporation or builder.

6. *Do I always have to stick to the subject?*
Never, never. If you bring in irrelevancies, who can dispute you? Talk about how long you've lived in the township, for example. Mention your opponent has been there a much shorter time. Quote J. Edgar Hoover on any subject. Give a harangue about how much traffic will increase if your neighbor is given that two-foot side yard variance.

7. *I'm getting the idea. Can you give me some examples of irrelevancies that are always good for any cause I'm advocating?*
Try veterans' groups, the Patrolmen's Benevolent Association, education (in the abstract). Try and quote some revered local man, but make certain he's been dead for a while.

8. *How about "bad" irrelevancies?*
There aren't as many as there used to be. "Atheist" or "Communist" or even "Creeping Socialist" are considered too strong for polite governmental conversation. But you might try Consolidation, Taxes, Liquor or "Hot-Rod Teenagers." There are a great number of things, however, that are looked upon as slightly nasty, and most of them are in the "diversion" line: drive-in movies, pinball machines, pool halls, billiard parlors, hamburger stands, night clubs, staying up late (as, for example, doing your wash after 11 p.m. at one of those all-night laundromats).

9. *You mentioned living in the town for a long time. What if I just moved in?*
Easy—make the reason you're before the government body the same as the reason you moved in. For example, "If I had wanted curbs and sidewalks, I would have stayed in X-ville. The reason I moved here is because you don't have them." Or, the variation, "The reason I moved here is because X-ville didn't have curbs and sidewalks."

10. *I feel almost prepared. But what do I do if I ever get elected or appointed to a government body?*
You remember everything I have told you. But never, repeat, never in any way, let on to anyone that you know it.

This satire speaks volumes about the dangers to be avoided in zoning administration and zoning board action. Our hope lies in more citizens, more community officials, being able to say to Finston—and even grizzled and battered practitioners like me who have seen the bitter truth of bad zoning administration—"Thanks for the lesson; we have made certain that it will not happen here."

9

The Relationship of Zoning to Other Planning Tools

Even though the emphasis in this book is on zoning and the vital role it plays in community development, the thesis that it is but part of a total package necessary for effective planning has been stressed. We have seen how zoning preceded planning during the earlier part of this century and how the philosophy changed after the need for a sound basis for land-use controls became evident and some influence was wielded by the federal government. That change involved a recognition that all phases of a community structure were founded on land use, that purposeful planning was the cornerstone for guiding and directing land development, and that zoning could perform its ascribed function equitably and reasonably only if it is viewed as a tool for implementing comprehensive planning. With the new philosophy came the perception that the design and organization of developing areas and the financing mechanism for the community infrastructure to service the new, as well as the older parts of an urban configuration created the need for additional plan-implementing tools. Thus, subdivision controls and capital improvement programming became a part of American local government's arsenal for guiding growth.

It Takes Four to Tango

It has been noted previously that the four primary elements of the planning process are the master plan, the zoning ordinance, the subdivision ordinance, and the capital improvements plan and program. In Chapters 1 and 2, a great deal was said about the correlation between the planning process, the master plan, and zoning. Here, I would like to emphasize that those four primary elements form a total planning package. Any other approach will fall short of achieving an integrated, efficient, economical pattern of land use, the hallmark of a desirable community. These four planning tools are like four pilings driven to solid bed-rock upon which a community structure can rest—that is, provided they are well prepared, well administered, and supported with a pro-planning attitude.

There Is a Definite Difference

Because there is frequently a misunderstanding as to how zoning and subdivision controls differ, the logical place to start in a discussion of the latter is with a delineation of that difference. Zoning controls land use; subdivision regulations control and direct the separation of one or more parcels of land from a larger parcel, setting standards for ultimate development. Technically, subdivision is defined as the division of any tract of land into two or more pieces, although state statutes differ in their legal definitions and in the exemptions from controls provided for certain classes of subdivision.

Just as is true with zoning, subdivision regulations are an exercise of the inherent "police power" of government, subject to the requirements of being reasonable and necessary to promote and protect the "public health, safety, and general welfare." Controlling the subdividing of land and establishing standards that are to be met when developing and using that land does not require government compensation to the owner, even though that owner may feel that those standards place an economic burden on her or him.

Because of the frequent use of the term "subdivision" in reference to housing developments, many people mistakenly assume that the regulations do not apply to business and industrial development. Indeed they should, and do. Some of the greatest benefits from having good subdivision regulations have accrued to communities faced with major industrial or business/office parks and shopping centers. Whatever the purpose of development may be, subdivision regulations apply and can provide the means of assuring a workable project that well enhance the quality of the community.

Community Development Is Two-Faced

All cities and towns have two development faces. The first is that which is already built on parcels established by previous subdivision—the "older" part of town. The other is the emerging new development that takes place on vacant, infill lots in the inner city and on larger vacant parcels at the fringes or on newly annexed land. Subdivision regulations may not play a major part in infill development, but they are the major means of establishing standards to assure quality in any area where new lots will be created. Zoning guides and directs development in the older, already platted areas, and the two together shape the pattern of land use and the organizational efficiency of the final product in the newer areas.

It is through subdivision and the resulting development, whether residential, commercial, or industrial, that the emerging physical pattern is created—a pattern that the community will have to live with for years. Zoning, based on good planning, will determine the contribution and the compatibility of the use of land. It will be up to subdivision controls to shape that physical pattern so that it becomes an asset instead of a liability. How will the new streets relate to present and future transportation facilities? Has adequate thought been given to plans for new arterial streets, for protecting residential streets, or for a mass transit system? Will the design of the circulation system add unnecessary miles and resultant additional costs to providing mail delivery, police and fire protection, and the collection of garbage, to say nothing of the public cost for street maintenance after the developer has gone? These are but a few of the concerns that reflect a public interest in how new areas are developed.

Subdivisions determine the demand for existing services as well as the necessity for their expansion or for building new facilities. Each new development calls for an extension of the infrastructure of the city, in addition to creating a new physical pattern in the way streets are designed and located. Water and sewer lines must be provided and must be adequate to carry the additional load. If the primary system of water or sewer lines is at or close to capacity prior to development of a major subdivision, the added demand may require the public to construct a new trunk sewer line, a filtration plant, or a new water well. The cost of doing so becomes a burden on the tax-paying public and a long-term financial obligation for all present and future property owners. It is, in effect, a subsidy to one landowner/developer who is in the business for personal gain.

The same situation exists with all other utilities and services that make up the infrastructure—the community lifelines. Electrical and gas ser-

vices are required. Fire hydrants and street lights must be installed. Provision for drainage and stormwater runoff must be made. Where these
items are not given enough consideration during the initial stages of
development, there is only one place where the responsibility for doing so will rest ultimately--that is the governmental tax coffers provided
by the public.

Planning Is for Kids, Too

An element of major importance to overall community planning upon
which subdivision development bears heavily, and one frequently given
inadequate attention, is the effect of new residential growth on the
school system. Far too many planning commissions labor under the
illusion that they cannot involve themselves in matters relating to school
boards. This attitude exists in spite of the fact that every state planning enabling act I have seen clearly gives the planning commission
the authority to review and make recommendations regarding the plans
of all public bodies, including school boards. Ignoring this has resulted
not only in misplaced schools, but also in subdivisions that have
generated the demand for new school facilities prematurely, thus requiring children to be subjected to the trauma of double sessions.

A graphic illustration of this mistaken belief that school location,
construction, and even closing, are the sole prerogative of school boards
was an experience of mine in Albuquerque. I had just arrived on the
scene as the new planning director and was attending my first planning commission meeting. One of the agenda items was a proposed
subdivision carrying with it a zone change request for higher density
residential use. The hearing room was packed with neighbors of the
area, all in opposition to the proposal. During the course of the presentation by the spokesperson for the opposition group, strong reference
was made to the effect of approval on the existing school, claiming that
it would be seriously overcrowded. The chairman of the planning
commission grabbed his gavel, banged the table, ruled the speaker out
of order, and in his most pontifical tone pronounced this most amazing
doctrine, "This planning commission has nothing to do with schools;
they are the school board's problem." Needless to say, the project was
approved, the school became overcrowded, and the people of
Albuquerque are still paying, both in taxes and the loss of community
character, for the mistake.

No Subdivision Is an Island

The obvious conclusion is that every subdivision shapes the physical form—the service delivery system, neighborhood and community character, the transportation network, and present and future property values of the entire jurisdiction. The ramifications of our carving up virgin land to accommodate either unplanned urban sprawl or well-planned new development reverberate throughout the total community structure. Thinking comprehensively seems to come hard for us in our affluent society—affluent at least up to now. Recognition that a community interest exists in how every piece of our land resource is used and developed comes even harder, yet it is essential if we are to do more than to repeat the mistakes of the past and to compound them as we are doing in the present. We have the tools, we only need to use them well. The regulation of the subdivision of land for the benefit of that community interest is one of those tools and a very important one. Comprehensive planning reflected in the framework of the master plan is the basis for policy formulation and direction, but, without the implementing twins, the zoning ordinance and the subdivision ordinance, it would be just that—nothing but a plan.

Subdivision control is vested primarily in the planning commission by state enabling legislation. This is an administrative, not legislative, authority or power. No planning commission can require that subdivision plans be submitted and approved unless the governing body has enacted a subdivision ordinance. As in zoning, this is a utilization of the inherent governmental authority to restrict and regulate that lies solely in the hands of elected officials and cannot be delegated, other than for administration and application within the parameters of the rules and standards set by an act of the legislative body. Also, just as in zoning, no subdivision ordinance should be adopted without careful research and study, which should utilize pertinent information contained in the master plan. When a governing body decides to consider an ordinance, the planning commission is the logical group to do the preliminary investigation and, with the help of an attorney, to draft a recommended ordinance. Input from the general public again is vital, and, before submitting a recommended ordinance to elected officials, the commission should conduct several open discussion meetings and at least one official public hearing.

When the final draft is ready to be referred to the governing body, much the same procedure applies. Each elected official reviews it, the municipal attorney gives an opinion on its appropriateness, comments are sought from city department heads, and public discussion meetings are held. Media publicity and public notice of discussion meetings, as well as the official public hearing, are essential, the latter being a legal requirement of state legislation. Prior to final passage of the ordinance, several options are open to the governing body. After hearing the public reaction, assuming there are worthwhile suggestions or legitimate criticisms, they may change or modify the wording. Whether the changed ordinance is sent back to the planning commission for review and comment is a matter of governing body discretion. (Presumably, the planning commission has been part of the meetings and hearings and has made its views known during the process.) A second option, if there is need for major change, is to refer the ordinance back to the commission for restudy, carefully noting the policy direction that is to be followed in making the detailed changes. The final option, of course, is to bite the bullet, determine that the ordinance as drafted speaks to the best interest of the total community in spite of the few objections raised, and pass it on final reading. You will note that I have not suggested total rejection as as option, since I am assuming a recognition of the need for this important planning implementation tool by any well-meaning governing body.

You Can't Tell a Book By Its Cover

Once the ordinance is passed, what should the interested citizen expect to find upon reading it? It should spell out, in reasonable clarity, all administrative responsibility, procedural steps, and standards of development and enforcement. In brief form, an outline for the major elements would be:

1. Statement of purpose and intent;
2. Definition of terms;
3. Procedure;
   A. Application procedure and process;
   B. Requirements for sketch plan review;
   C. Requirements for preliminary plan review;
   D. Requirements for final plat (plan) review;
   E. Procedure for approval and filing of final plat;
4. Design Standards;
   A. General design requirements and review procedure;

B. Streets, rights of way, and easements;

C. Topography and grading;

D. Sidewalks, planting strips, curbs and gutters;

E. Drainage and stormwater runoff;

F. Street trees and street lighting;

G. Utilities, both public and private;

H. Planting and landscaping;

I. Trails, walkways, and bike paths;

J. Open space and community areas;

5. Administration;

6. Performance and maintenance guarantees;

7. Inspection and enforcement;

8. Fees;

9. Violations and penalties.

Several of these merit additional comment. In the discussion of the zoning ordinance, I mentioned the importance of clear, understandable language and a carefully thought-out set of definitions. The same caveats apply here. The procedure section has included the words "plan" and "plat." This is because the final, approved document, which must be filed with the county recording officer before any lots can be sold, is legally termed a "subdivision plat." The sketch plan is general in nature. It shows the parcel that is to be divided, its natural features, and what is intended for it. The purpose of the sketch plan is to allow early discussion and mutual understanding between the developer and the planning commission or planning department. The preliminary plan begins to get into details of engineering, topography, street and lot layout, utilities, etc., for the entire parcel and is subject to public hearing and approval by the planning commission. If there is sizeable acreage involved, the final plat (plan) may be that of only a small portion scheduled for immediate development. Should this be the case, all subsequent final plats or parts of the total development should meet fully the terms and requirements of the preliminary plan approval granted the entire larger parcel.

The performance guarantee is a means of assuring the community that the development will take place as approved and that streets, utilities, and all improvements will be installed in accordance with community standards and subject to appropriate inspection. This guarantee can be in the form of a bond or cash or assets held in escrow by the local government. Any default on performance would permit the use of these funds to complete the improvements but not for any other purpose. Some of the more aggressive and progressive local governments are insisting on some assurance as to the quality of improvements by requiring the same type of maintenance guarantee that is expected of a home builder—that is, a warranty of quality work for a period of time after the project has been completed through a maintenance bond or other suitable surety.

Administration—The Key to Success

As in all other local ordinances, administration is the key to effectiveness. In the case of the subdivision ordinance, good administration requires a great amount of cooperation among municipal departments and staff. The larger cities may have placed all building and subdivision development inspection in the planning department, but the involvement and assistance of the public works department, the parks department, and others will be necessary. Smaller towns will not have all the separate departments, but there will be some division of responsibility for the delivery of services, and, again, coordination of inspection and enforcement is imperative. The major concern in smaller communities will be enough qualified staff to handle the inspections and administrative details. Fees can provide a large part of the financial support needed for this purpose. Courts have ruled that such costs can be met by fees charged; however, the municipality must be able to substantiate the equitable relationship of the fee structure to the cost of providing the services. Excessive charges beyond that necessary to provide administration of the ordinance will be considered to be illegal taxation.

One final point on the value of subdivision control and the subdivision ordinance to the master plan and the planning process concerns land dedication. It has long been accepted that dedication of rights-of-ways for streets, roadways, and alleys, as well as easements for utilities, can be a legitimate requirement for subdivision approval. The proper use of this provides the community with the means of carrying out its transportation plan and developing a coordinated network for circulation. In more recent years, the idea of requiring dedication of land for other public purposes as a requisite for approval of proposed major subdivisions has gained favor, both in local ordinances and in the courts. Such required dedications can include land necessary to protect stream flow or provide drainage; land for pedestrian paths and bikeways; land for parks and open space; and land for schools. A cautionary word is needed here, however. All such requirements, if they are to withstand any challenge, must be solidly founded upon documented planning studies showing that mandatory dedication will serve the public interest and that it is not unreasonable.

It Takes More Than One Tool to Build Anything

From this brief exploration of the subdivision control process, the correlation between the twin tools of implementation of planning readily can be seen; zoning creates the framework of land use and subdivision controls provide the means of weaving the fabric of the structure within that framework. To understand the reasonableness of the broad use of governmental police power contained within zoning and subdivision ordinance application to privately owned land, one must understand and accept the concept of community interest in all development that I have stressed in this book. There is a definite community responsibility to make certain that, as our towns and villages grow and new areas are developed, the taxpaying public does not have to move in to subsidize any subdivision when the developer moves out. This is where there is a community interest as well as private interest in any development of land. Through zoning and subdivision ordinances based upon comprehensive planning, development can be guided and directed, but any development will affect the need for the provision of public services. This leads to examining the fourth tool of the planning process, a partner with zoning and subdivision control—the capital improvements program (CIP).

Great Cities Don't Happen—They Are Made!

When the fabric of a community is studied in depth, when the question of what is the greatest determinant of sustained quality of community character is seriously approached, the vital role of capital improvements—facilities and services—becomes obvious. Great cities are made not just from physical form and good design, but also from the efficiency of that services delivery system and the adequacy of their cultural and social amenities. These are provided by the willingness of the people to support and finance public facilities, to provide the capital for improvements. Hence, the term capital improvements. Just as an industry cannot run and continue to prosper with faulty machinery and equipment and a business will not survive as a healthy operation without quality products and services, a city cannot be an attractive, economically sound community if its capital investment is ignored or allowed to deteriorate. Yet, how little attention is paid to this essential facet of local government by the general public, and how minimal is the knowledge of most people about the role that a capital improvements program and budget should play in efficient governmental administration.

The demand for and location of public facilities and services is determined by zoning and subdivision ordinances (or the lack thereof), but the overall quality of life in the community will be determined by the relationship of physical development to improvements that must be provided by the public sector. A misplaced or poorly planned subdivision can adversely affect existing facilities, result in new major public improvements becoming necessary, or throw plans for school locations out of kilter. Capital improvements are usually financed through borrowed money with a long-term commitment for repayment or, until recently, partially by grants from the federal government.

Faced now with major cutbacks in federal aid programs, states and cities must give even greater thought to the demands for facilities and services created by new development. Diminishing grants, fewer available dollars for public expenditure, and inflation should result in our placing added emphasis on long-range planning. Logic would dictate that, with fewer dollars to spend, we should want to make certain that we get the most for our money through careful, future-oriented planning. The ironic truth is that we are doing exactly the opposite in many places. For example, in an economy move, the Colorado General Assembly recently demolished the agency charged with long-range state planning at a time when planning for future growth is needed more than ever before.

From the standpoint of local or municipal government, whose responsibility is it to see that capital improvements are planned in advance of need and are related to the development and financial policies of any community? Again, the prime responsibility for whatever happens or doesn't happen rests with the elected officials. All planning enabling legislation recognizes the relationship of comprehensive planning to capital improvements planning and includes the authority for the governing body to delegate the preparation of a capital improvements program to the planning commission. This is also an administrative function, and the commission's role is advisory and recommendatory. After preparation, the program is forwarded to the governing body with the planning commission's recommendation and must be officially adopted as policy by the elected officials in order for it to mean anything.

The Problem Is Getting the Troops Together

This is not to say that the planning commission's function is perfunctory or that it does not have an important part to play. The commission is the key to relating improvements to the comprehensive plan and to coordinating the expressed needs of all departments with each other and with the goals of that plan. Each specialized department will have its ideas on what capital funds are required and how they should be spent. It is planning's function to evaluate these ideas in terms of total community need and dollars available and to recommend to the governing body priorities for inclusion and expenditures. Obtaining the understanding of this and the cooperation from the heads of these departments is one of the toughest jobs faced by any planning director or commission and will be next to impossible without the full support of the elected officials and the chief administrative officer, whether mayor or city manager.

Naturally, the parks director or the public works director are both apt to feel that the needs of their departments are important (in fact, the most important). They will fight for their departments and, as specialists, sometimes have the inability to accept the idea of a separate coordinating agency evaluating their priorities in the spectrum of total community needs. During my time as city manager in Albuquerque, I had some interesting confrontations with just such a public works director over the capital improvements program. To him, the only things important to the city were streets, water, and sewers. Everything else was just window-dressing and readily expendable in the final determination of where the limited funds should go. To make matters worse, he had held his position for 18 years and had built up a supportive political base more powerful than some of the elected city commissioners. Happily, this situation does not exist in every city, and it can be overcome in any city by strong governing body support. Even more happily, it no longer exists in Albuquerque.

To understand more fully why cooperation from each specialized department is needed, a look at what comprises a capital improvements program is helpful. To over-simplify: it provides the public with those facilities and services that are not paid for out of the day-to-day operating fund. Capital expenditures are thought of as being large sums necessary for land acquisition, construction, remodeling, or maintenance of all public improvements. They are an investment of the public's capital in the community's future. Typical candidates for such investment would be city halls, firehouses, libraries, museums, water and sewage disposal plants and systems, parks, golf courses, maintenance and storage buildings, community centers, major equipment, police stations, jails, and so on. A well-run community tries to avoid borrowing for maintenance or small investments for public improvements, but these, too, have been known to be included in the capital improvements program where prior neglect had caused an accumulation of problems or where there was to be a general program of improvement such as resurfacing all streets.

The essential thing to capital improvements programming is to include the word *planning*. To be effective, the program—in conjunction with the comprehensive plan, the zoning ordinance, and the subdivision ordinance—must look forward and anticipate what needs for public expenditures will be created for a workable and foreseeable future by the total planning and policy package of the community. These needs must then be balanced against the projected revenue availability over the same period, and, from that, a determination made of what is needed most and how it can be financed. Following this procedure is pre-active planning at its best, but too often local elected officials prefer to let a crisis develop and then react rather than plan ahead.

Putting It All Together

To provide a general understanding of the process and the difference between the CIP program and the capital improvements budget (CIB), we will take a look at how both come about. Assume that you were the city manager of a city of 250,000 people (as happened to me in Albuquerque), and you found that there was no long-range CIP program. All major public improvements were done on a pragmatic or crisis basis. Because of the "all growth is good" philosophy of the existing power structure, most of the bond issues for improvements in recent years had been for service facilities to new subdivisions, all furthering the empire-building of the public works director. Winds of change were blowing, however, with several groups seeking more emphasis on planning and zoning, and, at the last election, the voters had elected the first woman to the City Commission—something the "good ole boys" found hard to believe. She was planning-oriented, capable of stirring things up, and had the support in doing so of one of the other four commissioners.

Playing off of this, you begin your campaign for the establishment of a CIP. Working with the planning director, you establish the procedures, develop the necessary forms, and begin to indoctrinate the planning commission on the role that they must play. Throughout all this, stress is placed on the interrelationship of CIP planning with the comprehensive plan, the zoning ordinance, and the subdivision ordinance. Success of any one of these is proportionate to the existence and effectiveness of each in the total development picture. The hardest place to sell this idea or even the concept of a long-range CIP was, of course, at the staff meetings with the individual department heads. They each saw the process as a threat to their operation and to their ability to lobby individual commissioners for support of their projects. One advantage to a good manager/commission charter form of government is that the manager has the authority to hire and fire all heads of departments. This does play a part in helping to convince them of the merit of a manager's proposals.

When administrative procedures are ready, the development of the CIP is initiated. It is timed so that it can be presented to the governing body for their consideration well in advance of the review and adoption of the overall city budget. The planning department is responsible for the entire project, and all other departments are so informed. The objective is to assemble a workable, affordable program of capital needs projected over a five-year period. Individual components should be rated in terms of benefit to the entire community based upon the comprehensive planning process. After establishing these priorities, the year the specific project should be included in the capital improvements budget (CIB) is then determined in relation to the projected financial capabilities of the city.

The process proceeds as follows. The planning department, using standard forms, requests each department to list and justify all perceived capital needs over that five-year period and to rate each one as to their benefits to the community and necessity from the standpoint of public health, safety, and general welfare. Suggestion by the department as to the year for inclusion in the CIB is also required. The documents of each department are returned to the planning department and carefully reviewed in conjunction with the proposals of the master plan, other department's requests, and the information available to the planning staff about the most pressing needs for adequate services to present and future population. They next formulate a tentative five-year program, a suggested first-year CIB, and a careful defense for the reasons for their suggestions.

Planning Directors, Keep Your Bags Packed

From this point on, it is a matter of meetings, discussion, even arguments, and finally—that favorite word of American politics—compromise. Here the skill of the planning director is put to a real test. First comes a conference with each department head and his or her representative staff. Naturally, anything requested that has not been given high priority or perhaps not included generates pathetic cries and protests. Again, the success of the planning agency and the director depends on the support of planning by the chief executive officer and the governing body. Without this, the planning director can start looking for a new job.

Assuming that support is forthcoming, after consuming many hours in this give and take, the planning department reviews and revises the suggested CIP and CIB and readies it for presentation to the planning commission. This agency studies the recommendations, discusses them with its staff, and determines whether to allow any aggrieved department head a hearing prior to scheduling a general public hearing on the entire program. After a campaign of publicizing what is to be considered and hearing public suggestions and reactions—whether in one official hearing or several—the task of determining the final recommendation to the governing body falls to the planning commission. They may revise, amend, add to, or subtract from the program developed by staff. Then they forward to the elected policy makers their proposal for a capital improvements program over the next five years (it could be six years if a five-year plan sounds too Russian) and a capital improvements budget for the community for the next fiscal year.

As in the case of other implementing action for planning, the governing body is required to hold an additional public hearing or hearings and to take into account these public views before making the CIP and CIB official. In our political system, the governing body has final responsibility for what is contained in both. It is for this reason that more citizens should learn about the importance of capital improvements programming in the planning function. Governing bodies respond to public opinion, and organized citizen expression can be helpful to a planning commission and its staff in convincing elected officials to support community priorities instead of reacting to myopic special or vested interest appeals. With or without participation by interested and objective citizens, when the governing body has, by resolution or ordinance, passed the CIP, it becomes the blueprint for the vital lifelines and amenities upon which the growth of the city will depend.

And Then There's Next Year— And the Next—And the Next

What happens after the program is approved, the first year CIB is included in the next fiscal year budget, and the bonds necessary to pay for the improvements have been approved by the voters? Is the work of the planning commission and its staff on the CIP finished? Just as comprehensive planning is a continuous process, so is capital improvements planning. The planning department, after this first five- or six-year program has met with approval and its first year has been activated, immediately moves to add another fifth or sixth year to the package. In other words, each year the same process of updated department priorities, reviewing, discussing, and projecting takes place. The CIP always stays that number of years ahead of the community's general budgeting calendar. In this continual review, priorities of the original program are subject to reexamination and may be changed as conditions change. A project scheduled for three years down the road in the previous year's CIP may be replaced by something that has become more pressing. The principle of relating the public expenditures of the community to its long-range comprehensive planning, its goals and objectives, and to pre-active rather than reactive thinking remains the same, however, over the years.

In this brief examination of subdivision controls and capital improvements programs and the attempt to show how they relate to zoning as the major implementing tools of good planning, no one should gain the impression that I have presented a full explanation of the details, the advantages, the process, and the administration of each. For example, no mention was made, other than reference to the approval of bonds, of the complicated process of financing public improvements and relating this to the general city budget. It is not the purpose here to cover all the facets of municipal finance or application of police power regulations to the subdivision of land. Rather, the purpose of this chapter's discussion, and the entire book, is to give a broad overview and an understanding of the increasing importance of community interest in land development, public and private. The contention here is that this interest can be expressed best in a representative democracy only by meaningful land-use controls, authorized by zoning and subdivision ordinances, with needed public services and facilities systematically and economically financed through applied capital improvements programs and budgets.

10

Frequent Zoning Problems

About the only thing anyone can say in regard to zoning and be relatively sure of being free from contradiction is that it is an intriguing, complex, and constantly changing process. The most knowledgeable zoning expert will be the first to admit this and will say that there is no way to anticipate all the problems any community may face in adopting, amending, or administering a zoning ordinance. Zoning is ever-evolving, and this is as it should be. There is always a new concept or new technique to create uncertainty of legality or reasonableness and for which there is no precedent on which to rely. There is always the question that has never been asked before or, if asked, has never been satisfactorily answered. The best that anyone, concerned citizen or expert, can do is to understand the principles, have a general concept of good zoning practice, and be aware of the problems that arise frequently in zoning application.

Probably there have been more books, papers, and technical publications written about zoning than any other activity of local government. Many of these, such as the Planning Advisory Service reports of the American Planning Association, give a good insight into new techniques and problems to try to avoid, and they are valuable aids. My experience has been that no one publication—not even all the books written on the subject if put together—would be able to include all the questions and problems that may need to be dealt with. The purpose here is to provide an illustration of some of the more common problems and to emphasize their importance, but not to be all-inclusive.

Keep It Simple

Although zoning is a complicated matter, I have never been convinced that it is necessary for ordinances to be as complicated, and in some cases badly written, as most of them are. Over the years, I have read many zoning ordinances. With but few exceptions, the language makes it impossible for anyone to understand what was being said, much less the basic intent. Any ordinance is a legal document, but it does not need to be so filled with legalistic mumbo jumbo that the lawyers themselves don't understand it. Confusing and unclear ordinance drafting leaves the matter of interpretation—by zoning officers, zoning boards of adjustment, and even courts—wide open to arbitrary, discretionary decisions. If the language is not clear to citizen readers, how can they know when they have been treated unfairly by the interpreting individual or agency?

One of the greatest contributors to the number of zoning court cases is the ambiguous, indistinct wording of ordinances. The solution to this problem is for more attention to be paid to ordinance drafting and for people to demand readable, understandable ordinance language. If the insurance companies can simplify the language in their policies, as many have done, certainly it is possible to do so in zoning ordinances.

Just in case you may not have had the occasion to experience this problem or to see how bad it can be, and to enable you to accept more readily the idea that I am not exaggerating, I have included a page from what is, in my opinion, the worst-written zoning ordinance in the country—that of the city of Denver. It epitomizes all that I have been saying. As a specific example, just try Section .3-4(5)(b)(b-1) or Section .3-4(10), and see if you can determine what you can or cannot do with signs. Remember, this is only one page taken from the ordinance at random, and this document goes on like this for over 100 pages.

In contrast, although it is not as simple as it should be, also included is a page from the ordinance of Albuquerque, New Mexico, relating to some extent to the same subject. As you will see, you have at least a fighting chance of knowing what the drafters of the ordinance were talking about, and what they intended. Other illustrations of even more simple wording with the ordinances being even more effective can be found around the country, but these two serve to make the point: keep it simple!

Excerpt from the Denver, Colorado Zoning Ordinance
Permitted Signs
Section .3-4(5)(a). Hotels and Motels
On Zone Lots having a linear street frontage of 100 feet or less—100 square feet; on Zone Lots having a linear street frontage of more than 100 feet— one square foot of sign for each linear foot of street front; provided, however,

computations shall be made and sign area shall be determined on each street front separately, and provided, further, that in no event shall more than 300 square feet of sign area be applied to any one street front and no sign shall exceed 300 square feet in size.

Section .3-4(5)(b). Each Use by Right Other Than a Motel or Hotel.
50 square feet, or, the total permitted sign area of each Use by Right shall be determined by one of the following provisions; provided, however, that no sign shall exceed 200 square feet in area nor shall the total sign area of any Use exceed 600 square feet.

Section .3-4(5)(b)(b-1). For a Zone Lot Having But One Use by Right.
One square foot of sign area for each linear foot of street front of the Zone Lot; provided, however, that in computing the area of such signs, the measurement of not more than two front lines, one contiguous with the other shall be used.

Section .3-4(5)(b)(b-2). For a Zone Lot Having Two Or More Uses by Right.
For each Use by Right, one and one-half square feet of sign area for each horizontal linear foot of that portion of building frontage occupied by the Use by Right, for the first 200 feet of building frontage, then one square foot of sign area for each horizontal linear foot of building frontage thereafter.

Section .3-4(6). Permitted Maximum Height Above Grade.

Section .3-4(6)(a). Wall or Window or Arcade Signs.
40 feet.

Section .3-4(6)(b). Ground Signs.
32 feet.

Section .3-4(7). Permitted Location.
Shall be set in a least five feet from every boundary line of the Zone Lot; provided, however, wall signs may project into the required setback space the permitted depth of the sign. In no case shall there be more than five signs applied to any street front.

Section .3-4(8). Permitted Illumination.
May be illuminated but shall not flash, blink, or fluctuate, and all direct illumination shall not exceed 25 watts per bulb.

Section .3-4(9). Animation.
Shall not be animated.

Section .3-4(10). Temporary Signs.
Subject to the conditions hereinafter set forth and upon application to and issuance by the Department of Zoning Administration of a permit therefor, signs identifying or advertising new construction, remodeling, rebuilding, development, sale, lease, or rental of either a Use by Right or a designated land area; each such permit shall be valid for a period of not more than 12 calendar months and shall not be renewed for more than one successive period at the same location.

Section .3-4(10)(a). Permitted Sign Types of Temporary Signs.
Wall, window, and ground.

Section .3-4(10)(b). Permitted Maximum Number of Temporary Signs.
One sign for each front line of the Zone Lot or designated land area on which the sign is located.

Section .3-4(1])(c). Permitted Sign Area of Temporary Signs.

32 square feet for each front line of the Zone Lot or designated land area on which the sign is located. Computations shall be made and sign area shall be applied to each front line separately.

Section .3-4(10)(d).   Permitted Maximum Height Above Grade of Temporary Signs.
20 feet.

Section .3-4(10)(e).   Permitted Location of Temporary Signs.
Shall be set at least five feet from every boundary line of the Zone Lot or designated area.

Section .3-4(10)(f).   Permitted Illumination of Temporary Signs.
May be illuminated but only from a concealed light source; shall not remain illuminated between the hours of 11:00 P.M. and 6:00 A.M.; and shall not flash, blink, or fluctuate.

Excerpt from the Albuquerque, New Mexico, Zoning Ordinance

b.   An application must contain other studies as may be required to determine the effect of flooding on the proposed structure or activity and the effect of the proposed structure or activity on the arroyo or flood drainage channel.

c.   Prior to the issuance of a certificate of approval, the Enforcement Officer must examine the plans and land of the applicant. The Enforcement Officer must find that the building, structure, or activity will not constitute a hazard to persons or property, will not divert water from or obstruct the natural flow of water in the arroyo or flood drainage channel, will not cause flooding of land outside the natural drainage course, and will not reduce or endanger the water-carrying capacity of the arroyo or flood drainage channel.

d.   The applicant may be required to erect dikes, barriers, or other structures or improvements necessary to guarantee protection to the public as a condition to the issuance of certificate of approval.

3.   The issuance of a certificate of approval will not constitute a representation, guarantee, or warranty of any kind or nature by the city of Albuquerque or by any political subdivision, or by an officer or employee of any of them, of the practicability or safety of any structure or activity, and will create no liability upon or cause of action against any public body, officer, or employee for damage that may thereby result.

4.   In the event of a conflict between the location of a major arroyo as shown on the Zone Map and the actual location of the arroyo on the ground, the centerline of the actual location of the arroyo controls for the purposes of these regulations.

F.   Supplementary Regulations Applicable to Sign in or Near Residential Zones. The provisions of this subsection apply to all signs in a residential zone or within 40 feet of a residential zone. In the case of a nonresidential zone within 40 feet of a residential zone, the more restrictive of these regulations or the regular sign regulations in the nonresidential zone shall apply.

1.   No advertising sign shall be erected.

2.   No portion of an illuminated sign shall have a luminance greater than

200 footlamberts.

3.   No sign nor part of a sign shall move, flash, or rotate. No sign or part of a sign shall change its illumination more than once an hour.

4.   No more than one sign per premises shall be illuminated, apart from the general illumination of the premises, between 10 P.M. and 7 A.M.

5.   No sign shall be on the public right of way, except for name and address signs mounted on mailboxes.

6.   An apartment with more than 20 dwelling units, or a nonresidential premises, may have signs identifying the principal uses of the premises, as follows:

(a)   One free-standing sign per premises; provided, however, that premises with more than 750 feet of public street frontage may have one additional free-standing sign for each 500 feet of additional frontage or fraction thereof.

(b)   No free-standing sign shall exceed 16 feet in sign height or 20 square feet per sign face. No free-standing sign shall have overhead wiring to supply electric power. No sign of any type shall be within a clear sight triangle.

(c)   Wall signs, provided the sign area on any facade does not exceed 40 square feet and the total wall sign area on any premises does not exceed 100 square feet. No facade shall have more than five words which contain any character equal to or exceeding four inches in height; words consisting of characters all of which are less than four inches high may be used without limit as to number.

The Value of Zoning Case Reports

Each time a zoning board of adjustment is called upon to act on a variance request or a planning commission is faced with making a recommendation on a zoning amendment, the situation is an individual one. It is that particular request and its ramifications for comprehensive planning that must be considered and given objective treatment. No two cases will be exactly alike. How can the deliberating agency be assured that it has all the facts, knows exactly what conditions exist on the subject property and those around it, and how what is requested will relate to the comprehensive plan if approved? The answer, in addition to an on-site inspection and the personal knowledge of individual members, is a system of zoning case reports.

Regardless of the size of the community and whether or not there is a planning department with a professional staff, no action should be taken by either the planning commission or the zoning board without a complete and well-documented zoning case report. Naturally, this can be accomplished more easily and probably with more professional expertise when the city has a planning staff, or, at least, some competent personnel trained in planning. If this is not possible, a simplified standard form still can be used, with the responsibility for thorough completion assigned to one of the administrative officials or to a member of the planning commission.

One of the best explanations of just what a zoning case report should be and the importance of the policy of having them is contained in a booklet entitled, *Writing Better Zoning Reports,* by Duncan Erley (Planning Advisory Service Report No. 321, published by the American Planning Association). In his introduction, while addressing those communities with planning staff, Erley outlines the usefulness of these reports as follows:

> One of the most important functions of any local planning staff is to provide technical advice on zoning decisions to its planning commission and zoning board. Good zoning decisions depend not only on the quality of staff analysis and recommendations, but also on the staff's ability to communicate those recommendations clearly and effectively. Most staffs use written reports to relay their findings and recommendations. These reports allow commissioners to study each case before attending a meeting. In addition, the staff presents oral findings and recommendations at meetings.

It is my belief that following this practice can be beneficial in any community, although the professional knowledge may not always be the best. The act of formalizing study on each application will focus attention on possible problems and the importance of the deliberation. Having each planning commissioner expected to do one of the reports from time to time might even encourage a greater familiarity with the comprehensive plan and the planning process, something that would greatly benefit most commissions.

Regardless of how they are done, there are certain guidelines that should be kept in mind. The first is that there should be an adopted policy about what is to be included. The format should be standardized and kept simple. Included should be headings for general information, special information, relationship to comprehensive plan, analysis, and recommendations. The information should be well-organized, with facts and analysis clearly separated from opinion. Important documents, including a map(s) of the area, department reports, and pertinent correspondence, should be included as attachments. The preparer of the report should present a summary of its contents to the commission and the public at scheduled hearings. More detailed information on this process can be obtained from the report mentioned at the beginning of this section.

Exclusionary Zoning vs. Exclusive Zone Use

I have now lived and practiced long enough to see a number of zoning philosophies and theories develop, be accepted as desirable techniques, and then fall into question or disfavor. The opposite of this—a new idea being proposed, rejected by opinion or legal review, and then becoming not only legitimate, but all the rage—also has happened. This serves to emphasize the point made before, that zoning is a complex, changing process, and that no matter how long you have been involved with it, there is always something new around the corner. As an example of the change from being respectable to questionable, at least in the meaning of a phrase, is "exclusionary zoning" or "exclusive zoning." From the 1940s through the 1960s, when the philosophy was to separate types of land use to avoid incompatibility, this term was bandied about in the best of circles. Court cases that later became famous were filed in attempts to gain legal precedent for the idea that you did not need to permit more than one legitimate use in a zone. Area development specialists for power companies became circuit-riding evangelists, spreading the gospel of exclusionary zoning as an idea whose time had come.

In fairness, neither they nor any of us were talking about what has now become accepted as the meaning of exclusionary zoning. Instead, it was preached that, if a community really wanted to attract good industry, a shopping center, or office park, or other good ratable, it needed to get on the bandwagon and practice exclusionary zoning. That meant picking out the area best suited for such uses and zoning them exclusively for that purpose. In such an industrial zone, residences, offices, and commercial uses would not be allowed. Many attractive, well-planned industrial parks resulted from this idea and its practice. Now the concept of the meaning of the term has changed drastically.

This change was brought about by the idea of exclusion being extended to zoning for residential use. In some areas, this was an attempt to use exclusionary zoning to increase tax revenues from residential development by requiring only large lots and floor areas or enacting other requirements that can be interpreted as economic or racial discrimination. In the 1960s, at least a dozen of the client communities of my consulting firm insisted on zoning almost all of their vacant land with a minimum lot requirement of three acres, and one went as high as 10 acres. This attitude ran into rough sledding in the 1970s. First came a change in federal regulations pertaining to eligibility for federal funds that insisted upon an equitable housing policy, and then came some far-reaching court decisions regarding the idea that each community must be prepared to meet its "fair-share" housing needs for all economic strata within its region. The landmark case, and probably the most famous, was *Southern Burlington County NAACP v. Township of Mount Laurel*, 336 A 2nd 713 (N.J. 1975), which established that this type of exclusionary zoning would not be tolerated by the courts. This probably marked the beginning of the changed connotation of the term accepted today. The following definition (from *The Language of Zoning* by Michael Meshenberg, Planning Advisory Service Report No. 322) reflects this change:

> *Exclusionary Zoning:* Zoning that has the effect of keeping out of a community racial minorities, poor people, or, in some cases, additional population of any kind . . . .

Lest it be perceived that the idea of any type of exclusiveness has been case aside, it should be noted that zones for a single use are still acceptable when supported by good planning reasons. Thus, industrial parks and office parks, or other kinds of integrated, planned land uses, can be designated for those purposes and those alone. Just be sure to refer to this as "exclusive use zoning," not exclusionary zoning. Keep in mind, however, that there is another wind blowing that may strike at this concept. In view of the energy crisis, the cost of development, and the reaction against "ghettoizing" types of use, many communities, supported by planning professionals, are returning to the concept of mixed use or "a place to live, to work, and to play."

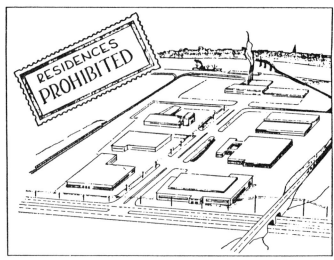

The Rat Race for Ratables

Somewhat related to the above is a problem of long standing in zoning effectiveness—the attempt to use zoning, and the willingness to alter it, to overcome the difficulty of financing local government. We long have relied heavily on the real estate property tax for local government financing, especially major capital expenditures. (See Chapters 1 and 8 for further discussion.) This causes local officials to make decisions based more on what a proposed development offers, or purports to offer, in terms of tax assessment potential than whether it is in keeping with good planning policy or will be beneficial to the entire community. This is now magnified many times over by the change in federal administration and policy and the drastic cut-backs in federally funded programs. After four decades of building up dependence on these federal programs culminated in revenue sharing, local government is finding itself being told that it has to kick the habit and do so almost "cold turkey." This portends ever greater likelihood of zoning based upon future planning being cast aside by politicians laboring under the delusion that a dollar gained in tax ratables today is better than a well-planned community of quality tomorrow.

Our very governmental structure, and our acceptance of it, contributes to this—no, that should be made stronger—*causes* this. For years we have accepted the idea of our government structure, designed in the eighteenth century, as being the best we can do. We nobly wave the flag for the division of jurisdiction—federal, state, county, and municipal—and for maintaining local control, whatever that means. In so doing, we have encouraged the creation and perpetuation of small, individual islands of government, each a parochial fiefdom unto itself when it comes to delivery of services and their financing. We have said to municipal officials, "There, that is your turf; you control the use of land there, and you have to finance the bulk of your operation from what you squeeze out of that turf." We have actually pitted municipal government against municipal government and municipal government against county government in the race for ratables. In so doing, we have thrown sensible regional patterns of development, equitable distribution of the economic generation potential of an area, and the opportunity to make sensible land-use planning effective right out the window.

As a consequence, not only do we have bad zoning decisions based upon short-range tax potential only, but we have to live with vast areas

overzoned for industrial or commercial use, shoddy development that
turned that way after approval was granted, leapfrogging pockets of
development that are expensive to service, and half-completed projects
resulting from persuasive fly-by-night entrepreneurs who went bust.
This situation will continue until we wake up to the fact that we have
been deluded, mainly by those holding office under the present structure, that there is not a better way of organizing government or, at
least, of equitably dealing with areawide land use and its economic
implications. One bright spot on the horizon is the action taken by state
legislation in Minnesota with the creation of the Twin Cities Regional
Council and its tax-sharing provision. There, when the major economic
generators locate, it is in a regionally planned area zoned for the purpose, with the resulting financial benefit shared with other communities
in the region. If Minnesota can do it, why can't it be done elsewhere?

Working Together

The above example from Minnesota illustrates that intergovernmental
coordination and cooperation are possible. As has been intimated, few
other state legislators have the courage to mandate such action between
municipalities or counties—all creatures of the state. Coordination of
zoning between jurisdictions, while all-important, is frequently difficult,
if not impossible, to achieve. This becomes a major problem for the
community that is serious about its planning if it is surrounded by other
municipalities or a county where the name of the zoning game is short-
sighted politics, or worse. It becomes a travesty when a town or city
is totally surrounded by an unincorporated county area and that county
has steadfastly refused to have any zoning. This situation can be
somewhat alleviated in those few states that have given their
municipalities the right to exercise extraterritorial jurisdiction zoning
three or five miles outside their corporate boundaries, but even this
is not complete assurance of the most orderly growth pattern.

If the county has zoning, unless it has been done in conjunction with
that of the municipality and strongly supported by elected officials of
both units, either one can destroy the other's good zoning intentions
by a single amendment or use variance. One of the greatest causes of
problems finding expression in zoning and creating competition instead
of cooperation is that of the ratable chase commented on above.
Shopping centers, industrial plants, and office buildings are coveted

uses of land, both in the inner city and the open county. It takes a lot of intelligent, objective cooperation between elected officials to end up with a land-use plan and zoning ordinances that transcend jurisdictional boundaries and preserve the economic potential of the older, developed incorporated area. An excellent example of how this can be done is the city of Boulder and Boulder County, Colorado.

When there is a municipal unit surrounded by an unzoned county in a state that does not permit extraterritorial zoning, all bets are off and chaos is invited. I have spent quite a bit of time in Durango, Colorado, over the last three years. It is a lovely little town, with an attractive main street and central business district. Even though one of its major industries is the tourist trade resulting from skiing, hunting, and a delightful narrow-gauge railroad, the main street still has department stores, hardware stores, specialty shops, and complete shopping services, as well as things for the tourists. I would classify its business district as one that is as economically sound and attractive as any small town I have been in anywhere in the country—that is, up 'til now.

Durango lies in LaPlata County in southwestern Colorado. Most of the people living in the unincorporated parts of the counties in this area do not believe in zoning. To be brutally honest, not only do they not believe in it, they are sure it is a communistic plot, and they don't take kindly to "flatlanders" or anybody else who tries to tell them otherwise. Zoning may be all right for the city folk, but "we ain't having none of it here in our county" expresses their feeling exactly. As a consequence, LaPlata County has no zoning ordinance. Within the last year, construction has started on two major shopping centers on a highway just outside Durango city limits. One of these will house a major chain discount store, and For Rent signs have already appeared along the main street because some of the merchants, long downtown stalwarts, are now planning to move to one of the shopping centers. There is a real danger that the vitality of what has been for years a substantial portion of the county's, as well as the city's, tax base will be sapped. All of this could have been avoided with intergovernmental cooperation in land-use planning and zoning.

The irony is that residents of Durango are LaPlata County residents and taxpayers also. The county has given little thought to the additional problems this haphazard growth will create in service provision, traffic circulation, and change of area character. In grabbing for the direct tax revenue, the county can well cause the solid base of downtown Durango to deteriorate and become depressed in real estate values enough to offset any short-term gain. Even worse, there is a real risk of destroying the attributes of one of the most pleasant "small-town America" places in existence anywhere, all from a misplaced attitude, competitive greed, lack of concern for the future, and worship of the "all growth is good" idol.

Stripping May Pay Off Some Place— But Not in Zoning

An easy trap in which to fall in first adopting zoning or even in or-dinance amendment is the one frequently set by property owners along highways or major traffic arteries. The bait is the philosophy that no use other than commercial is suitable for land along the sides of such roadways. The result, if those involved became convinced of this, is miles and miles of strip commercial zoning, 200 feet or so deep, on both sides. This is the personification of the exploitation of a public invest-ment for private gain and has been one of the greatest contributors to poor zoning over the years. The highway, street, or road came about because of a public need for the movement of people and goods, was built by public money, and any value for profiting from utilization of land for any purpose came as a result of that public investment. That investment should be preserved and protected, if not by access con-trol, by the exertion of the community interest in the public expression of what uses may occur and how development will take place.

Far too little use has been made in our planning and zoning of the service road concept or the reverse frontage idea of residential develop-ment as a means of combating commercial strip zoning. Just because a piece of land abuts a traffic artery does not give that owner the in-alienable right to exploit the existence of a public facility. Good plan-ning design can result in buffer strips and a separate development service road, with only designated access points to the main arterial. This same sense of design and respect for the public investment can allow residen-tial development with the backs of housing units turned to the major road and parking, garages, and service facilities adding to the shielding provided by a buffer strip or planting area. Such an approach is not unheard of, since it is found along turnpikes and parkways where all access is a matter of public control. Examples of this are the Merritt Parkway in Connecticut and the Garden State Parkway in New Jersey.

Succumbing to the plaint of real estate developers that "the highest and best use" (meaning the use that can return the greatest profit for the owner at the expense of the public is best) can lead only to proven woes in urban development. Invariably, the first will be extensive over-zoning for business use. A surplus of commercially zoned land leads to speculation, hodgepodge development, and ultimate deterioration. Landowners with residential property will be hesitant to invest in upkeep, preferring to wait for the pockets-full-of-money commercial developer sure to come their way some day! As lack of maintenance and rehabilitiation continues, character and values decline, resulting in a further subsidy from the general community being necessitated in order to overcome the loss in the tax base.

From the public viewpoint, yet another major problem, and a costly one, will occur. As the traffic artery strip zoned for business develops for that purpose (if it ever does), curb cuts and driveways will be required for access to developed properties. If there is to be any successful result for the business enterprises, traffic will increase with each developing parcel. As traffic increases and scattered turnoffs or driveways are created, congestion and traffic accidents will multiply. To attempt to deal with this, first will come the hue and cry for traffic lights, increased police control, and additional pavement lanes, all at public expense. Should the strip continue to develop, none of these measures will overcome the problems, and next will be the necessity of building a new highway or arterial at another location paralleling the one that myopic vision destroyed by ignoring the purpose for which it was built.

We have all seen this as we have driven around the country. A medium-sized city that is growing has a county or state highway skirting its border but inside its jurisdiction. Following the mistaken idea that no one wants to live on a highway and that all businesses regardless of the problems they may create will bring in beneficial tax ratables, the land on each side is zoned for that purpose. The highway becomes clogged, loses its ability to perform its basic purpose, and a by-pass is built. The mistake is repeated, the businesses on the "old road" go into decline, and we, the tax-paying public, are called upon for yet another solution, this time an expensive limited access freeway or throughway. An excellent example of this occurred in the Camden, New Jersey, area with New Jersey Highway 130. First, the close-in routing was quickly consumed by strip commercial, then the four-lane by-pass likewise was permitted to become a subsidy for private entrepreneurship, and, finally, the limited access New Jersey Turnpike was built—all paralleling each other, with the public paying a toll to drive on the latter.

Out, Damned Spot!

There are many terms in zoning bandied about but not really understood or clear as to meaning. Probably none fall into this category more firmly than that of "spot zoning." When a proposal for a change in zone classification from single-family residential to apartments is filed for almost any parcel, the first charge the opposing neighbors and their attorney will lodge will be that what is proposed is spot zoning and therefore illegal. Just what constitutes spot zoning and where it falls into the unreasonable and illegal area is something debated for years by zoning and planning experts, lawyers, and even the courts. A researcher can find hundreds of cases where the charge of spot zoning has resulted in municipal action being overturned, and can find a like number with similar action taken, similar charges filed, and the judgment of municipal officials sustained.

A definition of the term is included in the Glossary of this book but, again, another publication may define it in somewhat different wording. The key to understanding the concept is that the change made in the zoning map, whether by amendment or *use* variance, results in a use that is inharmonious with its surroundings and provides an undue advantage to a property owner over other property owners in similar circumstances. In the minds of many, the term has been related to the size of the parcel affected: for example, if a single, small lot surrounded by development of residential character is zoned for another use of a more intense nature; or an amendment is passed allowing conversion of a large structure on one lot in a primarily residential area to office use; or a use variance is granted for a lot to be commercially developed when all other parcels in the immediate area are residential. It is somewhat easier to see the inappropriateness of this type of zoning action as long as a small isolated parcel is involved. However, the charge of illegal spot zoning has been sustained by courts where large tracts and even several lots have been rezoned. Size is not always the determinant.

In *The Language of Zoning*, Michael J. Meshenberg says:

> Spot zoning is invalidated by the courts when it violates "in accordance with a comprehensive plan" requirements of state enabling legislation. The "spotness" is in the arbitrary and inappropriate nature of the change, rather than, as is commonly believed, in the size of the area.

A community that wants to avoid spot zoning and is interested in withstanding any challenge of their action where that charge is levied must have a good comprehensive planning program. If there is justification for a use change in the master plan, if the supporting documentation is well prepared, and if there is a recognizable need for the use allowed to serve the community good, governing bodies will avoid the expense of litigation and the possibility of being reversed by a court upholding the charge of spot zoning. As Meshenberg has stated in his definition, "Spot zoning, in sum, can be legal or illegal, but laymen generally think that it always is illegal and use the term loosely—and pejoratively—at public hearings when they oppose the change." The one thing that can be said with certainty about this problem is that there is a changing philosophy as to what properly can be termed illegal spot zoning and the best caveat for officials and citizens alike is handle with care.

How Are We Going to Keep Them Down on the Farm?

While we have grown from an agrarian country into an urbanized, or at least an urbanizing, country, we have overlooked the importance of one of the first types of land uses that occur anywhere. As we grow in population, we are facing an ever-greater problem of the production of food and the maintenance of agricultural lands, as well as the desirability of the preservation of open space around our built-up areas. Just as we can zone for *industry*, so can we zone for *agriculture*. Not only is it desirable from the standpoint of preserving land for farming, but it is one of the best ways to control orderly growth and development. Every community grows around a central core in which public services and facilities are provided. The orderly growth pattern should be such that it will enable that central core to be expanded on an economic basis and to have the municipal services and facilities extended as the need arises but not to have to provide them prematurely. A community that has a central core but at the same time has a vast amount of open, undeveloped land, whether it be used for agriculture or not, and which permits the indiscriminate, scattered development of this land, is asking for economic chaos.

On the other hand, if it is recognized that agriculture plays a vital role in our economy and that the growth pattern should have worked into it an element of timing, lands can then be zoned for agricultural purposes exclusively, thus discouraging scattered development. This should mean that the land will be used for agricultural purposes; only those dwellings will be allowed that are necessary to carry on basic farming, and they can be located on lots of sufficient size to ensure that they can provide their own services. In this way, the density pattern of the community is kept orderly, expanding outward from a well-serviced central core.

It is important to recognize that there is a relationship between this type of zoning and the tax structure of the municipality. Simply because one or two developments have already occurred on the extreme fringes of the community does not mean that the tax assessors can go wild and levy taxes against the surrounding farmlands based upon their potential for small lot development. To do so is not only unfair, but it will encourage opposition on the part of those people who are interested in maintaining a farming community. Perhaps the time has come to encourage the maintenance of open space and agricultural lands by allowing an adjustment downward in the taxes levied against lands where the owner has indicated a willingness to continue agricultural pursuits. This is certainly something worthy of consideration in view of the desirability of conservation as well as the preservation of open and green areas.

A more effective way to preserve agricultural land and its corresponding open space is by the public acquisition of a development easement or development rights. Here the public sector negotiates with the owner to arrive at a fair price to be paid, based on potential for development, and then buys the rights to more intensive use of the land. The owner is permitted to continue using the land for its present purpose, but a restriction running with the land prevents it from being developed for other uses, even if its ownership changes. Suffolk County, New York, puts this technique to use in preserving open space in its rapidly urbanizing area. It requires that a governmental unit and its people strongly support the concept of planning and the value of having open, undeveloped areas and maintaining agricultural uses. They must also be willing to provide the financial means for doing so. Transfer of development rights, discussed in the next chapter, is one of the newer techniques that may well offer a means of accomplishing the same purpose as acquisition of development rights by the public sector, but doing so in the private marketplace. Under this system, a farmer would be assigned a quota of development rights based upon the size of the farm, and these rights could be sold and transferred to other land where more intense development was desirable, had been planned for, and was permitted by local regulation.

A Sign of the Times

A problem in zoning that has been with us for many years is that of regulation outdoor advertising and signs. One of the most difficult aspects of preparing a zoning ordinance is anticipating the number and kinds of signs that are needed and that may, in fact, be essential to the economy of the community. It is difficult to set forth equitable standards and requirements that will permit necessary signs and yet prevent undesirable ones. Most large billboard sign owners are willing to locate them in industrial and business areas. It is relatively easy to keep this type of sign out of well-established and properly planned residential areas. With the evolution of the shopping center, new problems in signs have arisen. There is a need for identification signs, directional signs, individual shop signs, and directory signs, as well as parking and locational signs.

These matters must be dealt with carefully in a zoning ordinance. It is not enough arbitrarily to rule out all types of advertising in a community. Signs should be recognized as a legitimate element, and they should be anticipated with adequate standards established in advance. A number of articles and pamphlets have been written on the subject of advertising signs and can provide information for those people interested in seeing that this subject is dealt with properly in the zoning ordinance. Some of the more helpful ones can be obtained from the Chicago office of the American Planning Association.

Does It Have to Be a House to Be a Home?

Reference has been made several times to our changed social concepts and the high mobility of our society. The development of the automobile, combined with this social mobility, has greatly enhanced the use of mobile homes or trailers, as they sometimes are referred to, for living units. Mobile homes or modular units can be provided with less capital outlay than for the conventional home, especially given today's soaring costs and interest rates for residential construction. This type of housing as an alternative to on-site construction and as a means of obtaining more affordable housing is essential in this period of inflation and high interest rates.

Any municipality with zoning or contemplating the adoption of an ordinance should be aware of this kind of potential land use and have a clearly stated policy regarding it. It is up to each locality to make the decision of whether to permit such use and where, but that decision should be based on facts and planning principles, not emotion. Complete rejection and prohibition can run the risk of charges of exclusionary zoning, discussed earlier in this chapter. Indiscriminate allowance can create problems of impaction, traffic congestion, and poor design of sites.

Not every municipality should have a mobile home park or trailer court. I feel that they can be prohibited in a community where there is an adequate reason for doing so, and where this reason is clearly indicated by the planning and zoning studies available. On the other hand, there are a number of places now prohibiting such use that should not do so. The best way to approach this problem is to carefully survey your community, decide where mobile homes can be permitted without detriment to surrounding areas and with appropriate advantages to those who will occupy them, and *then* to establish adequate standards and provisions within the ordinance well in advance of the need. These provisions should deal with the density of the units; whether or not they can be on individual lots; whether they are to be stored in certain areas only temporarily; whether they must all be located in courts or parks, and what side yard, rear yard, and other area requirements and municipal services are necessary. Parking must be given careful consideration in establishing these standards.

We Can't Expect Everything to Fit the Pattern

When looking at common problems to be faced in the development and application of zoning, competing to head the list is nonconformance. While this was discussed briefly in Chapter 7, it is important enough to the zoning scheme to merit further elaboration. The term "nonconforming" is applicable to any use, structure, or lot that, after passage of a new ordinance or an amendment, does not conform strictly to the requirements and standards enacted. In developing an ordinance, for example, say that studies have shown an area to be predominantly developed as single-family residential at present, and the comprehensive plan developed prior to zoning calls for it to remain so. Within this zone or district the lot size pattern is 75 feet by 100 feet, the average setback from the center line of streets is 65 feet, and so on, with other lot area requirements based upon what is in existence and what is desirable. Close examination, however, shows that there are several parcels where they, or what has occurred on them, will not comply exactly with the standards best suited for the entire area. Rather than spot zoning these individual lots, the practice is to adopt those general standards and recognize anything not meeting them as being a nonconforming lot, structure, or use.

Thus, a structure in which a commercial use exists at the time of the adoption of the ordinance becomes a nonconforming use and is permitted to continue. A house with less than the required setback from the street or side yards below the minimum set by the ordinance becomes a nonconforming structure. If the lot requirement is for 7,500 square feet, with not less than 75 feet of width at the building line or street property line, and a lot exists when the ordinance is adopted with less than any of the required measurements, it becomes a nonconforming lot. In each of these cases, they are permitted to remain as they are, they do not have to be converted to conformance, and, in the case of the lot, the owner cannot be denied a reasonable use of the land.

Nonconformance runs with the land much like a deed restriction. The properties can be sold and the nonconforming classification passed on to successive owners, provided there is no change in any of the conditions present at the time the ordinance passed and the designation of nonconforming became applicable. Any change requested for a nonconforming use or structure must be turned down by the zoning officer, and the applicant can appeal to the zoning board of adjustment for a further variance from the requirements. The same applies to an owner of a nonconforming lot. The zoning officer cannot issue a zoning permit to allow building on it, but the owner may appeal to the zoning board for consideration. In this case, there is frequently an excellent example of the true intent of the variance procedure and the "good" variance diagrammed in Chapter 7. The zoning board has the authority to impose special conditions to protect the surrounding properties and the general area in all cases involving the granting of a variance to any nonconforming situation.

The subject of nonconformance in zoning is a broad and complicated matter. The intent here is to provide a general understanding of the term and to emphasize the care and attention that should be given to the subject by officials and citizens alike. Slipshod handling of nonconforming uses can lead to the destruction of the character and quality of a community, as well as excessive litigation. A zoning board that adopts the attitude that variance requests for nonconformance are to be granted automatically and without imposing protective provisions can destroy the intent of a good zoning ordinance. To understand all that is involved in this subject and its importance, the reader should refer to more specialized publications, inasmuch as this complex issue is a study within itself.

One final general comment concerning administration of zoning related to nonconforming lots, structures, and uses: when an ordinance is first adopted, a file listing and describing in detail all nonconforming properties should be established and kept current. All approved variances or changes should be noted. The major reason for this is to avoid later arguments and lawsuits about the existence of the nonconforming conditions at the time of the passage of the ordinance or any amendment.

11

Recent Developments and Emerging Techniques

Having entered the planning and zoning arena in the 1940s and experienced the the evolutionary changes through the years, I am astounded by the enormity of what has happened to the philosophy and concepts. This is so in both the dramatic advancement in ordinance techniques and experimentation and in the courts' acceptance of increased local regulation of land use. In that period, we have advanced from the rejection of any governmental intervention in the use of private lands by some state courts, as mentioned in an earlier chapter, to realization by most that changing conditions justify, even necessitate, the expression of community interest based on planning policies in how private interests may choose to develop land. If there is one underlying theme or trend through all of this, it would be the constant search for increased flexibility from the rigid, straitjacketed approach of the Euclidian zoning in applying land-use controls.

As we have seen, zoning began with the "use by right" principle, with certain permitted uses as a matter of right of ownership spelled out for each zone or district. If an owner of property wanted to do only what was included in the designation of allowable uses and within the stated dimensions for lot area and open space, permission to do so was a routine matter, and a zoning permit was issued based on the theory of "use by right." In many aspects of zoning, this principle is still followed, primarily in single-lot development by individual owners in residential areas. While this practice has proved worthy and use by right remains the fundamental precept in land-use planning and the designation of zone districts, the means for going beyond original zoning limitations in directing large-scale subdivision, commercial, and industrial development constantly have been sought. Thus, the technology

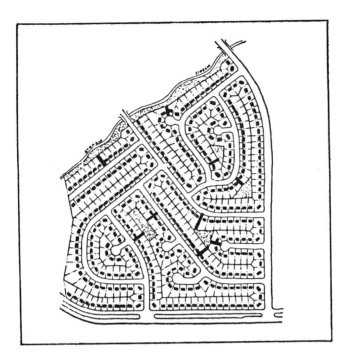

FIGURE 7. CLUSTER DEVELOPMENT
Plats show difference in development under typical lot-by-lot zoning (above) and cluster zoning. Both tracts have the same density, but clustering allows for more open space.

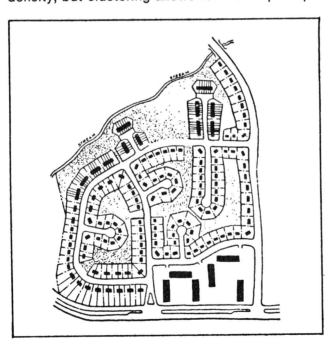

of land-use guidance and zoning of today is much different from that of the early days of my professional career. In view of the changing conditions and the increasing complexity of society, this is as it should be and offers support to the theory that zoning, to be effective, must be a dynamic, progressive, and ongoing process.

In this chapter, we will look at a few of the experiments that have become accepted practice, some of the older techniques that have been revived in different forms, and one or two of the newer methodologies that are being tested but have not gained full acceptance. No attempt will be made to explore these in great detail or to explain all the ramifications. There are other more technical publications available that provide in-depth discussion of all of the concepts included here and frequent reference will be made to sources for additional information. A list of these sources is included in the Bibliography.

Density Zoning/Cluster Development

Residential use zoning, with its area dimensions and the establishment of a fixed building envelope, has been with us since the enlargement of the Los Angeles ordinance establishing industrial zones to include other uses under land-use regulation. This being so, it seems logical to start this discussion of changing trends with a look at one of the earlier attempts to overcome rigidity of housing development standards that has been accepted practice for a number of years. In the ordinance of the earlier years of zoning, after a decision had been reached about the uses to be allowed, each was assigned numerical measurements for the size of the lot, where any structure could be located, and how tall it could be. A residential zone required a minimum size lot for each single-family home, with the same minimum requirements for yards for each lot. These provisions led to rather stereotyped development, especially in large tract developments by subdividers. Even the advent of curved streets, as opposed to the gridiron or rectilinear pattern, did not do a great deal to provide variety of design, usable open space, or flexibility of arrangement, with most speculative developers usually observing only the minimums required.

Density control and cluster zoning were innovations to try to overcome this. The idea of density control is to determine through future land-use planning the total number of dwelling units the municipality wants and can serve for a specified area and to key the zoning to that desired density. Flexibility of lot size becomes the appeal to inducing or requiring a developer to use this technique. This can be illustrated by the following example of how it worked on a tract of 100 acres. Studies had shown that the general area the parcel is in is suited for a density of four dwelling units to the acre, or a total of 400 units on the 100 acres. Allowing for loss of land for streets, drainage easements, and utilities, this would mean lot sizes of around 9,000 or 10,000 square feet, using traditional zoning. With a provision in the ordinance to allow density zoning, a plan could be approved with individual lots of, say, 6,000 square feet, but still limiting the overall total to 400 units. The remaining portion of the land becomes usable open space either dedicated to the local government or turned over for future maintenance to a homeowners association created within the subdivision.

Using the density zoning concept, it was a simple step to move into the idea of cluster development. With cul-de-sacs and loop streets, the smaller lots can be clustered together in residential nodes around the open space. There are advantages in this technique for everyone—the local government, the developer, and the homeowner—and it has become a widely accepted practice. Some of these advantages include: the ability to properly plan and utilize land with some areas unsuitable for development; less street construction and maintenance required; savings due to shorter lines for utilities; the provision of desirable open space; and encouragement of flexibility and attractiveness in site planning and general design.

In order to make the concept easier to understand, I have discussed only single-family residential development. This does not mean that density zoning is not applicable and useful for multifamily residential use, and, with conversion to other methods of intensity or impact measurement, the idea can be applied to office and industrial parks and shopping centers. Using an original theory developed by Byron Hanke of the Federal Housing Administration for residential development called Land Use Intensity, Frederick H. Bair, Jr., a planning and zoning consultant, has written a detailed pamphlet explaining the application of intensity (or density) zoning for all aspects of residential development in small or large cities. While Bair's explanation is far more complex than this discussion and involves technical measurement charts and fomulas, it is a helpful publication for those interested in exploring this approach further. (See Bibliography.)

Planned Unit Development

Once the technique of density zoning and cluster development became accepted practice, it was but a short step to planned unit development (PUD). Initially conceived of as a means of encouraging "master planning" for the long-range development of large residential tracts of land, the PUD idea has been extended far beyond that to become a very popular tool for greater local involvement in development of all types of land use and the creation of "mini-communities" or "new-towns" within a municipal or county area. In some places, such development

Figure 8. A typical planned unit development

Reprinted with permission from *Cost Effective Site Planning*, copyright 1976, National Association of Home. Builders, 15th and M Streets, N.W., Washington, D.C. 20005

is confined to residential use with mixed density (planned residential development, PRD); however, the prevalent application today allows mixed uses as well as residential mix and, in some cases, an increase in density over that of the applicable traditional zoning.

The first step in the PUD process is to provide specific procedures and standards in any newly prepared ordinance or amend an existing one. In accordance with the planning for future development, certain areas can be designated on a zoning map as PUD areas, with primary uses and densities allowed, or, as some communities have done, the process can be established, not specifically mapped, and treated as a "floating zone" to be applied as a map change after approval of an application. Under the latter approach, it is better to designate general areas where PUD's might be feasible, although not shown as predetermined sites, than to allow the possibility of an application anywhere under the ordinance's jurisdiction. The PUD technique was intended for and works best in large undeveloped sections of a community.

The processing of a PUD is more involved than a simple zoning application. Since there is a greater amount of review of all proposals of the project and more discretion allocated to them, local officials and agencies and many developers are critical of the idea. There are certain advantages to developers, however, such as the built-in stability of approval for a master-planned property over the longer period, allowing systematic partial development and financial outlay. It has worked well in many communities to provide advance long-range planning for sizeable areas, so well in fact that a goodly number of suburban municipalities and counties require all requests for large-scale developments to adhere to the PUD process.

Under "use by right" zoning, a 100-acre parcel, for example, might lie in one zoning category or in as many as two or three. Each would have established, possibly rigid, standards for use and area dimension. There might be a small commercial zone, a four-plex apartment zone, and a large, single-family residential zone. If a PUD ordinance exists, after a market study, a developer could propose to mix medium-rise apartments, townhouses, single-family units with accessible office or industrial uses and a commercial center, supplemented with a community center, a park, and open space, all in compliance with the terms and standards of the ordinance. Detailed drawings and information covering every aspect of the overall master plan would be submitted to the planning commission, reviewed by all departments and a site design review team, subjected to public hearing, and approved by the planning commission and governing body. After approval, the adopted "master plan" for the 100 acres becomes the permitted zoning for the parcel, superseding the underlying use by right zoning. Included in this process also would be all the steps necessary for any required subdivision approval.

As is the case with any flexible zoning technique, there are advantages and dangers. The advantage of PUD to the developer has been mentioned and, in addition to offering a greater opportunity for site plan and design review to local governments, this process can encourage long-range planning by major developers, provide an opportunity for flexibility in design and development while maintaining a unified scheme, and allow more efficient planning of roads, utilities, and services. The major disadvantages are the necessary negotiations and the potential for arbitrary discretionary action. Legal questions also have been raised by some who feel that the long-established precept that one governing body cannot commit or bind future governing bodies should be applicable, especially as it relates to land-use patterns and development policies. Although court decisions have been somewhat mixed where the PUD process has been challenged, in general the concept seems to have passed muster with the judicial. (For a more detailed discussion of PUD, see *Planned Unit Development Ordinances*, Planning Advisory Service Report No. 291, May 1973, American Planning Association, Chicago.)

Mixed-Use Zoning

The planned unit development idea is providing the opportunity for mixed uses in newly developing areas, but the desirability of this also is being seen in older areas. Like so many other things in our society, zoning seems to take pendulum swings from one extreme to another. Under the Euclidian zoning theory, each type of land use was to be separated as much as possible. Single-family residence zones should not include any commercial uses, other than the necessary continuation of a nonconforming use, and should be as far away from an industrial area as is feasible; apartments should be somewhere by themselves; and business uses should not be mixed with industrial. An extreme example of this is found in Denver where, until 1964, its zoning ordinances prohibited any residential use in its central business district, except for transients (hotels). Today, Denver is desparately trying to generate a downtown residential base to encourage continuation of its downtown stores and to house a rapidly increasing labor force of office workers.

There is no doubt that we went too far in total segregation of land uses, as was dramatically pointed out in Jane Jacobs's *The Death of Life of Great American Cities*, although I continue to take umbrage with Jacobs for her mistaken belief that this was all the fault of planners. Although no one could anticipate that the world situation would generate the energy crisis as it has, this phenomenon has changed our view of desirable urban organization far more effectively than Jacobs's plaint that we had lost and were losing a beneficial sense of community. Several additional factors, including the price of gasoline and single-family housing, have contributed to the change in the philosophy of urban planning and development to that of mixed land use. As a consequence, zoning ordinances are now encouraging residential/office/commercial intermingling by special districts, such as the Portland, Oregon, A-X Zone, and by bonus allowances and incentives, as found in many major cities.

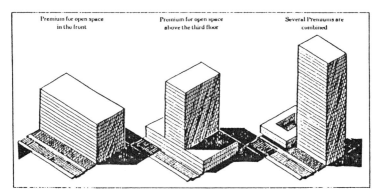

FIGURE 9. INCENTIVE ZONING
Additional floor areas may be offered to developers for providing certain kinds of desired amenities.

Incentives/Bonus Provisions

The idea of inducing desired amenities, sought-after types of land use, and additional design review by "carrot-dangling," instead of by stated specifications and requirements in zoning ordinances, began to appear during the 1960s. More recently, this idea of granting bonus density or floor area if certain things are done by a developer has grown in popularity and legal acceptance and is now found in most large city and urbanizing county ordinances. Although it closely resembles the idea of "contract zoning" (see later discussion) that was a zoning "no-no!" in the early days of my professional career, it can provide an effective tool for gaining increased community benefits when carefully and reasonably applied. The key, as is true with all flexible zoning, is to provide the foundation for such action in the policies and provisions of a comprehensive plan, clearly showing the reasons for it and the community benefit to be derived from achieving the objective.

The idea of the incentive approach is that the owner is encouraged to go beyond that which is required by providing something wanted by the community, rather than telling a property owner what must be done beyond a fundamental minimum requirement. In turn, that developer would be allowed to build beyond the use-by-right standards. If the policy of a city calls for increasing the housing units in the inner city, for example, a provision might be developed that allows a business or office building to exceed the stated floor-area ratio to the lot by a specified percentage, provided the structure includes some residential units. Another way this could be approached would be to rezone an inner-city area for multifamily residential use, with a minimum number of units required. Since the objective is to increase the downtown housing units, the incentive would be that, for a stated number of dwelling units beyond the minimum, the owner would be allowed a proportionate ratio of retail or office space on the lower floors. Incentive bonuses are now being used to achieve a wide variety of objectives— for plazas, open space, setting back upper floors, sky-walk development, arcades, and underground parking, to name just a few. San Francisco uses this technique to encourage access to its rapid transit system and to provide observation decks "at or above the twentieth story of the building." Arlington County, Virginia, is trying to encourage redevelopment of its Rosslyn area, using a 1961 redevelopment plan based on incentive bonuses.

An important aspect to note is that incentive zoning will be a license to destroy character and quality in any high-intensity area with existing liberal provisions of floor-area ratio, height, or density. To be used effectively, a basic zone change is needed to strengthen the primary requirements and the use-by-right provisions. As Richard F. Babcock and John S. Banta have said in *New Zoning Techniques for Inner City Areas*,

[Cities] have been eager to attract development in their urban core, resulting in such loose zoning restrictions that they have already given away whatever floor-area ratio or density increment over existing uses that the market might support. In those cases, a zoning rollback, with attendant practical and legal problems, is necessary before any realistic discussion of incentives can begin.

A perfect example of the importance of these words and the damage that can be done by not heeding them can be found in "beautiful" downtown Denver where a local administration succumbed to the first part of that quote, but totally ignored the latter before joining the incentive parade.

Downzoning/Inverse Condemnation

Putting the terms "downzoning" and "inverse condemnation" together is not intended to imply that they are inseparable or that there can be no downzoning without inverse condemnation. Rather, the intent is to emphasize that changing the zoning of an area from one type of use by right and intensity to a different use with less intensity—while desirable, sometimes necessary, and being increasingly practiced—is to be done very carefully. Any downzoning or increasing restrictions is an action that will usually be opposed by property owners, stir up conflict, and be a political hot potato. Charges of inverse condemnation or taking away private property rights—that is, denying use of land without compensation for lost value—will be made. Yet, this is a valuable and essential endeavor for sound planning where conditions change, new pressures have been created, and community goals and objectives have been revised.

The cardinal principle in land ownership has always been that any of us hold land subject to the proper and reasonable restrictions enacted by present and future governments. Changing those restrictions for justifiable reasons does not mean that an owner is to be compensated for the loss of a greater economic gain as long as that owner is left with a reasonable use of the land and the government action has been in good faith and for proven community good. Nevertheless, a property owner subject to reduced development potential will feel justified in bringing forth the "taking of land" issue or inverse condemnation.

Such was the case in the city of Tiburon, California, when an area was rezoned to allow one dwelling unit per acre. The landowner of a five-acre tract, acquired prior to the passage of the ordinance, filed suit declaring that it constituted a taking of property without just compensation. The case was finally heard by the U.S. Supreme Court, which ruled in favor of the city stating that "it could not be said that the ordinance so affected the property's value as to destroy reasonable investment expectations" (*Agins v. City of Tiburon*, 447 U.S. 255 (1980).

Probably the greatest need for the application of downzoning falls in the older, inner-city areas. The necessity for establishing a base for effective incentive zoning is a case in point, as is the need for correcting outmoded overzoning for business along major streets. Where there is a central business district that has maintained its character but has been overzoned, the residential fringe will be damaged by leapfrogging and spotty intensification without the protection downzoning can provide. Just such an area is the Curtis Park neighborhood in Denver. Comprised primarily of modest single-family homes and lying almost immediately adjacent to the ever-sprawling central business district of the city, it is a beautifully integrated, rapidly rehabilitating community that was facing the threat of loss of character from economic pressures and the office and apartment high rises spilling over from downtown. Neighborhood leaders, working with an organized neighborhood association, petitioned the city for downzoning. Not everyone owning property in the areas was in support of this proposal, and many discussions and meetings were held before enough consensus could be built to influence the city council to take action. To their credit, they did, and a valuable, older neighborhood has a better chance of surviving as just that.

Impact Zoning/Performance Zoning

One of the newer techniques resulting from the search for flexibility in zoning is impact—or performance—zoning. Several years ago, planners began experimenting with the idea of adopting general standards and then allowing broad flexibility of uses and densities, depending upon what effect projects would have on physical, social, economic, and environmental conditions within an area or community. A rating or point system was formulated for scoring major items of concern in each of those four categories to ascertain how the development would affect each one. The lower the score of impact or adverse effect, the more likely was the project to fall within the allowable total for favorable consideration. In some cases, where impact measurement was high, approval would be granted if the developer could show a means of mitigation and was willing to undertake it. The local community would thus be saved the cost of later correcting problems with public money.

Many of these approaches have followed the idea of the environmental impact analysis that has been required on all projects involving federal dollars over the last several years. Performance zoning, however, carries the question of impact beyond natural environment into manmade environment. An excellent example of its use is found in the Bucks County, Pennsylvania, zoning ordinance and its provisions for the development of open areas for residential purposes. The thesis is that the option of the type of housing permitted in specified areas should be largely in the hands of the developers and the economic marketplace. In an attractive publication entitled "Performance Zoning," they have taken one hypothetical land parcel and shown how it could be developed under the ordinance for any one of 11 residential structure types, including mobile homes. There are rather detailed standards to be met and formulas to be used for impact measurement and mitigation evaluation, but the opportunity for a wide choice in housing types by the developer and a greater variety of development character for the county offers a distinct advantage to both.

Growth Management Plans/ Land Development Codes

The impact zoning idea has been a decided influence on the movement toward growth management plans. For many years, local governments and counties have struggled with the problems inherent in growth and sought ways of controlling and managing it. Since the advent of planning and zoning, most jurisdictions have had the regulations for directing land development; but, over the years, responsibility for their administration has been divided between various departments and officials. The processing of a subdivision permit, for example, might require visiting and negotiating with as many as a half-dozen municipal officers. In extreme cases, it has even reached the point where the requirements of one office might be in conflict with those of another office—all within the same administration. Needless to say, this has caused a great deal of criticism of local controls by landowners and developers and, in some instances, has been the basis for moves to get state legislatures to intervene and limit land-use authority of local government.

Partly in an attempt to streamline the process and partly as a means of controlling growth better, the growth management plan idea is being used by more and more communities. Whether from the desire to keep growth within manageable limits each year by setting building permit limits, as has been done in Petaluma, California, and Boulder, Colorado, or in response to the need for a more efficient management system, growth management plans appear to be the wave of the future. Having said that, it would be wise to point out that they are not for every community. Any local government learning of the technique and thinking of instituting it should recognize that, while it may centralize the process, it does not simplify it. Instead, it creates a more sophisticated system that requires a greater amount of professional expertise from all agencies of government working cooperatively with the processing agencies. In other words, do not tell your planning department or community development department to draw up a growth management plan, adopt it, and expect them to administer it unless elected officials are willing to support it fully, both with policy and money for adequate, well-qualified staff.

An oversimplified definition of growth management planning is that it is a consolidation into one system of all requirements and control techniques necessary to carry out the intent of a comprehensive plan. Its fundamental principle is that all growth is not inevitable and that the rate and type of development are subject to determination by public policy and action. Thus, another word of caution: do not even consider the idea unless a well-established pro-planning attitude exists in the community. Where this is so, and where there are readers interested in finding out more about growth management planning, I would suggest *Urban Growth Management Systems* as a source of additional information. (See Bibliography.)

The combination of growth management and impact measurement has led to some communities combining zoning, subdivision, and other regulations and policies relating to land development into a land development code. Breckenridge, Colorado, for example, a resort town with a small permanent population, has done this. Their application of this approach has been very successful, thanks to the genuine concern of the town council, an understanding and supportive town manager, and an excellent community development department and director. All development is based on a point permit system that not only includes the principles of zoning and subdivision controls but also incorporates 10 other codes by reference and a complete list of planning and design standards. The statement of purpose in the adopted code is well done and is included here to emphasize what I have said about the attitude that should go with the adoption of any growth management plan.

B. Purpose

The purpose of this chapter is to ensure that future growth and development which occurs in Breckenridge is in accord with the wishes of the residents hereof; to identify and secure, for present and future residents, the beneficial impacts of growth; to identify and avoid the negative impacts of growth; to ensure that future growth is of the proper type, design, and location and served by a proper range of public services and facilities; and in other respects to achieve the goals and implement the policies of the Breckenridge Comprehensive Planning Program, as amended from time to time.

While the Breckenridge code is a good one for that community, and it could serve as a guide to other smaller, especially resort, communities, the bible for general reference to any local government interested in exploring this idea is *A Model Land Development Code, Complete Text and Commentary*, published by the American Law Institute in 1975. Assembled over a number of years by a distinguished Advisory Committee chaired by Richard F. Babcock, this volume is an attempt to modernize the approach to land-use regulation, something desperately needed. The purpose of the ALI and its committee was to prepare an adaptable model act that could be adopted by state legislators after modification to fit any particular state's needs and problems. The model Standard State Zoning Enabling Act (1922) and the Standard State City Planning Act (1928), prepared and suggested for adoption by the U.S. Department of Commerce, have been the guides for state legislation for over 50 years. Now the ALI hopes that the Model Code will encourage states with a real interest in guiding future development by helping municipalities to replace legislation based upon those outmoded 1922 and 1928 models. This is a valuable service, and I urge any person seriously interested in the future to become familiar with the ALI model and, even more important, to encourage state legislators to do so.

Zoning for Energy Conservation and Solar Development

Just as the change in our energy situation has had a decided effect on our attitudes about urban form and has encouraged mixed-use development, so has it introduced the new concept of zoning with consideration for energy conservation. This should become a significant concern and should find means of expression in industrial park, central business district, and residential zoning. In a sense, it also creates some contradictions. To conserve energy, we need to encourage a mixture of work place and residence, create greater density, place buildings closer together, encourage mass transit, while encouraging and providing for alternate energy source uses, such as solar. On the surface, the use of solar systems, which depend upon open access to the sun, would seem to be in conflict with other types of zoning that might help in energy conservation. But both are important, and effecting their compatibility will require recognition of the existence of a community interest in how land is used and how development is shaped.

The time may come when, in areas of intensive high-rise development, the use of an alternate energy source such as the sun by one building establishes a "prior right" to unobstructed exposure to that source that other buildings nearby would be required to respect. To an extent, this is already being included in some solar access ordinances relating to new construction. Notable among these are ordinances in Davis, Santa Clara, and Sacramento Counties, California, and Albuquerque, New Mexico. The regulations in such controls not only require careful site planning but also establish controlled building heights correlated to the angles of sunlight, plus standards for location, shape, and height of vegetation to assure protection of sun access. Progressive concern for this valuable energy source of the future will require greater involvement of the public sector in directing land development and, as such, may meet with resistence and political difficulties.

Once this hurdle is passed and a community moves in the direction of energy conservation measures and solar energy development, there are many opportunities available for public sector action both in zoning and other land development tools. First of all, the local government should make certain that it has its own house in order regarding conservation in public facilities and control of physical development of streets, street trees, and landscaping. Then comes the need for developing a clear statement of public policy and the enactment of implementing codes and ordinances, all carefully interrelated. The concept of a consolidated land development code is an efficient way of ensuring this. However it may be done, the most essential element is recognition of the need for energy conservation in the zoning and subdivision standards and complete coordination between the two. Fundamental to this will be increased participation by public agencies in the design review process in all development, especially subdivisions.

There are a number of helpful publications on energy conservation and solar development relating to planning and zoning, some of which are listed in the Bibliography. The most complete source of general information comes from the American Planning Association, and *Protecting Solar Access for Residential Development*, prepared by APA for the U.S. Department of Housing and Urban Development, is worthy of special mention here.

Transfer of Development Rights

One of the newer and most controversial ideas pertaining to land development controls is the transfer of development rights (TDR) from one piece of property to another. Used initially as an attempt to encourage preservation of historic structures in high-density urban areas, this technique is now gaining attention as a density control measure in suburban and rural areas. The principle involved is relatively simple; however, the application and implementation can be highly complex and difficult, and there are legal questions to be dealt with. As a result, TDR to date is somewhat like the weather—it is much talked about, but not too much is being done about it. While it may be an idea whose time has come, there are problems to be resolved concerning legislation, methodology, and equitable base determination, and there will have to be greater public understanding and acceptance before it becomes a matter of general usage and utility.

The TDR idea, simply put, means that each piece of property has specified development rights, and these rights are transferable to another parcel. Extension of this same principle was used recently to allow a property owner to sell the unused air rights of that property to someone else—as in the Grand Central Station transaction in New York City. In such built-up areas, rights of development are created by the provisions of a zoning ordinance establishing the bulk and height of the structure permitted on each lot. When such an ordinance is passed, there

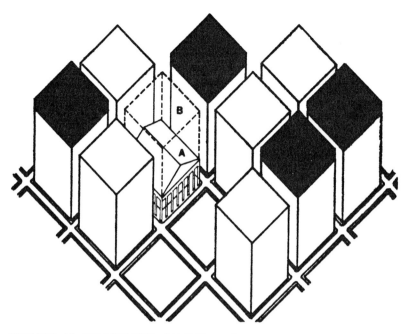

FIGURE 10. TRANSFER OF DEVELOPMENT RIGHTS
In this illustration of the use of TDRs for historic preservation,
the rights to be transferred (B) from a landmark building (A) are
given to other sites and appear as zoning density bonuses (C)
on other buildings.

are existing buildings—some historic, some not—of less bulk and/or
height. Those buildings can be demolished and new ones built to the
allowable maximum; the older structures can be added to within the
"rights" limit set; or, using TDR, the unused height or square footage
of floor area can be sold in the private marketplace and transferred
to another lot adjacent thereto or somewhere in the same district or
zone, and, in some cases, another designated area in the city. Thus,
the owner of a historic structure five stories high, located in a zone
district allowing heights equivalent to 60 stories, could be encouraged
to retain the historic building by selling the unused 55-story bulk to
another owner or to several other owners. To make this work, however,
the buyers would have to be allowed to exceed the set limits of height
or bulk for the zone in which their property is located by a stated percentage. The question then arises, if, as has been mentioned before, the
city has loose controls and has already allowed excessive bulk or height,

what does transfer of additional "privileges" do to the character of development? An excellent discussion of the use of TDR for preservation of historic buildings can be found in *New Zoning Techniques for Inner-City Areas,* referred to previously.

The use of TDR in suburban and rural areas to preserve agricultural land and open space or to control density is even more complicated. The best and simplest explanation of the process appeared in *Practicing Planner* (March 1977, American Institute of Planners, now American Planning Association). It is reprinted below.

What Is Transfer of Development Rights?

Transfer of development rights (TDR) attempts to achieve preservation of private property in the public interest without the expenditure of public funds for land acquisition. Put simply, TDR is a process by which the right to develop a parcel of land is separated from the land itself. Each remains private property and can be sold separately. The development rights can be sold to another party and used on a different parcel of land, thereby adding to the amount of development or density that can be built on the receiving parcel. Usually in suburban and rural jurisdictions the transfer is not to an adjacent parcel. Rather it is to a different area of the community.

Naturally, density limits on receiving parcels have to be clear or there would be no advantage to buying development rights to add to the allowable density. This usually is accomplished by zoning.

Usually, the system is proposed with specific areas for preservation of agricultural or environmentally sensitive land and with specific areas in which development is desired. The former is called a preservation district, or sending zone; and landowners in this zone are encouraged to sell their development rights. The latter is called a receiving zone or reception district, and developers are encouraged to buy development rights from landowners in the preservation zone to take advantage of added densities by using the rights. Usually, a developer can build as of right in a receiving or development zone. But, use of the development rights allows added density, up to a limit, beyond that zoned as of right.

Here's a simple example. Farmer X lives in an agricultural preservation, or sending, zone. He wants to keep farming, and he wants to sell his development rights. He sells them to Developer Y. The development rights have been set as one right per acre. The farm is 25 acres, and the farmer sells all 25 rights to Developer Y. Developer Y then gets approval to build a multifamily project in the development, or receiving, zone. It is zoned for five units to the acre as of right, up to 10 units per acres with development rights. His proposal is approved for a five-acre development of 50 dwelling units. He was able to build 25 units as of right under the normal zoning, and he added the 25 development right units he purchased from the farmer, for a total of 50. The sale of the rights is recorded and becomes, in effect, a deed restriction on the property of Farmer X. He can no longer build one unit per acre nor sell his development rights again.

So far, most TDR systems adopted are voluntary and would not force Farmer X in the above example to retain his land as a farm. Nor would the systems require that Developer Y build in the development zone on-. ly if he had purchased development rights. Thus, Farmer X had the choice of selling his land to a developer who wanted to build one unit per acre selling it acre by acre for single-family construction or remaining on it and farming but selling his development rights. The latter point is seen as attractive in many agricultural areas where people are inclined to keep farming but find it hard to resist sale of the land for a good price when developers move in.

In other situations where wetlands or other environmentally sensitive land is in the preservation zone, development may be more restricted as of right. In these cases, sale of development rights may be the only real economic alternative for a landowner.

Most of the TDR programs adopted to date are based on preservation of agricultural land. There are at most a dozen of them across the country. Most have seen little in the way of transactions so far. Also, there are a few places where TDR is allowed to preserve a single site (urban historic landmark, private park, etc.) as in New York City.

Basic to any consideration of TDR, remember, is a thorough, completely documented comprehensive plan and a well-staffed, professional planning agency, fully supported in the community.

Inclusionary Zoning

In Chapter 10, the possibility of charges of exclusionary zoning being a problem was discussed. Here we move to the other side of the coin and examine the new technique called inclusionary zoning. It is used to implement a public policy aimed at diversifying economic strata within a community and providing affordable housing to do so. This concept came about as a means of combatting the tendency of developers of major subdivisions to build only for the higher priced housing market. The method falls into the category of contract zoning discussed in the next section. To apply the principle of inclusionary zoning, the community adopts the policy of encouraging housing for moderate- and lower-income families, establishes percentages of market price and subsidized housing units to the total number, and requires the developer to agree or "contract" to provide the desired mix before project approval will be granted.

It has been said that inclusionary zoning came into focus as a means of responding to the charges of exclusionary zoning and that it is not seriously pursued in the day-to-day administration of some municipalities where it exists in name. Boulder, Colorado, on the other hand, is an example of a community that has made a serious effort to avoid becoming "a one class town" by using this technique. Some local jurisdictions, instead of having mandatory requirements, have gone the incentive or bonus route to show that they favor inclusionary zoning. For example, a developer will be offered additional density or number of units or the possible reduction of subdivision requirements as an inducement to provide an economic mix. Courts in general have been favorable to the idea embodied in inclusionary zoning but have not looked kindly on the use of the incentive approach.

The need for doing everything that can be done to encourage affordable housing for as much of our population as possible, regardless of their income, is a definite reality. As Meshenberg says in *The Language of Zoning*, inclusionary zoning is "a positive and active policy and program of a community to attract racial minorities or low- and moderate-income residents. Such policies, analogous to affirmative action in job recruitment, go beyond the avoidance of techniques which discourage certain classes of people from moving into an area; they actively seek to invite such groups."

Contract Zoning/Special Permits/ Conditional Rezoning

We now move into some of the most frequently challenged discretionary aspects of zoning that, nevertheless, are gaining in popularity, especially in communities using growth management techniques. For years, courts held that zoning as a use of governmental police power could not be bargained for by a developer and that all requirements had to be spelled out in detail or, at least, specific standards of measurement provided. This was the basis of the acceptable practice of special exception or conditional uses in traditional zoning ordinances. It was recognized that certain uses might be desirable in a single-family residence zone, but, because of certain characteristics, they might best be allowed only after proving their ability to meet standards not required of any use by right. The procedure required the applicant to present plans, and proof that all conditions could be met, in a hearing before the zoning board of adjustment or, in some instances, a planning commission. The provisions might imply a degree of discretion by the local agency by a phrase saying something like, ". . . may impose any other terms and conditions necessary to protect the general character of the area and preserve

the intent and purpose of the zone plan and ordinance." Other than
that, any indication of bargaining or contracting with an individual
property owner was a definite taboo.

With the advent of the planned unit development concept and its
acceptance by courts, the rejection of any kind of negotiation and
bargaining between municipal governments and developers became a
less likely result in case of a challenge. Even though this represents the
most discretionary aspect of zoning action by elected or appointed local
government officials, its use in some form is occurring more and more,
and provisions allowing contracting are being added to zoning ordinances all over the country—and being upheld by courts in some
cases. While, as a traditional, old-school zoner, I may have trouble
accepting this principle as being anything other than "blue eye and
brown tie" (meaning you get what you want because I like your blue
eyes, but he doesn't get what he wants because I don't like brown ties)
discretionary zoning by men/women, instead of by law, it may be as
Nancy H. Lieberman has said in a recent article in *Urban Land* entitled,
"Contract and Conditional Rezoning: A Judicial and Legislative
Review."[8]

> Traditional devices, including variance and special permits, are no
> longer sufficient. Innovative techniques, such as floating zones, planned
> unit developments, and overlay zones, have been added to zoning or-
> dinances to provide more flexibility. With a variety of land uses, an im-
> portant consideration in approving rezoning requests is the impact the
> development will have on neighboring lands. Among the techniques to
> accommodate land-use changes is the concept of contract and conditional
> zoning.

Lieberman goes on to indicate that there is not total acceptance that
the technique is legal. The argument continues over whether there is
a difference between contract rezoning and conditional rezoning or
whether they are synonymous, and such actions still are being struck
down by courts in some states. It would appear that most of the judicial
approvals of bargaining action, whether called contract or conditional,
have come in states where specific legislation allows municipalities this
discretion (as in Virginia and California). In other situations where such
action has been upheld, the courts have not squarely faced the question of an illegal contract and instead, as in Washington State, have
treated negotiated terms only as "agreements concomitant to a zoning
change."

[8]*Urban Land,* Urban Land Institute (Washington, D.C., November 1981) p. 10.

The issue remains unclear and, while ordinance provisions allowing the negotiation of terms and conditions are a reflection of concerned communities wanting to have a greater degree of flexibility in directing an orderly pattern of growth, a highly desirable objective, such zoning requirements must be approached with a great deal of care and caution. Any community doing so is wise to seek clarification of state legislation, have exemplary reasons for doing so based upon its planning policy and process, and—finally—have good zoning advice from its professional planner and an attorney specializing in zoning.

Site Plan and Design Review

Site plan review and design standards are two other terms to add to the compendium of techniques for more flexible administration of land-use controls. The former has been around in modified form since the advent of subdivision regulations by local governments. Requiring a developer to submit plans and specifications of what is proposed in a major development in the way of street alignment and arrangement, topography, lot configuration, and landscaping in order to obtain approval is site plan review. In earlier years, this carried with it no discretion. The terms and conditions to be met were stated clearly in an ordinance and the meeting of those requirements theoretically carried with it almost automatic approval, even though some give and take negotiation went on between developer and the planning agency and its staff. Other than the design of the general layout of streets and lots, no aesthetic aspects of buildings, types of materials, or service facilities such as street lighting, signs, etc., were considered to fall within the purview of local governmental authority.

Some attempts to add design considerations were made over the years. Special historic zones were created with design review commissions, and a few places, like Princeton, New Jersey, added a design review provision to the zoning ordinance for their central business area. However, it was not until the big leap in discretionary or flexible zoning known as planned unit development became accepted that substantial progress was made in putting local government squarely into the negotiated site plan and design review process. Today, the approval of a major development under PUD goes much further than the review of general use locations, density, and physical conformity of terrain, streets, and lots. Some PUD ordinances require detailed architectural drawings showing facades of typical structures and elaborate plans for planting, landscaping, and signage, and they provide the reviewing authority enough flexibility to impose aesthetic ideas or at least to negotiate them with the developer.

As a means of measuring basic impact, communities using the impact zoning technique include a complete review of the site plan, and some go so far as to have design evaluation as one means of determining favorable or unfavorable impact. In other areas using different approval methodology, more local governments are moving to require that all major developments follow the PUD application process because of the greater opportunity for the application of design criteria and municipal review. In industrial or office parks, shopping centers, or major residential subdivisions, the effective and sophisticated way to approach total review, including design, is to require that each PUD application incorporate a set of development guidelines that the developer has proposed and agrees to uphold.

One of the best examples of this is contained in the "Southpark Development Guidelines," a major office and commercial project of EMKAI Development Company, Inc., and ALCOA, Denver, Inc., in Littleton, Colorado. In this case, the design requirements are incorporated in the covenants running with the land, but conformance is subject to community review. Standards are included covering all aspects of individual project design, from the inception of the site plan to the completely finished product. Some 17 categories are listed, with design guidelines for each in written form, supplemented by illustrative graphics. The range of these categories goes so far as to include fencing, storage areas, site utilities, site lighting, site signage, and plant materials. This is an outstanding example of what a forward-looking, planning-oriented community can do to shape a more attractive environment through flexible zoning techniques reasonably and properly applied.

Zoning Hearing Examiner

At this point, it has probably become clear that I an not one to go around singing the praises of the zoning board of adjustment system for granting variances and exceptions. To put it simply, in most cases, I think it stinks. Seldom, if ever, have I encountered a zoning board whose members had any concept of good zoning principles, any sense of their responsibilities and duties, or even any ability to run a good hearing. The blame for this, however, should not be laid at the feet of the board members. Rather, it should be hung around the neck of the elected officials who appointed them either because they were loyal political supporters, would do as they were told, or were known to be sufficiently uninformed or lacking in intelligence that they would not or could not rock any boats or upset any political apple carts. Now to protect myself, I will quickly state that I know that there are zoning board members and elected officials somewhere out there in this vast country who are exceptions to that general rule. In truth, however, the zoning board of adjustment system has been the greatest single cause of harm to sensible land-use controls.

There are others who have recognized this over the years, and, for several decades, devices have been suggested to remedy problems in zoning administration, as well as to provide some improvement in the efficiency in granting minor map changes and keeping such action related to comprehensive plans. The best method devised so far is to create the position of zoning hearing examiner. This can be done in home rule cities, unless prohibited by state legislation, or by a general enabling act passed by the state permitting statutory cities and towns to do so. Under this administrative method, the responsibility for receiving applications for variances and minor zoning changes, processing them, conducting hearings, swearing in witnesses, and rendering decisions or making recommendations would be given to one (or several, if in a large city or county) qualified person known as a hearing examiner. In some instances, communities initiating the hearing examiner procedure have used lawyers, but, as of this writing, about one-half of the hearing examiners are trained planners. Whichever professional—planner or lawyer—is given this important job, he or she will need to work closely with someone skilled in the other profession.

Some cities, like Albuquerque, have instituted this process and, in so doing, have abolished the zoning board of adjustment function. An appeal of the decision by the hearing examiner may be taken to the planning commission in some cases and to the elected council in others. The normal appeal of any final decision—to the courts—remains. It should be pointed out that Albuquerque is a home-rule city. In states where the legislature has taken steps to grant this authority to all cities, the duties, authority, and process is detailed in state statute. To further explain how the office is created and to provide some understanding of this technique, here is a section of the Oregon zoning enabling act:

75. Oregon Revised Statutes, § 227.165 (1975).

76. § 227.165. A city may appoint one or more planning and zoning hearings officers, to serve at the pleasure of the appointing authority. Such an officer shall conduct hearings on applications for such classes of permits and zone changes as the council designates.

§ 227.170. The city council shall prescribe one or more procedures for the conduct of hearings on permits and zone changes.

§ 227.175 (1). When required or authorized by a city, an owner of land may apply in writing to the hearings officer, or such other person as the city council designates, for a permit or zone change, upon such forms and in such a manner as the city council prescribes.

(2) The hearings officer shall hold at least one public hearing on the application and within 60 days after receiving it deny or approve it. However, at the option of either the city or the applicant, the proceeding on the application may be extended for a reasonable period of time, as determined by the hearings officer.

(3) The application shall not be approved unless the proposed development of land would be in compliance with the comprehensive plan for the city. The approval may include such conditions as are authorized by ORS 227.220 or any city legislation.

(4) Hearings may be held only after notice to the applicant and other interested persons.

§ 227.180 (1). A party aggrieved by the action of a hearings officer may appeal the action to the planning commission or council of the city, or both, however the council prescribes. The appellate authority on its own motion may review the action. The procedure for such appeal or review shall be prescribed by the council, but shall include a hearing at least for argument. Upon appeal or review the appellate authority shall consider the record of the hearings officer's action. That record need not set forth evidence verbatim.

(2) A party aggrieved by the final determination in a proceeding for a discretionary permit of zone change may have the determination reviewed under ORS 34.010 to 34.100. Oregon Revised Statutes, §§ 227.165, 227.170, 227.175, 227.180 (1975).

Zoning by Referenda

A recent trend of judicial decisions and state legislative changes concerning the right of the general citizenry to have a say in land-use policy expressed through zoning is worthy of comment. For years, the attitude of courts has sustained the idea that the exercise of the police power pertaining to land use in a representative government is not subject to vote by the general public. This position has been supported strongly by local elected officials and state municipal leagues (the local government lobby existing in most states). Their position and their strongest argument has been that zoning is a "quasi-judicial" action and therefore exempted from constitutional provisions letting citizens challenge the legislative decisions of local governments by initiative and referendum. With the growing complexity of zoning, the advent of more flexible, and sometimes discretionary, provisions being added, the rising strength of neighborhood organizations, and the increasing general interest in zoning action by all citizens, it was almost a certainty that some change in this philosophy would be brought about, either by the courts or the legislatures.

The idea of neighborhood zoning districts suggested in an earlier chapter has been tried in varying forms in Buffalo, New York; Columbus, Ohio; and Baltimore, Maryland. The Indiana legislature enacted what has been referred to as a "minigov" bill in 1972, although the final version was watered down considerably from the original intent of its supporters. The states of California and Ohio have taken legislative action permitting zoning to be changed through referendum. Now comes a unanimous decision by the Supreme Court of Colorado saying that that state's constitution does not prohibit the right of citizens to demand referendum review of a zoning change to which they object.

Greenwood Village, a Denver suburb, annexed 90 acres in 1979, rezoned a portion as commercial, and placed the remainder in a residential category with the lot size requirements considerably less than those in the surrounding areas. At about the same time, the cities of Lakewood and Arvada, also part of the Denver metro area, had rezoned land for additional commercial and office use. In each community, the decision of the governing body was challenged by citizen groups, taken to court and, upon reaching the Supreme Court, consolidated into one case by that body. The decision rendered will have far-reaching effects in Colorado and may well be of influence in other states. The opinion written by Associate Justice Robert B. Lee and supported by the other members of the court leaves little doubt that Colorado communities now must recognize the right of citizens to voice their opinions on land-use development through initiative and referendum as indicated by this language in that opinion:

> In view of the purposes for which the referendum and initiative powers were reserved, and the nature of the acts themselves, we find that zoning and rezoning decisions—no matter what the size of the parcel of land involved—are legislative in character and subject to the referendum and initiative provisions of the Colorado Constitution. One of the unquestioned purposes of the referendum and initiative powers is to permit the total and free exercise of legislative power by the people. Thus, the power to call referendum and initiative elections is a direct check on the exercise or non-exercise of legislative power by elected officials. Indeed, a

heightened community sensitivity to the quality of the living environment and an increased skepticism of the judgment of elected officials provided much of the impetus for voters exercising the powers of initiative.

One or two more decisions like this one, and I may have to change my opinion about the courts in Colorado—at least the Supreme Court. Power to the people!

In these pages, I have tried to pick out a few of the more important concepts and ideas that have emerged or are emerging. What has been covered is by no means all inclusive. As I have indicated often, zoning is challenging, constantly changing, never static, but extremely important to our future—far too important to leave to politicians!

12

Is Zoning Here to Stay?

Other than taxes, there is probably no single term or concept that has been subject to more criticism and attack than zoning, yet it has continued not only to survive, but to thrive. This is to be expected, since both deal with the twin great American gods, money and profit. An examination of zoning's history since the day of its inception indicates that, much like the income tax, there have been those dedicated to its demise. From the first attempts at land-use regulation by government, the constitutionality, the reasonableness, and the logic of the public sector exercising any say as to what individuals may or may not do with their property have been questioned. This questioning has supported the economic well-being of many lawyers, kept courts busy, and divided communities into diverse camps of opinion. It seems clear that zoning has survived and has continued to be more broadly used in the face of its controversial nature and will continue to last because it is a necessary element of organized society.

A closer examination of that troubled history shows that, in most cases, the opposition to zoning has come from individuals and organizations whose motives were based on possible personal gain at public expense or from those who don't understand the need for land development guidance. While some respected professionals in the planning field have been known to make unkind remarks about zoning's lack of success, their seeming willingness to abandon it or totally make over the process has probably come more from a sense of frustration than opposition to public involvement in the development of land. Several years ago, for example, Cornell professor John Reps presented an oft-quoted paper entitled "A Requiem for Zoning" that has been used by some to say that "even planners don't think zoning works." Having heard his speech, I would dispute that interpretation of Reps's intent but would argue that he was one of the early voices crying out for better procedures for achieving orderly patterns of growth.

It is my contention that serious attacks on zoning—the ones pre-

venting its adoption or ending in a court challenge—come from those
who say:

1. "Profit at all costs, the public be damned";
2. "This is a free country, and nobody's gonna tell me what to do
   with my land"; or
3. "You can't trust anybody in government."

The first category has been rather widely discussed in this book, and
some aspects do not need too much elaboration. Although I have singled
out developers and the construction industry, in fairness I have to add
that almost all of us fall into this category in some ways or at some
time. We have been conditioned to think this way by our great amount
of space, our formerly abundant resources, and our rags-to-riches
dreams. Our mores all have worked to foster the illusion that we can
continue to consume a disproportionate amount of the world's resources
and that we are all entitled to take advantage of the capitalistic system
to become rich. After all, isn't that the American Way?

Reality is very difficult to perceive and to accept. In spite of irrefutable
facts, how many of us believe that we face a national and a world crisis
because of limited energy sources and food supplies, and unwillingness
of the nations to live together? Believing would dispel the illusion to
which we cling so assiduously. We would have to recognize that there
is a difference between standard of living and true quality of life. Then
would come the realization that we are not going to be able to maintain our huckster-imposed standard of living and that we are going to
have to work together to maintain *any* acceptable quality of life. And
it cannot be done if we exploit or condone exploitation of our resources,
our land, or society in general.

When we begin to think realistically in a society with representative
government—especially about government operations, whether they
be about land-use controls in a local community or the appointment
of a U.S. Secretary of the Interior—we cannot avoid seeing the need
for individual responsibility. It shouts at us! It is there pointing an
accusing finger at us when we gripe about what "they" are doing or
when we try to make money at the expense of society or complacently
allow others to do so. Our lack of willingness to accept personal responsibility is everywhere—in the beer-can-and-rubbish-littered highways,
our crime rate, our slums, our poorly organized urban form, and the
small number exercising the privilege of voting in an election. Many
of us are the victims of society, but all of us are the cause of that society being what it is today.

Now, to say a word about the second category. I love individual freedom as much, if not more, than the next person. It should be treasured and protected. But the notion that land ownership carries with it the "freedom" for the owners to do whatever they please with the land is an anachronism in today's crowded world. The problem is that the message has not gotten through to a lot of people; it has not been recognized and espoused by our politicians and has not been accepted as reality by many of our citizens.

There is no middle ground to the position that zoning is a mistake because it tells people what they can or cannot do with their land. You cannot resist governmental regulations on the one hand and then expect any help in preserving the value of your property on the other hand. Granted, many would rather take their chances on diminished property values than have government (or society, actually) have anything to say about what they may do. This is another example of our unwillingness to face reality. The rancher or farmer in LaPlata or Delta County, Colorado, who struggles to send his kids to college or to build up a nest egg for the future epitomizes the American dream, but the major source of adequate income for the college education and for the nest egg is the land. To gamble that someone else won't lessen or totally destroy the value of that land by opposing all zoning is like playing against the house odds in Las Vegas.

In an earlier chapter, a quote was included from an opinion written by Judge Waesche that makes the point that zoning, rather than being a denial of rights, is the only process we have for protecting land values from harm by others. This is an important concept. The Constitution does not say that you and I by virtue of land ownership have the right to do as we like to the detriment of someone else or society. Nor does it guarantee us protection from some other private owner's action that may adversely affect what the marketplace considers to be the value of our land. Rather, it is a broad legal framework with built-in restraints to keep laws from being unreasonable or unjust as measured by current conditions. These conditions are changing constantly, and, as they change, the wisdom of the drafters of the Constitution in providing this flexibility proves its worth.

Underlying all of the above is a little bit of the thinking of those falling into the third category of "aginers"—the lack of trust in government, or at least in those running it. At no time in our history has this been more prevalent, and at no time in our history has distrust been more justified. We have managed to get through some very sad and disheartening days involving the executive branch of the federal government only to have similar problems arise in the legislative branch. It seems to have become commonplace to have national and state representatives expelled, forced to resign, or marched off to jail for criminal acts. Local government is not immune from this disease, as illustrated by a very recent situation of embezzlement, favor buying, and dishonesty that has shaken up a small suburb in Denver.

We cannot permit criminal actions to be commonplace, to be accepted, or to be shrugged off as simply being a way of life. We have to go back to the idea of the responsibility of an individual in our society and our form of government. Our government and the people conducting it are what we make them or what we allow them to be. The more people who disassociate themselves from any involvement or rationalize their failure to vote or participate in any decision making, the more corruption, ineptness, and inappropriate action (or inaction) is invited. We pride ourselves on self-government—as long as things go the way we like and we don't have to involve ourselves. What is being said by those who oppose zoning or any other government program on the grounds that government cannot be trusted is that our system has failed, that you can't trust people. They are really saying that they don't trust themselves.

All of this is not being said because I believe or advocate that the continuation of self-government or its success depends on zoning. It is not a penacea for the world's, this country's, or a single community's problems. Zoning is but one example of community action among the hundreds that can be taken by society working collectively to make tomorrow better. The difficulty of getting acceptance of zoning—zoning that is meaningful and effective— is symptomatic of many of the problems of our society in doing *anything* collectively to make that better tomorrow. As long as we allow ourselves to be convinced by those who would profit from the view that good zoning does not make sense, we will continue to repeat the mistakes of the past in community development. Zoning, or some adaptive use of the police power of government to express a community interest in how we grow and develop, may not be perfect, but the alternative of abandoning such controls is frightening to contemplate.

This chapter was headed with the question, "Is zoning here to stay?" We have looked at a great many reasons why the answer to that question is in the affirmative. When populations increase, so do problems. When problems multiply, voices are raised to demand a solution. The use of government restraint and regulation of land use came about because undirected freedom of choice had led to abuse after abuse. Zoning has not happened because a few people wanted to be able to tell others what they could or could not do with land. It came about as a reaction to that abuse. In truth, it was made a necessity by those whose voices are raised most loudly in opposition.

As we have seen, many things have caused more people to understand the value of zoning and why it is necessary. Regardless of the lapse in federal interest, I believe there is growing citizen understanding of the value of conservation in all forms—conservation of human resources as well as natural resources and quality of life. One vital tool, zoning, speaks to this as probably no other governmental function can. There is no way that we can conserve energy without relating that objective to the use of land and how that use is developed. Other than outright public ownership, a philosophy very much out of vogue at present, there is no avenue available for conserving natural resources, protecting natural assets, preventing unnecessary flood damage, or encouraging agriculture, except through zoning. Our greatest asset of all, land, cannot produce the maximum benefit for the community unless it is fitted into the total picture through comprehensive planning translated into the provisions of zoning or some adaptation of its principles. We are overwhelmed by mediocre development, not because zoning as a process has failed but because we have failed to use that process effectively.

As we have moved through this examination of the zoning function, its adoption, and its administration, we have seen how changes in all of these areas have occurred. There has been a push toward greater flexibility and maneuverability within the broad confines of regulatory standards by both private interests and the public sector. Changes have taken place, some for the better and some questionable. Those that have strengthened the ability to express community interest based on sound planning principles in the quality of land development have been beneficial. Personally, I feel that any of the new techniques that diminish the right to express community interest are a mistake. I reiterate that with the right to express that interest goes the responsibility of justifying any action taken through a thorough planning process that clearly demonstrates the merit of that community interest. Any jurisdiction not doing so should be denied the right.

The changes that have been mentioned, if carefully thought through and expertly administered, have the potential for good results for both the private and the public sector. The permit or point system and performance zoning can provide flexibility in design, type of structure, and/or use, and still affect a local community's development policies and how its planning objectives are carried out. Land development codes and growth management plans can incorporate the above and, at the same time, coordinate controls and streamline the process. Incentives and bonus provisions, unless used extremely carefully and only where appropriate, can offer some greater potential for erosion of community protection. They are the most questionable of the newer techniques in terms of legal application and avoiding inequitable discretionary allocation. As in most matters of zoning, the quality of the administrative practices may well determine whether these are good or bad.

These and other new techniques are evidence of the ongoing efforts to find better ways of achieving what has been, or should have been, zoning's objective for the last 65 years—making our cities and towns better for all of us. The system may not have been as successful as desired, but zoning's detractors have failed to come up with something better. When asked to do so, the most frequent recommendation is to leave it to the marketplace. Frankly, I had rather send a fox in to guard the chicken coop.

Zoning has had and will always have its detractors. Some will be sincere, whether their opposition is based on misinformation, emotion, or lack of understanding. Others, whose motives may be subject to some question, will play on our penchant for thinking we can make things better by doing away with one system and adopting another. Their rallying cry is that zoning hasn't worked, as evidenced by hodgepodge growth, therefore, we should throw the system out and try another. Just because comprehensive zoning has been around for over 65 years doesn't necessarily mean that it should not be changed or that it cannot be improved. Many of zoning's failures can be blamed on the people responsible for implementing the system and on the abdication of responsibility by all of us as citizens. Most responsible for its failures, however, are those who advocate its demise and ensure its failure by misuse and manipulation for their own ends.

My conclusion is that the principles and processes now embodied in zoning are here to stay. The crisis conditions we face, the self-centered society, and the over-extension of our financial and environmental capabilities to absorb uncontrolled growth will necessitate it. The name and the format may change, but the principle of the right to express community interest in how every remaining piece of land is developed will remain and even grow stronger. This increased weight of community interest over private interest will become increasingly important to more people, and a greater understanding of the concept will keep the functions of zoning around in some form for a long time.

The fundamental question is not Will we have government regulation of private use of land? but, rather, Who will do it? Who will have a say in it? and How will it be done? We long have said that, theoretically, land-use controls are best allocated to local governments—the grass roots. Yet, the federal government has had more influence on land-use patterns, economic pressures shaping growth, and the reshaping of urban development than all the state and local governments combined. The policy of the interstate highway builders, for example, completely changed the pattern of development in any city lying near one of the routes. This network with its convenience of urban area travel did more to contribute to urban sprawl than even the Federal Housing Administration with its unwise policy of making guaranteed loans available only to single-family housing. The administration and policies of urban renewal funding by the federal agencies led to pragmatic projects that totally ignored comprehensive planning and necessitated adjustment in pre-active planning for orderly growth just so a community could qualify for some of that "free" federal money.

If we look carefully at the past 40 years, we can see that, while we have paid lip service to the notion of "local control," the major shapers of urban form have been the federal and, in some cases, state governments. While local governments struggle with the problems created by higher levels of government and wrestle with the impossible task of financing solutions to these problems, we mistakenly congratulate ourselves that we have maintained local control over land use. As economic pressures from these forces build up, so does the hue and cry of the exploiters for zoning changes and less-restrictive standards. The human factor enters the equation, and, with typical lack of foresight, the policy makers succumb to the pressures, and they whittle away at sensible planning and zoning policies because of all those nice "ratables" that can be generated. A few years later, after recognizing the difficulty of financing solutions to the problems created by traffic congestion, utility extension and expansion, and increased service costs, the cry goes up, "See, I told you zoning has failed."

There is no question that something has failed in situations like this, which have been repeated all around the country. It is a failure founded on our forgetting, or perhaps even losing, a fundamental concept of how our governmental process was structured. Representative government is founded on the theory of participatory democracy. It, and any system attempted within it, will work only if there is this participation in selecting those who lead, determining the policies under which the business of government operates, and overseeing the administration of those policies. Any system, especially one relating to the profit potential in land and its use, will fail when the element of participatory democracy is weak or entirely missing. But the system hasn't failed: the system is sound and needs only some adjustment and proper use.

Assuming that comes somewhere close to being the truth and that we can move toward improvement in the necessary involvement and participation, what are some of the changes that might help in making zoning more effective? As I have indicated, a number of the newer techniques offer excellent possibilities. Other methods of application and administration will be developed over the coming years. Rather than confine any suggestions for needed changes to techniques and methodology, I prefer to finish with some comments about some things that I feel to be more basic to our success in the future, not just in zoning, but also in governmental structure. It seems to me that fundamental philosophies are what determine the direction we take in the legislative and administrative functions of government. I believe that a number of these are outmoded and inadequate for the times in which we live. The ability to adjust or change philosophy when this happens may well be a determinant in the survival of a society.

If we really want the system of land-use controls and zoning to work and to improve the results, I would suggest the following adjustments in existing fundamental policies:

1. We need to enunciate a national policy making it clear that the ownership of land does not carry with it the right of exploitation. The public investment in infrastructure is to serve all people and not just to provide the opportunity for private profit in land investment and development.

2. The sacred cow of our present taxing policy should be melted in flames of rethinking and revision. The way that Thomas Jefferson and Alexander Hamilton conceived that governments should be financed is not adequate for today, and certainly not for tomorrow. Other than looking for additional things to tax, there have been few changes in the system, which has seemingly been revered because it is the way

we have done it all of these years. Tax revision is a political hot potato, but a necessity nevertheless.

The revision must be aimed at overcoming the real estate ratable sickness that destroys all attempts to obtain orderly growth patterns. A start toward improvement would be the institution of more tax-sharing or tax-redistribution systems if we must suffer along with our present antiquated real estate property-taxing system. If states have to start collecting real estate taxes for redistribution to prevent the incessant ratable wars from which we now suffer, then so be it.

3. We must eliminate the exaggerated emphasis placed on the phrase "local control." It has been used to defeat intergovernmental cooperation, regional land-use planning, and state land-use policy development. Even worse, it is the method for perpetuating isolated power bases for local politicians. Local control is an excellent theory when applied properly, but this does not mean that it can only be applicable within the confines of an arbitrary municipal boundary around a square-mile area. We can have local control in regional and state government if we accept and support the idea of participatory democracy in those forms of government.

4. Our present national administration and James Watt not withstanding, we should work for the establishment of a national land-use policy. An excellent beginning would be the restoration of something like the National Resources Planning Board of the 1940s, with the responsibility and authority to survey the entire country's resources, determine priorities of need, and recommend an implementing national policy for land development. This policy should then be put in legislative form, with states required to devise their own land-use policies and plans applicable to their particular problems and needs within that broad national framework.

5. Accompanying this would be a concentrated effort to modernize and strengthen state legislation pertaining to land development. This should include broadened state planning activity, especially in areas of regional or intergovernmental concern such as a major airport or rapid transit system. State legislators must recognize that they have a responsibility to lead, to establish the direction in which the entire state should go, and to accept the fact that individual, parochial, municipal governments will invariably create inefficient and uneconomic land-use patterns.

As a correlative concern, states must revise and improve the tools they now provide to all local governments to enable them to do planning and zoning. Statutes based upon the recommendations of the U.S. Department of Commerce some 60 years ago are becoming limiting straitjackets to local jurisdictions trying to cope with present problems. As has been said, the American Law Institute's publication should become the model for today.

6. If we could accomplish some of the above, we would be able to move toward an attitude of federal/state and state/regional partnership in guiding land-use development—a much-needed approach. At present, we are saddled with a nonconstructive "us versus them" psychosis with regard to national, state, and regional cooperation, not only in land use, but also in many other areas that are the cause of pressures that create problems in orderly land development. One such effort at interstate and regional cooperation, although largely dependent upon federal financial aid that may no longer be available, has been the Four Corners Commission in the Southwest. While it has not solved all of the problems, it has been able to establish a dialogue and to illustrate the effectiveness of a commonality of purpose.

7. Going a step further, I would advocate moving toward requiring regional land-use plans that take precedence over local plans. General state land-use policies and plans would serve as the basis for space allocation and density patterns by regional planning agencies. All municipal zoning would be required to adhere to regional plans and policies. To maintain participatory democracy, regional councils should be broad, their membership elected from designated districts, and the adoption of the plan or amendments thereto should require approval of a district council in each of the affected districts.

This would be in keeping with a proposal recently made by the Roles of Government Workgroup of the Colorado Front Range Project. Here, a representative group of citizens found the present governmental structure in need of drastic change and urged that consideration be given to calling a constitutional convention to do a complete revamp of the form of local government! Their suggested model proposed elimination of counties and municipalities and the division of the state into localities, districts, and regions, each based upon population.

8. Throughout these pages, I have made comments about and suggestions for strengthening neighborhood involvement in zoning decisions. The recent decision of the Colorado Supreme Court on initiative and referendum rights supports this concept, and several states have recognized its desirability by amending legislation to allow neighborhoods a say in zoning affecting them. The approach deserves

further consideration since it might help in encouraging a return to participatory democracy. Nothing seems to get people involved quickly better than a good zoning issue.

9. Finally, back to the beginning—we must return to the principle that land is first and foremost a community asset before it is allowed to be an individual commodity.

> In the long run, it is the sum total of the actions of millions of individuals that constitute effective group action; . . . get involved in political action. Otherwise, we shall all eventually find ourselves stranded in space on a dead Spaceship Earth, with no place to go, and no way to get there.
>
> Dr. Paul R. Ehrlich

APPENDIX A

Glossary of Terms

NOTE: A number of these definitions of terms originally appeared in the American Society of Planning Officials (now American Planning Association) Planning Advisory Service Report No. 322, entitled "The Language of Zoning," by Michael J. Meshenberg. Where notations such as [PAS 204] have been included, the reference is to another Planning Advisory Service report. It is recommended that the reader consult these for further, more detailed information on the topic and on zoning in general.

accessory building or use　A building or use which: (1) is subordinate to and serves a principal building or principal use; (2) is subordinate in area, extent, or purpose to the principal building or principal use served; (3) contributes to the comfort, convenience, or necessity of occupants of the principal building or principal use; and (4) is located on the same zoning lot as the principal building or principal use. (Here, ordinances sometimes make exceptions, as in the case of accessory off-street parking facilities or storage facilities permitted to locate elsewhere.) Early ordinances would simply allow accessory uses that could meet this or a similar definition. Regulatory experience, however, has led to spelling out in more detail types of accessory uses permitted in individual districts and development standards. Examples of accessory uses are private garages, storage sheds, play houses, and swimming pools. [PAS 248]

aesthetic zoning　The regulation of building or site design to achieve a desirable appearance. While making cities look nice has always been a purpose of zoning — setbacks, height limits, bulk regulations have all been appearance-related — regulations exclusively to control aesthetics have had rough going, with most courts finding them an inappropriate use of the police power. Recently, however, many courts have relented and granted approval to greater control over design.

air rights　The rights to the space above a property, for development, usually for a dissimilar use. Common law grants the owner of a piece of real estate ownership of a vertical space extending an unlimited distance above the ground. An owner who either has chosen to build at a very low intensity or not at all may sell or lease his rights to build higher. Common sales of air rights are above transportation facilities such as highways or railroad tracks or yards.

　　Examples of major air rights developments include New York City's Pan Am building and Madison Square Garden and Chicago's major office, residential, and open space development over the Illinois Central Railroad tracks adjacent to downtown.

area requirements   The designation given to the specific requirements set forth in a zone or district by the zoning ordinance text. Area requirements refer to the numerical standards established for a lot or yard in a particular zone. Area requirements can also refer to structures, and, in some ordinances, a minimum dwelling size is established and is considered to be an area requirement of the zoning ordinance. (See Figure 11.)

as-of-right or use-by-right (self-executing) zoning   Uses and development standards that are determined in advance and specifically authorized by the zoning ordinance. The ordinance, as a result, is largely self-enforcing because no flexibi..y is involved and no discretion occurs in its administration. For example, a single-family zone would allow single-family detached residences as of right; so long as site development standards are met (e.g., height, yards, bulk), the zoning permit must be granted. (See also permitted use.) This is the traditional Euclidian zoning system based on the earliest comprehensive ordinances and the Standard State Zoning Enabling Act.

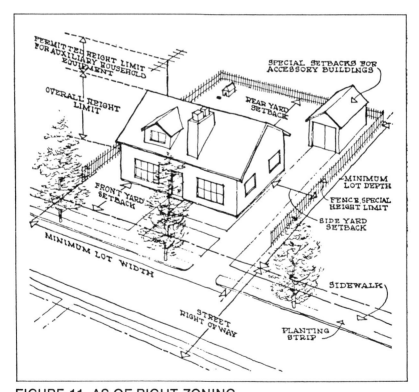

FIGURE 11. AS-OF-RIGHT ZONING
A property owner in this residential zone knows in advance exactly what and how he or she is permitted to build because all the requirements are spelled out.

buffer strip or zone   An area established to protect one type of land use from the undesirable characteristics of another. Usually applied between industrial and residential zones with the requirement being that the industrial zone must provide a buffer strip between its boundaries and that of the residential zone. The purpose is to screen any potential objectionable features resulting from the more intensive utilization of land from neighboring, less-intensive use areas.

bulk regulations   The combination of controls establishing the maximum size of a building and its location on the lot. Components of bulk regulations include: size and height of building; location of exterior walls at all levels with respect to lot lines, streets, or other buildings; building coverage; gross floor area of buildings in relation to lot area (floor area ratio); open space (yard) requirements; and amount of lot area provided per dwelling unit. Their purpose is to assure sufficient light, air, and open space on the ground and at all levels of a building and, secondarily, to maintain a compatible and pleasing appearance. The bulk envelope is the three-dimensional space defined by the bulk regulations, within which a building can be built on a lot.

case law   A term used to refer to the accumulation of judicial interpretation of zoning principles. These are founded on the enabling act passed within the state, the state constitution, and the United States Constitution. As each zoning case is brought before the judicial bar and a decision is rendered, we are, in effect, building up a series of opinions that form the accumulated case law which gives us the interpretation of both the individual ordinance and the legislation. Case law is extremely vital to determining what can or cannot be done in zoning in a particular state.

certificate of occupancy (compliance)   A certificate that is issued by the zoning officer to indicate that, after construction of a building has been completed or a use in an existing building has been changed, the purpose for which the building was constructed is being carried out in accordance with the terms of the zoning ordinance. This is a check and balance system on the zoning procedure. It means that an inspection has indicated that the use being carried on at the time of occupancy and the condition of the structure at the time of occupation, meets all of the requirements and legitimately can continue. No structure can be occupied until a certificate of occupancy has been issued if such is required in the zoning ordinance. Some ordinances do not require a certificate of occupancy, but all probably should.

comprehensive zoning   A zoning ordinance and map, based on sound comprehensive studies and investigations and, preferably, a development or master plan for the municipality. This term is used to distinguish zoning that is comprehensive in nature, dealing with all aspects of the community development, from zoning that is piecemeal or haphazard. Comprehensive zoning will be founded on thorough studies dealing with land use, population, traffic circulation, economy, and municipal services and facilities, as well as a projected future land-utilization plan.

conditional rezoning   The attachment of special conditions to a rezoning which are not spelled out in the text of the ordinance. Along with other devices to assure compliance, it may bind the developer to the conditions through filing a covenant. While frequently invalidated by the courts, its recent legal history has been more favorable. Conditional rezoning is considered to be a form of contract zoning and therefore is often found illegal by the courts. The distinction between conditional zoning and contract zoning is fuzzy and seems to revolve around which is emphasized more, the conditions or the contract. [PAS 318]

density controls   A technique used in zoning to establish the number of dwelling units of any kind that may be developed in a given area of land. A minimum lot size is established, but this can be reduced as long as the density of units does not exceed that which has been established as desirable for the area. In other words, a 100-acre tract which would nominally be zoned for half-acre lots would probably result in some 160 to 170 dwelling units, with allowance for streets and roads. Density control will permit the 100 acres to be developed with the individual lots being perhaps 12,000 to 15,000 square feet, as long as the overall density of the 100 acres does not exceed the 160 to 170 families. The remaining portions of the land left in the 100 acres is then set aside for public purposes, usually recreational in nature.

development rights   A broad range of less-than-fee-simple ownership interests, mainly referring to easements. Thus, an owner can retain complete or absolute (fee simple) rights to his or her land and sell the developments rights to another. The owner would keep title but agree to continue using the land as it had been used in the past, with the right to develop resting in the holder of the development rights. Such rights usually are expressed in terms of the density allowed under the existing zoning. In transfer of development rights, the amount may not exceed the difference between this total and that which actually exists on a given parcel of land, expressed in dwelling units per acre or square feet of building area.

   Some jurisdictions have developed programs to acquire development rights in order to keep land open. These programs were originated because it was felt that total public ownership was undesirable and, typically, infeasible politically. The purchase of only selected rights would be substantially less expensive than total purchase and would still allow the owner to continue making economic use of his land. In practice, though, public acquisition of development rights has often cost up to 95 per cent of the full market value of the land. [PAS 204]

downzoning   A change in the zoning classification of land to a classification permitting development that is less intensive or dense, such as from multifamily to single-family or from commercial or industrial to residential. A change in the opposite direction is called upzoning.

exception   A term applied to a function of the zoning board allowing the granting of an exception to the provisions of the ordinance rather than a variance. The word exception is usually preceded by the modifying word, special. This implies that within the framework of the ordinance an unusual circumstance is anticipated and special provisions are set forth in the ordinance text which state that, when certain things happen, an exception can occur. Illustrative of this is the fact that a residential zone would probably be the best place for the location of a private school. The zoning ordinance text can anticipate this and establish the fact that a private school can be permitted as a special exception by the zoning board. The zoning board then has the responsibility of investigating the matter and making certain that the requirements set forth in the ordinance are met.

floating zone   A term applied to designate the establishment of a zone which has not been mapped. In adopting the zoning ordinance, a community may decide to permit industrial use but at the present time is sufficiently undeveloped that it does not feel it can determine just exactly where this use would be best located. While it is adopting its ordinance, it wants to recognize the potential of industrial growth and have standards established that can be used as a guide. It is easy enough to determine certain areas in which the industrial use would not be permitted, but large areas of open space may be very similar in character and such a use could occur in any one of them. The ordinance will then state that anywhere in a certain area within the municipality where anyone can assemble a tract of a minimum size, usually as much as 50 or 100 acres, the floating zone may be brought into play and the area then designated whatever designation is given to the zone itself. A procedure is established to permit careful study of this matter by local authorities before such action can take place. The floating zone technique is extremely tricky and must be used only with care and with the advice and assistance of professionals, as well as the substantiation of careful studies.

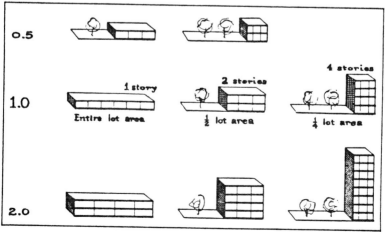

FIGURE 12. FLOOR AREA RATIO
Using the same floor area ratios, a developer is able to choose from several development options.

floor area ratio   The ratio of floor area permitted on a zoning lot to the size of the lot. Thus, a permitted floor-area ratio of 6.0 on a 10,000 square foot lot would allow a building whose total floor area is 60,000 square feet. FAR provisions may be used in combination with other bulk regulations, such as bulk planes, open space, and building spacing requirements. When used alone, they give developers great flexibility in deciding whether to build a low building covering most of the lot or a high building covering only a small part of the lot or, in some places, a combination of buildings, so long as the total allowed is not exceeded. [PAS 111]

growth management (growth control; land-use development management)   The use by a community of a wide range of techniques in combination to permit it to determine its own amount, type, and rate of growth and to channel it into designated areas. Comprehensive plans often form the backbone of the system; devices used to execute growth management policy may include zoning, emphasizing flexibility, capital improvements, programming, adequate public facilities ordinances, urban limit lines, population caps or ceilings, and many others. Some of the sophisticated systems have departed dramatically from the traditional land-use controls, using a variety of innovative devices to achieve particular policies. Conceptually, growth management differs from conventional approaches in that it does not accept likely population growth and its rate as inevitable; these are open to question and are subject to determination by public policy and action. [PAS 309/310]

hardship   An unusual situation on the part of an individual property owner that will not permit the full utilization of property that is given to others within the community. A hardship exists only when it is not self-created or when it is not economic in nature. In other words, a true hardship exists only when the literal interpretation of the requirements of the ordinance would place an individual in an unusual circumstance and would deny the right to use property for any purpose, or create an unnecessary burden, unless relief is granted.

hearing examiner (zoning examiner; zoning adjuster)   A public official who usually has authority to hold public hearings in connection with applications for variances, special use permits, and small parcel rezonings and, occasionally, has the authority to make approval or denial decisions. The purpose of the office is to professionalize the making of such decisions and free the process from many of the political pressures to which boards of adjustment are now subject. Due process procedures, if established, are usually stricter than those used by boards of adjustment. [PAS 312]

highest and best use   The use of a property that will bring to its owner the greatest profit if offered for sale. In theory, the economics of the real estate market establish a maximum value for each parcel of land at any given time. Except in developed areas or along transportation corridors where there is pressure to develop, this "highest and best use" is likely to be agricultural or residential. Zoning, by placing each property in a particular district, may interfere with market operations and raise or lower the value of property. Thus, while a gas station built on a particular site might give the owner the greatest return, zoning might allow only single-family houses. Thus, one purpose of zoning is to *prevent* the "highest and best use" where it is inappropriate.

incentive (bonus) zoning   A system under which developers are given bonuses in exchange for providing amenities the community feels are desirable. This is in contrast to zoning's traditional, more negative effect of limiting or restricting development. Bonuses granted usually are in the form of higher permitted densities or floor area ratios to improve a development's profitability; amenities received have been plazas, more open space, certain desired site designs, and access to transit stops. Wider use of the incentive device, for example, to promote the development of low- and moderate-income housing or to protect sensitive natural areas, is only now being explored. It appears that there are considerable opportunities for expansion of an incentive zoning system to achieve many more desirable public objectives.

There has been some objection to incentive zoning on grounds that, if it is to be effective, base densities or floor-area ratios must be set lower than would be justified by location in the urban pattern. [PAS 257]

inclusionary zoning   A positive and active policy and program of a community to attract racial minorities or low- and moderate-income residents. Such policies, analogous to affirmative action in job recruitment, go beyond the avoidance of techniques that discourage certain classes of people from moving into an area; they actively seek to invite such groups. Inclusionary zoning devices usually include offering incentives or bonuses to developers for building low- or moderate-cost housing or exceptions to traditional controls. Such practices are rare, but they are being experimented with in a number of places. While some courts have accepted the idea of inclusionary incentives, they have generally invalidated the techniques. Inclusionary policies are a response to the challenges being levied at exclusionary zoning.

inverse condemnation   The effective taking or reduction in value of a property as a result of public action, in contrast to a direct taking through eminent domain. For example, by building a dam that inundates a property, the public will have destroyed its value, and the law requires that the landowner be reimbursed for the amount of the loss. There is extensive debate about how far government can go in using police power regulations that diminish property values before compensation must be paid (the "taking issue"); for example, the anticipation of government action, such as building a new highway or a renewal project, may cause blight, which could be interpreted as inverse condemnation. These arguments have become heated recently as growth management devices have placed stringent controls on land use. Compensable regulations have been developed partly as a way of mitigating the problems of inverse condemnation.

land use   A term used to indicate the utilization of any piece of land whether it be lot, plat, tract, or acreage. The way in which land is being used is the land use. This is the basis for a study that results in the formulation of the district boundaries for a zoning ordinance. Land use is an indication of the existing development within a community.

land-use plan   The proposed or projected utilization of land resulting from planning and zoning studies. This is usually presented in map form, indicating areas in which it would be most desirable to have residential, commercial, industrial, or other types of usage to occur. It is supported by documentation and written text explaining the underlying development policy behind the plan and the principles upon which it is based.

master plan   A comprehensive plan for the physical, social, economic, and environmental development of the municipality, including studies of land use, circulation, etc., and a report presenting the objectives, assumptions, standards, and principles that are embodied in the various interlocking portions of the plan. A master plan is usually a composite of one or more mapped or written proposals recommending development policies for the municipality which is adopted by the planning commission, either as a whole or in part, after public hearing. A master plan may include proposals for various stages in the future development of the community.

mixed-use zoning   Zoning that permits a combination of usually separated uses within a single development. Many PUD ordinances specify permitted combinations of, say, various residential types and local businesses. More recently the term has been applied in a more limited way to major inner-city developments, often with several high-rise buildings, which may contain offices, shops, hotels, apartments, and related uses.
　　While zoning traditionally has separated land uses, improved performance controls and some rethinking of old values on the part of planners and their critics has led to a loosening up of narrowly defined districts to permit appropriate mixtures, such as local shopping in residential areas, and therefore more interesting, livelier neighborhoods.

nonconformities   Lots, structures, uses of land and structures, and characteristics of uses, that are prohibited under the terms of the zoning ordinance but were lawful at the date of the ordinance's enactment. They are permitted to continue, or they are given time to become conforming. The continuation of such nonconformities is based on the principal that laws cannot be applied retroactively unless there is a compelling reason — such as imminent danger to health — to do so. While ordinances permit legal nonconformities to continue, they prohibit the substitution of a new or different nonconformity, nor do they permit the extension or enlargement of nonconforming uses. Many ordinances permit the rebuilding of a nonconforming use when destroyed by fire but, if a use is abandoned for a specific period of time, it cannot be restored, and the future use of the premises must conform to the zoning. Some ordinances provide for the abatement (amortization) of all or some nonconformities at the end of a prescribed period. Increasingly, ordinances are distinguishing among classes of nonconformities to include: nonconforming lots; nonconforming buildings or structures; nonconforming uses of land with minor structures only; nonconforming uses of major buildings and premises; and nonconforming characteristics of use; and are providing for their individualized treatment. [PAS 281, 248]

performance standards   A minimum requirement or maximum allowable limit on the effects or characteristics of a use, usually written in the form of regulatory language. A building code, for example, might specify a performance standard referring to the fire resistance of a wall, rather than specifying its construction materials. Performance standards in zoning might describe allowable uses with respect to smoke, odor, noise, heat, vibration, glare, traffic generation, visual impact, and so on, instead of the more traditional classifications of "light" or "heavy" lists of uses. It is a more precise way of defining compatibility and at the same time is intended to expand developer's options. The performance standard approach is based on the technical ability to quantify activities (e.g., how much noise) and to measure them to see if they meet ordinance requirements. The most advanced work in performance standards has been in the area of industrial emissions. (Local requirements in many fields, especially pollution control, have now been superseded by federal or state regulations.) Because such measures require technical skill and often some expensive equipment, small communities have tended to prefer the more traditional specification standard approach. In such places, clear statements of purpose or intent often are substituted for precise measurable standards. [PAS 272]

permitted use   A use by right that is specifically authorized in a particular zoning district. It is contrasted with special permit or conditional uses that are authorized only if certain requirements are met and after review and approval by the board of adjustment or other public body. (See also as of right.) [PAS 248]

planned unit development (PUD)   A form of development usually characterized by a unified site design for a number of housing units, clustering buildings and providing common open space; density increase; and a mix of building types and land uses. It permits the planning of a project and the calculation of densities over the entire development, rather than on an individual, lot-by-lot basis. (See cluster development.) It also refers to a process, mainly revolving around site-plan review, in which public officials have considerable involvement in determining the nature of the development. It includes aspects of both subdivision and zoning regulation and usually is administered either through a special permit or a rezoning process.

While PUD has most commonly been used for housing developments, it also is frequently applied to other forms of development such as shopping centers, industrial and office parks, and to mixed-use developments, which may be any combination, depending on local ordinance. Planned unit development allows the unified, and hence potentially more desirable and attractive, development of an area, based on a comprehensive site plan. PUD can have a number of advantages over conventional lot-by-lot development including: mixing building types and uses to create more heterogeneous and "alive" communities; combining often unusable yard space on individual lots into larger common open spaces; offering greater opportunities for incentives to building lower-cost housing; lower street and utility costs resulting from reduced frontage; and the possibility of increasing the density of a development while keeping desired amenities.

On the other hand, there are some critics who fear that the flexibility offered by PUD, and the negotiations that virtually always accompany the approval process, permits communities to extort higher cost amenities from developers, thereby using it as an exclusionary device.

Other terms for PUD include planned development, unitary development, or community unit plan. [PAS 291]

precedent   The term precedent is applied in several ways in connection with zoning. First, it may be applied to a particular court case, and it can be said that the opinion rendered is a precedent establishing opinion. By this is meant that, in future judicial determinations, the decision will probably have a great influence and will be followed. Precedent is also used as a term to describe action taken by local governing bodies and zoning boards. A zoning board is frequently cautioned that it may be establishing a precedent if it grants a zoning variance without due reason. This will mean that anyone else who wants to do something not permitted by the zoning ordinance would have the same right to demand to be permitted to do so as the individual who has been given the improper variance. Even a properly granted variance can sometimes establish a precedent that will be difficult to overcome in the future administration of a zoning ordinance.

principal use   The main use of land or structures as distinguished from a secondary or accessory use. A house is a principal use in a residential area; a garage or pool is an accessory use. Zoning ordinances will often establish a general rule that only one principal structure or use will be permitted on each lot. Drafters of such language generally have single-family areas in mind; but, unless application is clearly limited to such use, it can lead to unnecessary complications, such as requiring land to be subdivided in multifamily, commercial, or industrial districts where there is to be more than one principal structure or use on a lot or tract or requiring buildings to be joined merely to avoid the subdivision requirement.

public notice   Almost all zoning ordinances establish procedures for conducting public hearings to amend or change an ordinance. In each case, there will be a provision requiring public notice. This means that the public is to be informed and given an opportunity to be heard before the official action can be taken. In the case of a zoning amendment, public notice is usually publication of the amendment itself, with an announcement that it will be considered for passage at a certain time and place. In the case of a zoning variance, public notice may consist of a newspaper announcement, the mailing or delivery of a personal service of notice upon all property owners within a certain distance of the property to be affected, or the posting of a sign on the affected property.

revision of ordinance   A revision of a zoning ordinance is distinguished from a zoning amendment in that the revision is considered to be more comprehensive. A revision usually results in a total reorganization of the ordinance and the map. The entire zoning process within the community is subjected to study, and, as a result of changing conditions either in the region, the area, or the municipality itself, a number of basic changes are proposed in the ordinance and map. Rather than do this on a piecemeal basis as an amendment, it is frequently found to be easier to do it as a comprehensive revision, which, in essence, means a rewriting of the ordinance and at least a re-examination of the map itself.

rezoning   Rezoning is a familiar term applied to both zoning amendments and zoning revisions. It is the commonly accepted term that refers to any change in the zoning ordinance. Newspapers frequently refer to a simple, minor amendment as rezoning of an area. Rezoning can apply to a small area, a large portion of the municipality, or the entire community. The process that must be followed in rezoning is the same as for a zoning amendment or a zoning revision.

special permit   A term coming into more frequent use because of the inclusion within zoning terminology of the special use permit technique. This is similar to the exception, but rather than being a permitted use as an exception, a degree of discretion is built into the ordinance by the terms that are set forth, giving either the zoning board or the planning commission the right of determination as to the compatibility of the proposed use with the comprehensive plan of the municipality, as well as other stated considerations. The special use permit will be indicated in the terms of the ordinance, and an elaborate procedure of application and review will be established. The idea is that the use of a special nature can be permitted in a zone in which it would not ordinarily be a permitted use because of the additional safeguards that have been placed in the special requirements.

spot zoning   The amendment to a zoning ordinance that, by its very nature, is offensive to the comprehensive scheme of zoning. This may be an amendment dealing with one lot, several lots, or a large area. The determination of spot zoning is based more upon the resulting detriment to the comprehensive scheme of development than it is on the area to which the zoning is applied. As it is much more difficult to apply comprehensive zoning thinking to a small parcel or to one lot, there is a tendency for the designation of spot zoning to be applied to one-lot zoning, far more than to larger area zoning. As a result, the mistaken philosophy has been created that the term spot zoning applies only where you have amended a zoning map to draw a district boundary around a lot in one ownership. This does not necessarily hold true. If the zoning amendment can be shown to be a part of a comprehensive plan and it can clearly be indicated that it is a phase of a coordinated scheme of development, it is, in all probability, not spot zoning.

strip zoning   Any zoning for any purpose, usually found along a major roadway, that is placed in a pattern that follows the outline of the road and that is not based on the results of comprehensive study or fact finding. Strip zoning most frequently is commercial strip zoning along highways. The mistaken philosophy is that, simply because land is located along a highway, the frontage has the right of being developed for commercial purposes. This usually results in a strip, 200- to 300-feet deep, being established as a business or commercial zone on both sides of the highway. This is one of the most destructive misconceptions in zoning. Strip zoning will lead to blighted conditions and a deterioration of the community.

subdivision   The process (and the result) of dividing a parcel of raw land into smaller buildable sites, blocks, streets, open space, and public areas, and the designation of the location of utilities and other improvements. Subdivision regulations usually come into play where a subdivision is above a certain number of lots, varying from two to about five, or when a new street is built.

transfer of development rights (TDR)   A relatively new concept, enacted in only a few locations, in which the development rights are separated from the land in an area in which a community (or state) wishes to limit development, and permits them to be sold for use in an area desirable for high-density development. It has been promoted as a way to retain farmland, preserve endangered natural environments, protect historic areas, stage development, promote low- and moderate-income housing, and achieve other land-use objectives. Considerable research currently is underway to determine whether the TDR concept, which appears to offer such vast potential, can be applied to actual situations. A good deal of attention is being focused on the few states and localities that have enacted variations on the scheme. (Also called development rights transfer.) Density transfer within a single property or on adjoining properties has been fairly widely used and serves as the jumping-off point for the long-distance transfers proposed under TDR schemes. [PAS 304]

transition zone   A designation of an area frequently found on the fringe of a downtown built-up section. It implies that the area itself is in transition, probably changing in character from residential to semi-business. Transition zoning is extremely important to provide proper guidance. It will be impossible to continue the area as a one-family residential zone, so, in order to make a transition, provision is made in the ordinance to allow for the conversion of large homes into apartments or to allow for the introduction of business and professional offices. In this way, the transition from a residential area into a central business district is started and can be made on an orderly basis.

variance   A device that grants a property owner relief from certain provisions of a zoning ordinance when, because of the particular physical surroundings, shape, or topographical condition of the property, compliance would result in a particular hardhip upon the owner, as distinguished from a mere inconvenience or a desire to make more money. A variance may be granted, for example, to reduce yard or setback requirements, or the number of parking or loading spaces, or to increase the permitted size of a sign. Some ordinances specifically preclude the granting of a use variance. Authority to decide variances usually is vested in the board of adjustment. Though intended to serve as a safety valve to protect against unfair treatment of any property owner, variances have been used (or abused) by boards of adjustment to change significantly the character of an area in violation of plans and policies.

vested right   A right is vested when it has become absolute and fixed and cannot be denied by subsequent conditions or change in regulations, unless it is taken and paid for. There is no vested right to an existing zoning classification or to have zoning remain the same forever. However, once development has been started or has been completed, there is a right to maintain that particular use, regardless of the classification given the property. In order for a nonconforming use to earn the right to continue when the zoning is changed, the right must have vested before the change. If the right to complete the development has not vested, it may not be built, no nonconforming use will be established, and the new regulations will have to be complied with.

Vested rights are often established by showing that some development permit has been obtained and substantial construction on the project started. How much construction or land improvement must have been completed before the rights are vested varies among the states. In some states, application for a building permit or other development approval may be sufficient to establish a vested right to complete a project. Others may require substantial investment and beginning of construction on the land, with completion of structures that are unique to the planning project. (See also nonconformities.)

zoning amendment   A change or revision of the zoning ordinance or map. This must be done by legal process established by the enabling legislation of the particular state in which the municipality is located. There will be the necessity of drafting the amendment, submitting it to the governing body, conducting the public hearings, and official adoption before it can be made a part of the zoning ordinance.

zoning appeal   An appeal filed by an individual who has applied to the zoning officer for a zoning permit and who has been turned down for noncompliance with the requirements of the ordinance. The zoning ordinance itself will set forth the procedure that must be followed in filing such an appeal. A time element is stated, and the applicant must take his action within this period. An appeal must also be filed on appropriate forms that have been adopted as part of the zoning policy within the community.

zoning board   The term used to refer to the zoning board of appeals in some states or the zoning board of adjustment in others. Regardless of designation, it is a group of individuals, usually five in number, created officially by the adoption of the ordinance and appointed by the mayor or by the governing body. Their purpose and function is to review applications for variances or exceptions and to decide whether there is a legitimate reason for granting the applicant the desired relief, or the exception requested.

zoning commission   A group of citizens of a community appointed by the governing body for the purpose of formulating the zoning ordinance text and map in the initial stage. Their job is that of study and investigation of the existing development and the problems of the community in order to prepare a recommended zoning ordinance that can be referred to the governing body for finalization and adoption. After careful study, they conduct the public hearings thereon and make a final recommendation to the official governing body. When the zoning ordinance is adopted, their work is completed, and the zoning commission goes out of existence.

zoning district   A geographic area in which the designation of the zoning ordinance sets forth requirements dealing with all uses that may be conducted therein. A zoning district is a part of the community that has an indicated boundary on the zoning map and to which the provisions of the ordinance apply. The theory is that each property and each person within a given zoning district must be treated alike. There can be no discrimination between individuals within the district itself. Zoning districts should be established only after careful consideration of existing development and future planning principles for the municipality.

zoning map   The graphic depiction of the zones or districts within a municipality, region, or area for which the zoning ordinance is applicable. The map itself will include all of the area within the boundaries of the governmental sphere of operation. It will also include an indication of the boundaries of each of the zones or districts, as well as a legend showing the type of uses that may be permitted in each of the districts. It will include names of streets, streams, and other places, as well as dimensions indicating the boundaries between districts. It is adopted as a legal part of the zoning ordinance and should be designated as the official zoning map of the municipality.

zoning officer   The individual appointed to enforce and administer the zoning ordinance. It is his or her duty to receive applications for zoning permits, as well as certificates of occupancy permits, and to check against the ordinance to see whether such permits can be issued. The zoning officer cannot make discretionary determinations, but must go by the terms of the ordinance itself. If an applicant does not comply with the conditions set forth, the zoning officer has no choice but to deny the request, in which case there may then be an appeal made to the zoning board for relief.

zoning ordinance   This text, together with the zoning map(s), spells out the terms and conditions of zoning within the municipality. It is put together as a written document, setting forth all of the standards, procedures, and requirements and is placed in legal form to be adopted, after a public hearing, by the local governing body. The preparation is the responsibility of a zoning commission or a planning commission that should base it on sound and carefully prepared planning studies. It must be published before it is adopted so that it can be generally known within the community, and it will consist of several pages of text containing technical terminology and phrases.

zoning permit   A permit issued by the zoning officer showing that the plans submitted are in compliance with the zoning ordinance and that the use or structure proposed is allowed by the ordinance or has been allowed by the granting of a variance by the zoning board. No use or structure can take place unless it has obtained a zoning permit where a zoning ordinance is in effect. There is usually a fee charged by the municipality for this permit.

zoning policy   The policy that the governing body and members of the official family of a community should adopt as the basis for its zoning ordinance and map. It should set forth the kind of community that is desirable, the procedure that will be followed to obtain that type of community, and the aspects that will be considered to be important in reaching decisions on zoning administration.

APPENDIX B

Bibliography

American Society of Planning Officials (now American Planning Association), 1313 E. 60th St., Chicago, IL 60637. Planning Advisory Service Reports. *The Administration of Flexible Zoning Techniques.* Michael J. Meshenberg. PAS Report No. 318. 1976. 62 pp.

-------. *The Hearing Examiner in Zoning Administration.* Daniel Lauber. PAS Report No. 312. 1975. 26 pp.

-------. *Intensity Zoning: Regulating Townhouses, Apartments, and Planned Developments.* Frederick H. Bair, Jr. PAS Report No. 314. 1976. 40 pp.

-------. *The Language of Zoning: A Glossary of Words and Phrases.* Michael J. Meshenberg. PAS Report No. 322. 1976. 40 pp.

-------. *Neighborhood Zoning: Practices and Prospects.* Efraim Gil. PAS Report No. 311. 1975. 44 pp.

-------. *New Zoning Techniques for Inner-City Areas.* Richard F. Babcock and John S. Banta. PAS Report No. 297. 1973. 60 pp.

-------. *Performance Controls for Sensitive Lands: A Practical Guide for Local Administrators.* Charles Thurow, William Toner, and Duncan Erley. PAS Report Nos. 307, 308. 1975. 156 pp.

-------. *Planned Unit Development Ordinances.* Frank S. So, David R. Mosena, and Frank S. Bangs, Jr. PAS Report No. 291. 66 pp.

-------. *Urban Growth Management Systems.* PAS Report Nos. 309, 310. 1975. 141 pp.

-------. *Writing Better Zoning Reports.* Duncan Erley. PAS Report No. 321. 1976. 8 pp.

-------. American Planning Association, 1313 E. 60th St., Chicago, IL 60637. Planning, 1981. Colorado Chapter. *The Law of Planning and Land-Use Regulation in Colorado.* Available from Gordon Apell, Denver City Planning Office, 1445 Cleveland Pl., Denver, CO 80202. 1975. $5.

Breckenridge Community Development Department, Breckenridge, CO 80424. *Development Code.* 1980.

Bucks County Planning Commission, Doylestown, PA 18901. *Performance Zoning.* 1973.

City of Albuquerque, New Mexico, City Hall, 400 Marquette Ave., N.W., Albuquerque, NM 87102. *Albuquerque Zoning Ordinance and Zoning Atlas.* 1974.

City and County of Denver, Colorado, 1445 Cleveland Pl., Denver, CO 80202. *Zoning Ordinance Text; Revised Municipal Code.* 1956, with amendments to 1981.

EDAW, Inc., 240 E. Mountain Ave., Fort Collins, CO 80524. *South Park*

Development Guidelines. Prepared for EMKAY Development, Inc; ALCOA Denver, Inc.; and City of Littleton, Colorado. 1981.

Friedmann, John Rembert Peter. *Retracking America: The Theory of Transactive Planning.* 1973; reprinted 1981 by Rodale Press, Inc., Emmaus, PA 18049. 289 pp.

Gallion, Arthur B., and Eisner, Simon. *The Urban Pattern.* Van Nostrand Reinhold Co., 135 W. 50th St., New York, NY 10020. Third edition. 1975. 451 pp.

International City Management Association, 1140 Connecticut Ave., N.W., Washington, DC 20036. *Local Planning Administration.* Mary McLean, ed. Third edition. 1959.

Jacobs, Jane. *The Death and Life of Great American Cities.* Random House, 201 E. 50th St., New York, NY 10022. 1961. 458 pp.

Scott, Mel. *American City Planning Since 1890.* University of California Press, 2223 Fulton St., Berkeley, CA 94720. 1971. 767 pp.

Smith, Herbert H. *The Citizen's Guide to Planning.* Planners Press, American Planning Association, 1313 E. 60th St., Chicago, IL 60637. 1979. 198 pp.

THK Associates, Inc., 40 Inverness Drive, East, Denver, Colorado. *Energy-Conscious Planning.* Prepared for the Office of Energy Conservation, Office of the Governor, Denver, Colorado.

U. S. Department of Housing and Urban Development, Washington, DC 20410. *Streamlining Land-Use Regulation: A Guide for Local Governments.* 1980.

--------. *Protecting Solar Access for Residential Development: A Guidebook for Planning Officials.* 1979.

Urban Land Institute, Suite 300, 1090 Vermont Ave., N.W., Washington, DC 20005. *Urban Land,* July/August 1981, "Structuring The Implementation of Transferable Development Rights," by George M. Raymond, p. 19; and November 1981, "Recent Trends in Conditional Rezoning Validation," by Annette Kolis Eagleton, p. 21.

Utah League of Cities and Towns, 10 W. Broadway, Salt Lake City, UT 84101. *Planning and Zoning Administration in Utah.* Herschel G. Hester III.

Index

vested right, 233–34
Village of Euclid v. *Amber Realty
Co.* (1926), 25–26, 31–32, 45
Virginia, zoning in, 187

Waesche, Donald M., 34, 209
water faucet principle, 21
Watervliet, New York, zoning
  map in, 85
Whitnall, Gordon, 116
Williamsburg, Virginia, land
  value in, 14
Wisconsin, zoning in, 117
Writing Better Zoning Reports, 164
Wyoming, land-use policy in, 10

zoning, abuses in, 34, 211;
  constitutionality of, 28–29, 36;
  as controversial issue, 2–3, 43;
  criticism of, 207, 209, 210, 212;
  definition of, 30–32; and
  democracy, 36–37; effects of
  no, 1, 2; and eminent domain,
  27–28; enforcement of, 91–92;
  exclusionary vs. exclusive zone
  use, 165–66; for energy
  conservation, 193–94
  fundamental principles of, 27–43;
  future of, 207–17; human factor
  in, 212–13; and ignorance, 35–43;
  importance of, 1, 8, 10–12; and
  independence, 37–38; and land
  development, 39, 40; need for
  changes in, 214–17; need for
  intergovernmental coordination
  in, 51, 168–70, 216; need for
  national policy in, 50, 214, 215,
  216; opposition to, 34–43; and
  police power, 28–29; and politics,
  39–40, 48–49, 102, 120–21; and
  protection of little people, 37;
  purpose of, 69; relationship of,
  to housing costs, 41–43;
  relationship of, to other codes
  and ordinances, 38–39;
  relationship of, to planning,
  33–34; rumors on, 1–2;
  understanding role of, 4–5;
  value of, 211
zoning administration, 91–108;
  appeal procedures in, 102–3, 234;
  policy making in, 92–93; politics

in, 102; role of citizen in, 98;
  role of planning commission in,
  93–94; role of zoning boards in,
  99–102; role of zoning officer
  in 94–98
zoning amendments, 93–94, 234
zoning board(s), 234; advice for
  members of, 121–22; basis for
  decision of, 131–32; duties of
  members, 135–36; function of,
  100–2, 107–8; granting of
  variances by, 113–14; guidelines
  for procedures in, 122–24;
  importance of, 99–100;
  membership of, 103–5; and other
  zoning bodies, 105–7;
  qualifications of members, 103–5;
  relationship of, to governing
  body and planning commission,
  105–7; relationship of, to
  planning commission, 93–94;
  relationship of, to state courts,
  105–7; role of, 99, 107–8
zoning by referenda, 203–5
zoning case reports, value of,
  163–64
zoning commission, 234–35;
  relationship of citizen's advisory
  group to, 54
zoning controls, 144
zoning district, 235
zoning hearing examiner,
  201–3, 225
zoning hearings, 129–41; attendance
  at, 3, 132–33; citizen conduct
  at, 136–39; function of, 129;
  importance of holding, 132–33;
  need for, 56–57; role of
  attorney in, 133–34
zoning map, 235; as enforcement
  tool, 97; as essential element of
  zoning, 80, 85; examples of,
  81–84
zoning officer, 235; and appeal
  procedures, 102–3; qualifications
  for, 96–98; role of, 94–96
zoning ordinances, 143, 235–36;
  adoption of, 57; basic ingredients
  for development of, 68–72; as
  enforcement tool, 97;
  implementation of, 33; need for
  clarity in, 65–66, 74–75, 159–60;

outline of typical, 72–74;
schedule of requirements in,
85–88
zoning permit, 236
zoning policy, 236
zoning regulations, attorney's role
in 62–63; citizen's role in, 58–61;
development of, 45–64;
governing body's role in, 61–62;
professionals' roles in, 63–64;
steps in development of, 52–57

zoning variances, 109–28; definition
of, 112–13; determining
differences between good and
bad, 116–17; and flexibility,
119–20; function of, 113–14;
guidelines for obtaining, 139–41;
legality of, 109; making
application for, 130–31; misuse
of, 109; need for change in
method of handling, 124–26;
and politics, 120–21